Cuisine Grandmère

by the same author

THE STUDENT'S COOKBOOK

VEGETARIAN STUDENT

SIMPLY FISH:
A Guide to Identifying, Buying and Eating Fish

SIMPLE FRENCH CUISINE:
From Provence and Languedoc

KITCHEN SUPPERS

Cuisine Grandmère

From Brittany, Normandy, Picardy and Flanders

JENNY BAKER

Illustrated by James Baker

ff

faber and faber

LONDON · BOSTON

First published in Great Britain in 1994
by Faber and Faber Limited
3 Queen Square London WC1N 3AU

Photoset by Wilmaset Ltd, Birkenhead, Wirral
Printed in England by Clays Ltd, St Ives Plc

A CIP record for this book
is available from the British Library

ISBN 0-571-16877-9

2 4 6 8 10 9 7 5 3 1

To my fellow Francophiles

Acknowledgements

A cookery book is always a joint effort. It depends on the enthusiasm of so many people and I would like to offer special thanks to all those who have helped and encouraged me on the way. This begins with family and friends on whom I am always experimenting to all the people at Faber and Faber who are involved with producing the final result. A special mention must go to all those grandmothers, mothers and daughters and their menfolk who have kept the tradition of the regional cooking of Brittany, Normandy, Picardy and Flanders alive and upon whose recipes this book is based.

Contents

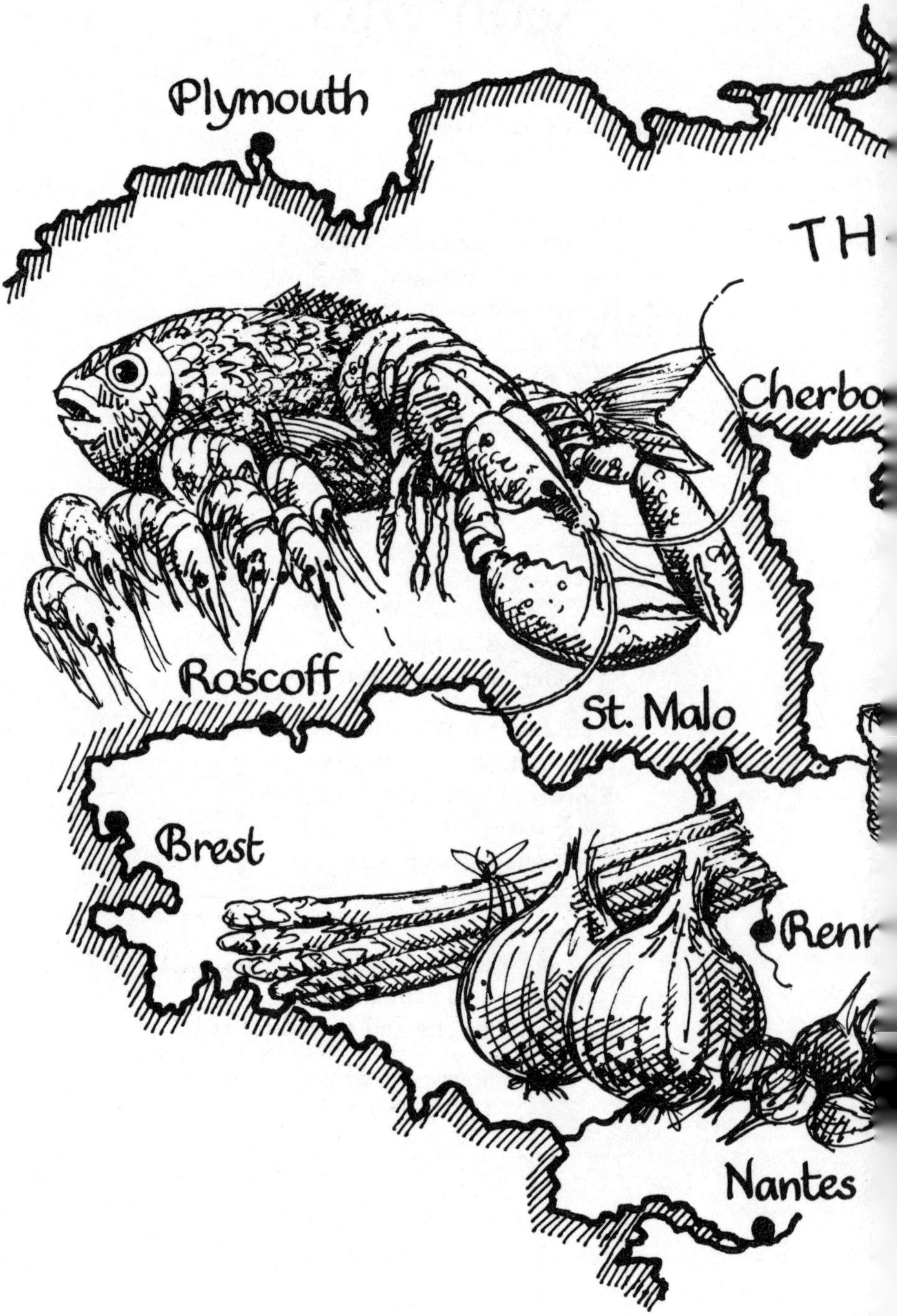

Plymouth
TH
Cherbo
Roscoff
St. Malo
Brest
Renn
Nantes

Dover
rtsmouth
Calais
Boulogne
Lille
IANNEL
Dieppe
Amiens
Havre
Rouen
Caen
CALVADOS
CRÈME FRAÎCH
Cidre Bouch
BIER

Introduction

I always seem to be about to arrive at or to be leaving the north of France. Over the years my family and I have made the crossing from here to there dozens of times. At first we always travelled to Boulogne or Calais but more recently to Le Havre, Caen and St-Malo. Now all these places evoke a peculiar sense of time suspended – as if they are caught between the knowledge that the holiday is about to begin and all is before me, or the realization that somehow those weeks have slipped away and I am turning my back on the delights of France, the French and the food they eat.

Each time we cross, we spend a day, a night, a long weekend, sometimes even a week, enjoying the countryside and food of one of the northern regions, Brittany, Normandy, Picardy or the Nord, before turning south and making for the Midi. We always leave the region with that wish that life was twice as long and we were several times as rich, so that we could get to know more of each of them.

So I began to collect my kind of souvenirs in the form of strings of Breton onions, Normandy cheeses, jars of duck or goose *foie gras*, pickled *salicornes* and cherries, *sel gris*, a bunch of artichokes, a pear or apple tart glistening with apricot glaze. And, of course, recipes. Whether to be tried out in France or in England, I culled them from the places where we ate and the cookery books I dug out from the bookshops of the towns we passed through. This last was not always easy because French regional cookery books are thin on the ground and seldom stay long in print. I suppose this is because the French automatically cook in the style of their region, the art having been handed down from mother to daughter and nowadays kept alive by the demands of the men for food like Grandma used to prepare. So the sort of cookery books the French demand are of a more general nature.

Like every food lover who crosses from Britain to France, I was struck by the contrast between the vigour of their cooking traditions and the demise of our own. How can it be that with a climate and countryside that so closely mirrors ours, they should remember so much of their culinary past, while most of us are hard pressed to unearth more than a handful of recipes? I began to feel that I was not only discovering northern French cooking but that I was also uncovering what once might have been our own.

I soon found that, although a few dishes overlap from one area to another, each of France's northern regions has its own distinctive style of cooking, which has evolved from the nature of the people, the land and its produce.

Of the Bretons it is said they are born with the water of the sea flowing around their hearts and this sort of poetic description is typical of the region with its Celtic beginnings which go back long before the birth of Christianity. Then the coastal region was known by the Gallic name of Armor and the wooded interior Argoat. It was to this haven that Cornish and Welsh Celts fled in the fifth century AD to escape the persecutions of the Angles and Saxons, bringing with them their legends of King Arthur, Merlin and the Holy Grail, Tristan and Iseult. They called their adopted land, so like Cornwall with its rocky shores and windswept landscape, Cornouaille or Little Britain, which later contracted to Brittany.

The cooking of Brittany is simple and homely and with its 750-mile coastline, it is no wonder that seafood plays a big part. Here you will find warming fish soups and stews, fresh fish and molluscs, seafood platters overflowing with variety, dishes of beans and chestnuts, mountains of artichokes and cauliflowers, onions, shallots and garlic, tomatoes and spring vegetables, big fat strawberries, cherries, apples and pears. And of course *galettes* and *crêpes*, those sweet or savoury pancakes which took the place of bread at every meal. This is not surprising in an area where the staple crops are buckwheat, chestnuts and dried beans, none of which lend themselves to breadmaking. But it is not all unsophisticated; the Bretons claim to have invented béchamel sauce, *beurre blanc* and Châteaubriand steak.

If our connection with Brittany goes back to the Celts, our common bond with the Normans is a Viking ancestory. At the same moment in history when they were invading the Anglo-Saxons' territory, these men from the north were doing the same to the peaceful inhabitants of the Seine valley, until they were tamed in the tenth century by the Frankish king known as Charles the Simple. His straightforwardness so disarmed them that they were persuaded it would be more pleasant to settle down than spend their days pillaging and looting. Thus Normandy was founded. The descendants of these Norsemen became landowners and wonderful administrators, whose prosperity increased after William's English Conquest in 1066. When he divided England among his followers his cook, William de Percy – who had gone into battle wielding a hefty soup ladle – was given Northumberland. Normandy was finally lost to England but the title Duke of Normandy is still held by the Queen. This area of France, with its rich pastures and orchards, hedgerowed fields, chalk cliffs, sandy beaches and wooded hills was left virtually unmarked by the horrors of the First World War, but then suffered appalling destruction after the D-Day landings in 1944.

As a race the Normands are strong and robust, taller than the average Frenchman and with gargantuan appetites. Not for them *nouvelle cuisine*. Like my West Country forebears, their diet is based on apples and cider, butter and cream, fresh seafood and shellfish, lamb raised in salt meadows, pheasant, chicken and pork from pigs fed on apples and pears. These are all accompanied with an abundance of vegetables: potatoes with leeks, sweet garden peas, carrots, succulent green beans and early spring vegetables. The meal invariably ends with an array of the best of French cheeses and exquisite fruit tarts, dumplings and turnovers or a generous helping of sticky rice pudding.

And what of Picardy and the Nord, separated from England by the narrowest part of the Channel? Our constant links with these flat lands seem to have been trade, intrigue, smuggling and war. Perhaps especially on a wet and windy day when the clouds hang low over the landscape, I always feel a sense of sadness as we drive down those long, straight, poplar-lined roads, bordered with the carefully tended cemeteries of two world wars. These are set at the edge of vast arable fields in which little villages sit in clusters of trees, the grey slate or red-tiled roofs topped by a church steeple pointing heavenwards.

Yet there's nothing sad about the cooking of these northern regions; rather it is down to earth and lusty. The Nord, which includes part of Flanders, is strongly influenced by the Belgians, whereas that of Picardy with its canals and market gardens owes more to the French, especially the Normands. Curnonsky described the Nord as a land of beer and bricks, and beer certainly plays a large part in the cooking. Gin is the presiding spirit and coffee strongly flavoured with chicory is a favourite breakfast drink.

Inevitably by choosing such a large area I have had to leave some recipes out. So I have let myself be guided by my own personal taste and concentrated on the things that I like. Just because I write about cooking doesn't mean that I'm the sort of person who wants to spend all day in the kitchen, so I have avoided complicated recipes. I feel those dishes that require every saucepan you own should be left to the professional chef, and that the whole pleasure of eating out is to be able to go for things you wouldn't normally make at home.

You have to drive far south before you come to the wine-producing areas of France and of the regions covered in this book, it is only when you reach the Loire in Brittany that you will see a patchwork of vineyards. French people cook with what is readily to hand which means seasonal and local produce, so although wine does play a part in northern cooking, its place is often taken by cider or beer. And when they want to flame a dish or add an extra vigour, they rely on apple brandy or, further north, on gin. All these can of course be bought in England and now that customs duties have been eased they can be brought back from France without breaking the bank.

A few words about crème fraîche and butter. They feature in many of the recipes because they are produced in northern France, and regional French cooking is all about using what is readily to hand. It's a curious fact that although the French are nothing like as health-conscious as we are, their incidence of heart disease is lower than ours. Perhaps it is all a question of balance. It goes without saying that they are great advocates of garlic and enjoy a glass or two of red wine with their meals, both of which are supposed to lower the risk. Fresh salads and fruit figure daily on their menus, and butter is used in the kitchen rather than spread on the copious amounts of bread eaten at every meal.

But if you are cholesterol-conscious, don't feel these recipes are not for you. Instead of butter you could use a good quality oil, such as olive, and go for low-fat crème fraîche which is being introduced by at least one supermarket chain (though, unlike the thicker version, it does curdle when added to hot sauces). In recipes which don't call for it to be heated, you could of course simply leave it out and perhaps use yoghurt in its place. The purists will raise their hands in horror at this sacrilege and say that by changing ingredients you lose the authentic flavour. True, up to a point, but I like to think that cooking is like language, it should evolve with the times.

For those who want to use the real thing, it's interesting to note that Normandy butter is always unsalted, and that the best comes from

Isigny, Cormeilles and Neufchâtel, whereas that of Brittany is usually slightly salted – in the old days it used to contain much more salt and was stored in stoneware jars so that after several months it developed a somewhat rancid taste which the Bretons liked.

Like my first volume of French recipes, *Simple French Cuisine from Provence and Languedoc*, this is a book for people cooking in both Britain and France. The ingredients are readily available in shops, markets and supermarkets on either side of the Channel. You do not need any special pots and pans to do the recipes but I swear by cast-iron enamelled cookware, which is especially useful because it can go from the top of the stove to the oven. I use a gas hob and an electric double oven and find I much prefer the conventional small oven to the larger fan-driven one. I like using a mortar and pestle and a *mouli-légumes* but also have and use a food processor. I like sharp knives.

Unless otherwise stated, all amounts are for four people.

I enjoy cooking seasonally and like to begin with a simple ingredient which plays an important part in a dish. So I have followed the format of *Simple French Cuisine* and set the book out in seasons with sections devoted to flavours, herbs, fruit and vegetables. Recipes should not be absolutes, as every cook gives them something of themselves, and the ones in this book are written from my personal experience of the cooking of northern France. I would like to think you would treat them as a guide and let them work for you by adapting them to your own style and taste. That way perhaps they might really have their place in our own cooking.

Jenny Baker
Wandsworth and La Marie-Thomas
1991–1993

The Flavour

Facing us across a sea, which the French call *La Manche* but which we insist is the English Channel, is northern France, a land of contrasts that sweeps from the wide, open fields of the Nord, through the marshes and networks of canals and market gardens of Picardy, across the rich and varied landscape of Normandy with its lovely old timbered farms and barns, to the granite cliffs, sandy beaches and mysterious past of Brittany, where the country people still speak their ancient Celtic tongue.

The sea divides us and crossing – or going under – it brings us immediately the sensation of entering a more interesting world. A world of different language, tastes and smells. Yet the sun over there is no hotter. Days which begin bright are just as likely to give way to a chilly greyness when the mist comes down and blots out the divide between earth and sky. It rains just as much. There's nothing strange about the produce. Going round the shops and markets in Brittany, Normandy, Picardy or the Nord we can recognize almost everything, yet no one would dispute that the way the French cook it is altogether more interesting. And no one would argue that we could not do the same.

Let's begin with the flavour. Onions, shallots and garlic. Fresh garden herbs. It's impossible to do without them. They are the base of all French country cooking and northern France is no exception.

Once, not so very long ago, the Breton onion boys, the *Johnnies de Roscoff*, crossed over from France every autumn to sell their strings of onions and shallots. They also brought their bicycles, pedalling them from door to door selling their wares. They probably sold garlic too but those were the days when the English hardly used more than a whiff, so perhaps they left it at home. In the sixties, living in Barnes in south London, I remember those 'boys', who were mostly middle-aged, grizzled and wiry, dressed in their blue working clothes with berets on their heads. In the evening we would see their bikes parked outside the decaying barn that was their headquarters and imagine them all inside, exchanging gossip and cooking a meal and wondered if this annual trip was for them a grand holiday or if they missed their wives and families.

We used to buy their plaited strings of onions and shallots, the more worldly haggling over the price, and hang them in the kitchen for decoration as well as for practical use, and now in retrospect I wonder if it was their romantic journey or their superior flavour which made them seem so much more special than onions bought by the pound from the greengrocer's shop. Those days are over, the barn has long since been demolished and made way for flats, the onion Johnnies are no more and their place has been taken by Bretons who are firmly part of the twentieth century and who ship their vegetables from Roscoff to Plymouth via their own Brittany Ferries which was started for that purpose, before it also became one of the leading cross-Channel ferry companies.

Onions, shallots and garlic may now be transported in bags woven of different coloured plastic string, but when you cross the Channel in the autumn, you'll still find them sold in plaits on at least one stall in every French market. Or you might buy them direct from a local producer, as we did coming across a lonely barn on the road from Dol-de-Bretagne to Mont-St-Michel, where they hung line after line from the beams, almost overpowering the air with their concentrated, pungent smell. And for the seriously interested there is the onion market at Plouescats, close to Roscoff, or the September fairs at Bapaume and Arleux in Picardy where they sell the local speciality: russet-red heads of smoked garlic.

If members of the onion family are the base of all French cooking, it is the herbs and flavourings which determine the character of each region. Those of the south – rosemary, wild thyme, sweet basil and fennel – evoke not just the smell of the food but sun-baked arid hills, warmth and the long, heady days of summer. Those of the north – parsley, chervil, tarragon and chives, tied in a bunch or chopped and scattered as a flavour or a garnish – suggest a temperate land where rain is as welcome as the sun, a land of varied shores rich in seafood and of fertile fields, lush meadows and orchards, where vegetables, dairy cows, sheep and pigs flourish. It is said that the meat from cattle grazing in Normandy's Caux region has a slight flavour of parsley, the carrots taste of seaweed and the lambs, which are raised in the salt meadows of Brittany, Normandy and Picardy, have a flavour all their own.

Then there are the soft leaves of northern-grown thyme which is as strong in flavour but lacks the woody stems of Provence's wild variety;

the subtle bitterness of sorrel; garden angelica, mustard, capers and salt, all of which play some part in the cooking of these regions, whether it is to flavour soups or sauces, fish dishes and salads, roasts of lamb or pork, poultry and game, vinegars, frogs' legs or snails, boozy liqueurs or perhaps a rhubarb tart or buttery Breton cake.

Onions, shallots and garlic

Onions have been cultivated since the earliest civilizations and flavours vary from mild to strong depending on the species. In Britain, onions are always sold simply as onions, so there is no ready guide to determining how they will taste, but the cooking process does affect the flavour and whether sweating onions or gently cooking until golden, don't let them brown, because it will coarsen their flavour. If peeling and chopping onions makes you cry, try cutting off the stalk end before cutting the root. It seems to work. Don't ask me why. Really obstinate onion skins can be removed more easily if you steep the onions for a short time in boiling water.

Shallots are a variety of onion but instead of producing a single head, the plant forms a cluster of small bulbs. They are easy to grow, and traditionally are planted on the shortest day to be lifted on the longest! They can then be kept, plaited like garlic and hung in a dry atmosphere, for up to a year. The flavour of shallot is more delicate than onion, sweeter and less pervasive and is much favoured in the north of France. Never brown shallots, as it completely spoils their flavour, turning them bitter and unpleasant.

For many people garlic is synonymous with French cooking and perhaps it explains how the French can eat so much, yet apparently remain less prone to some of our heart-related diseases. Garlic has been known for centuries as a medicinal plant, reputed to cure all sorts of ills from bronchitis to blood pressure. Soldiers and cocks were fed it before going into battle, sailors took it to sea, and the French peasant believes that not a day must go by without garlic because not only is it an antidote against sickness but it ensures longevity.

When in France in the autumn it is worth buying a string or two of onions, shallots or garlic and hanging them up in the kitchen. Apart from looking decorative, they will keep well into the next year.

Onion boys' soup
Velouté Johnny

This soup, called after the onion boys from Roscoff, is heartwarming on a cold winter's day. Serve it with croûtons of French bread either fried or sprinkled with oil and baked for 10 minutes at the top of a hot oven Gas 7/425°F/220°C.

25 g (1 oz) butter	salt
450 g (1 lb) onions, chopped	freshly milled black pepper
350 g (12 oz) potatoes, cut in chunks	1 egg yolk
1 litre (1¾ pints) stock	1 tablespoon crème fraîche

Melt the butter in a saucepan and gently fry the onions until soft but not brown; this takes 5–10 minutes. Add the potatoes and stock. Bring to the boil, season with salt and pepper and simmer, covered, for 30 minutes. Liquidize or purée. Beat the egg yolk with the crème fraîche and stir in a ladleful of the soup. Tip this mixture into the pan and heat through without boiling, stirring all the time.

Haricot bean soup
Soupe à la bretonne

In this warm and nourishing winter soup, the rather bland beans are made full of flavour with the addition of onion, garlic, spinach and herbs. Serve with fried bread croûtons.

225 g (8 oz) dried haricot beans, soaked (see Etceteras)	1 bay leaf
1 onion	25 g (1 oz) butter
2 cloves garlic	150 g (6 oz) spinach, chopped
3 potatoes, peeled and quartered	salt
sprigs of parsley and thyme	freshly milled black pepper

Put the drained, soaked beans into a large saucepan and add 1 litre (1¾ pints) water, the onion and garlic (both left whole), potatoes, parsley, thyme and bay leaf. Bring to the boil and simmer, covered, for 1½–2 hours. Purée and return to the pan. Melt the butter in another pan and add the chopped spinach, let it reduce to a purée and stir into the soup. Season with salt and pepper and simmer for 5 minutes.

Marinated bloaters
Les gros bouffis marinés

In northern France every fish counter stocks silvery-bronze bloaters, which are whole herrings soaked in brine and cold-smoked. The French give them curious names such as *sauret*, *gendarme*, *bouffi* and *craquelot*. Here they are not so easy to find, but you could use kipper fillets instead. The fish soak up the flavours of the onions, oil and peppercorns in which they are marinated and make a quick and cheapish starter or a main course if served with boiled potatoes and sliced raw carrots. To skin and fillet the bloaters, put them in a bowl, pour over boiling water and leave for a minute or two. Peel away the skin. Split each fish down the front from head to tail. Gently open out a little and stand the cut sides on a board. Press carefully along the backbone to flatten the fish and ease away the bone. Turn over, snip the bone near the tail and, with the point of a knife, ease away the backbone. Use a good quality oil such as olive, walnut, corn or sunflower.

4 bloaters, skinned and filleted
2 onions, finely sliced
1 teaspoon peppercorns
2 bay leaves
6–8 tablespoons oil

Lay the fillets in a dish in layers, topping each layer with slices of onion and peppercorns. Lay the bay leaves on top and pour over the oil. Keep for at least 24 hours in a cool place before eating.

Mussels with onions and shallots
Moules à la cancalaise

Cancale, in the western corner of the bay of Mont-St-Michel, is famous for its oysters and mussels and, like every other place along the French coastline, it has its own version of *moules marinière*. Here the mussels are steamed in a little white wine flavoured with onions, shallots and herbs. The sauce is finished with butter. In St-Malo they add crème fraîche, as they do in Normandy, where they often stir in an egg yolk too, *à la poulette*. Wash the mussels ahead of time so that they can soak for several hours in water with a little flour. As they open to eat the flour, they will release any sand in the shells. Tap sharply with a wooden spoon any mussels that are open, if they fail to close, discard them as well as any with broken shells, as they will be dead.

1 kg ($2\frac{1}{4}$ lb) mussels
1 tablespoon sea salt
1 tablespoon flour
50 g (2 oz) butter
2 onions, chopped
2 shallots, chopped
sprigs of parsley and thyme, tied in a bunch
1 bay leaf
2 tablespoons white wine
freshly milled black pepper

Wash and scrub the mussels under running cold water, removing the beards and barnacles. Leave them to soak for several hours in a bowl of water with the salt and flour. When ready to cook, melt half the butter in a large pan and fry the onions and shallots for a few minutes until golden. Add the herbs, wine and mussels. Season well with pepper. Bring to the boil and boil fiercely, covered, for 5 minutes. Transfer the mussels to a warm serving bowl, add the remaining butter to the pan and when it melts, strain the liquid over the mussels. Provide another bowl for the shells.

Oysters with shallot vinegar
Huîtres à la sauce pauvre homme

All along the coast of Brittany and Normandy, you'll find oysters on the menu all the year round, although they are best between September and April. An oyster in good condition should be full of water when it is opened. If you are unsure of its freshness, touch the extreme edge of the flesh lightly with the point of a knife or a drop of lemon juice. If it retracts, it is fine.

In Cancale they are served at every café and restaurant, either as a separate course or to garnish fish, chicken, salads or soups. They are most often eaten raw but those who are perhaps jaded by such an abundance can order them poached on a bed of spinach, or baked with garlic butter, or stuffed with mushrooms in a garlicky flavoured béchamel sauce, wrapped in bacon and grilled on skewers or simply fried in hot oil and garnished with lemon and parsley.

The cheapest way of eating them is to buy them from one of the stalls on the promenade overlooking the oyster beds and sit on the sea wall discarding their shells on to the sands below, which are already littered with hundreds of thousands of shells. Here, too, you can watch the oyster growers, riding their tractors like modern-day cowboys out over the mudflats when the tide is out. And always with the oysters, which if not quite two a penny are incredibly cheap, you will be served a small bowl of shallot vinegar with which to sprinkle them.

The oysters themselves look most attractive if served on a bed of seaweed with crushed ice. There is a knack to opening them which involves inserting the tip of a short knife under the hinge and severing the muscle, taking care all the time not to lose any of the juices surrounding the oyster. Get your fishmonger to give you a lesson. They will keep for several days, in a temperature between 2 and 5°C (34–40°F), if packed together and weighted down so they can't open and spill their water.

Just before serving, open the oysters, discard the flat upper shell and arrange them on a large platter. Accompany with a small bowl of wine or cider vinegar to which a finely chopped shallot has been added. Season well with pepper.

Breton garlic butter
Beurre breton

Use this butter to make garlic bread or to stuff mussels, clams, oysters and other shellfish. It can also be used to stuff snails, the *petits escargots gris* from Rennes and Cesson, which are the same prized variety as the snails which haunt the vineyards of southern France and our own English gardens, where they are not prized at all.

- 1 shallot, chopped
- 1–2 tablespoons white wine or lemon juice
- 225 g (8 oz) slightly salted butter, softened
- 2 cloves garlic, chopped
- handful parsley, chopped
- freshly milled black pepper

Put the chopped shallot into a small bowl, add the wine or lemon juice and leave to infuse for several hours. Cut the butter into chunks and put it into a mortar or bowl and mash until soft. Gradually mash in the garlic, parsley and shallot. Season well with pepper.

Frogs' legs with garlic butter
Cuisses de grenouilles

No one who is adventurous can miss the opportunity to try frogs' legs at least once in a lifetime. They sell them in France in packets in supermarkets alongside the frozen peas and *langoustines*. They taste like tender chicken with just a hint of fish. One of the simplest ways of cooking them is in this Breton recipe.

24 frogs' legs
150 ml (¼ pint) milk
2–3 tablespoons flour
oil for frying
50–75 g (2–3 oz) Breton garlic butter (see above)
2 lemons, quartered

Heat the oven to Gas 5/375°F/190°C. Dry the frogs' legs with kitchen paper. Put the milk and flour on to two separate plates. Dip each leg first in milk then in flour so that they are coated all over. Heat about 2 cm (1 in) of oil in a frying pan and when it is sizzling, quickly fry the legs until golden on both sides. Drain them on greaseproof paper. Dot them with the Breton garlic butter and put into the oven for 5–10 minutes. Serve garnished with the lemon quarters.

Pumpkin pie
Flamique à l'chitrouille

Flamique or *flamiche* is a typical savoury pie from Picardy. In this version the filling is made with a mixture of pumpkin and onions but you'll come across ones made with leeks or the local pungent Maroille cheese. The French call the bright-fleshed orange pumpkin *potiron*, while the pale yellow kind are known as *citrouille* or *chitrouille*. In this recipe I am suggesting puff pastry but use shortcrust pastry if you prefer. It can be eaten hot but is nicest when it is set aside to cool a little and served warm with a simple green salad.

75 g (3 oz) butter
700 g (1½ lb) pumpkin, peeled, de-seeded and cubed
100 g (4 oz) onion, chopped
sprigs of parsley and thyme, tied together
1 bay leaf
pinch nutmeg
salt
freshly milled black pepper
450 g (1 lb) puff pastry
1 egg, beaten

Melt the butter in a saucepan. Add the cubed pumpkin to the pan with the onion, herbs and nutmeg. Season with salt and pepper. Cook over a gentle heat until soft, which should take about 20–30 minutes.

Meanwhile, divide the pastry into two pieces. Roll one into a circle and line a 20 cm (8 in) tart tin. Roll the other piece into a circle to form the top. Cover the pastry and put into the fridge until needed. When the pumpkin is soft, mash it well and raise the heat to evaporate as much of the water as possible. Set it aside to cool. Heat the oven to Gas 7/425°F/220°C. Fill the pastry base with the cooled pumpkin mixture, lay on the pastry lid and press all round to seal the edges. Brush the lid with beaten egg, cut a slit in the top and bake the pie for 20 minutes. Lower the heat to Gas 4/350°F/180°C and bake for a further 15 minutes until puffed and golden.

Puréed onions
Purée d'oignons à la bretonne

Breton onion purée is a delicious accompaniment to grilled or roast meats, especially lamb or pork, and makes an interesting alternative to our mint or apple sauces.

900 g (2 lb) onions, quartered
salt
1 tablespoon oil
½ teaspoon caster sugar
100 ml (4 fl oz) Muscadet or other dry white wine
freshly milled black pepper
25 g (1 oz) butter

Put the onions into a pan, cover with water, add a little salt and boil until they begin to soften and break up, after 15–20 minutes. Drain well. Wipe out the pan and add the oil. Heat it, return the onions to the pan, sprinkle over the sugar and fry over a medium heat until they are golden brown, shaking the pan from time to time. Add the wine, and season with salt and pepper. Cook uncovered until the onions are soft and have absorbed almost all the liquid, which will take 10–15 minutes. Put into a food processor or liquidizer, add the butter and purée the mixture. Serve in a small bowl or sauceboat.

Breton onion sauce
Sauce aux oignons

Onions stirred into a béchamel sauce make a delicious accompaniment to roast lamb and this Breton recipe is just like the one my mother used to make whenever she roasted lamb or mutton. The only difference is that the Bretons add a dash of *lambig*, apple brandy, and a touch of crème fraîche.

450 g (1 lb) onions, sliced
salt
300 ml (½ pint) béchamel sauce (see Etceteras)
2 tablespoons apple brandy or calvados
3 tablespoons crème fraîche

Cook the onions in salted water for about 30 minutes, until tender. Meanwhile make the béchamel sauce. Drain the onions very well. Stir them into the sauce, taste and adjust the seasoning. Stir in the apple brandy and crème fraîche.

Picardy's onion sauce
Sauce picarde

In the marshy regions of the Somme they serve this unctuous onion sauce with wild duck. It differs from the Breton version in that the onions are cooked in the sauce, which is made with water and not milk.

50 g (2 oz) butter
50 g (2 oz) flour
450 ml (¾ pint) water
2 tablespoons wine vinegar
450 g (1 lb) onions, sliced
salt

Melt the butter in a saucepan, mix in the flour and let it cook for a couple of minutes, stirring all the time. Gradually mix in the water and wine vinegar. Bring to the boil, lower the heat and simmer for 5 minutes, stirring often. Add the onions and season with salt and pepper. Cover and simmer for 1 hour until the onions have reduced almost to a purée. Check from time to time and if the sauce seems too thick and in danger of burning, add a tablespoon or two more water.

Fishwife's squid with onions
Morgate à la sinagote

Morgate is the Breton name for squid, which the French call *calamar*, and this way of cooking them comes from the little port of Séné, once famous for its two-masted fishing boats, known as *sinagots*. Nowadays it is possible to buy squid already cleaned but if you have to do it yourself, follow the method they use in French markets. Cut off the tentacles just above the eye and set aside. Pull off the head and discard. Slit the body in half with scissors, open it up and wash away all the jelly-like innards and the curious quill which looks exactly like plastic. Eat the squid either with rice or steamed or boiled potatoes.

700–900 g (1½–2 lb) squid
50 g (2 oz) butter
2 onions, finely chopped
1–2 tablespoons chopped parsley
1 teaspoon dried thyme
2 cloves garlic, chopped
100 ml (4 fl oz) Muscadet or other dry white wine
salt
freshly milled black pepper

Cut the squid into strips or cubes. Melt the butter and soften the onions in it until golden. Stir in the parsley, thyme and garlic, then add the squid. Leave over a low heat for 10 minutes, stirring occasionally. Pour in the wine and season with salt and pepper. Simmer for a further 30–35 minutes until the squid is tender and most of the liquid is absorbed.

Pork with onions
Caqhuse picarde

Caqhuse is a famous dish from Picardy in which a joint of pork is roasted or braised with onions. The French don't go in for crackling, preferring to remove the thick layer of fat from their pork and use it to wrap round leaner joints of meat before roasting, or it goes into various pâtés, terrines and sausages.

1½ kg (3 lb) boned, rolled leg of pork
salt
freshly milled black pepper
450 g (1 lb) onions, chopped
4 tablespoons oil
50 g (2 oz) butter

Heat oven to Gas 7/425°F/220°C. Season the pork on both sides with salt and pepper, sprinkle half the onions over the base of an earthenware oven dish and lay the pork on top. Scatter over the remaining onions. Pour over the oil and dot with the butter. Put into the oven and bake, allowing 25 minutes per 450 g (1 lb) and 25 minutes over. Lower the heat to Gas 6/400°F/200°C after 15 minutes. Baste five or six times during the cooking time and if the onions begin to get too brown, cover the dish loosely with foil. The pork is ready when the juices run clear when pierced with a skewer.

Steak with garlic
Beefsteak à la bretonne

When grilling steak, I often use a cast-iron ribbed grill pan which goes on top of the stove. When cooked the steaks are attractively striped and the pan itself is ideal for making the buttery, garlic sauce which accompanies them. To make sure the steaks will be tender, an hour before grilling remove them from the fridge and marinate them in the juice of a lemon with a generous sprinkling of freshly milled pepper.

4 sirloin or rump steaks
oil
salt
freshly milled black pepper
50 g (2 oz) butter
1 teaspoon mustard
3 cloves garlic, finely chopped
1 tablespoon chopped parsley

Heat grill for 5–6 minutes until very hot. Brush the steaks lightly with oil and grill them, allowing 2–3 minutes on each side for medium rare, 3–4 minutes more for well done. Put them on a serving dish and season with salt and pepper. Melt the butter in the grill pan, stir in the mustard, garlic and parsley and pour immediately over the steaks.

Beurre blanc

Beurre blanc, the white buttery sauce flavoured with shallots and vinegar, is said by the Bretons to have been invented in a little village close to Nantes. It goes wonderfully with poached river fish like pike and perch, but is also good with the more easily obtained rainbow trout. You must use very good, slightly salted butter and it should be at room temperature. Before you begin, cut it into pieces the size of a walnut. Make sure you make the sauce in a heavy-based pan and don't use any utensils containing aluminium, which may or may not damage your brain cells but will turn the sauce an unappetizing shade of grey.

2–3 shallots, chopped finely
4 tablespoons white wine vinegar
2 tablespoons crème fraîche
225 g (8 oz) butter, cut in cubes

Put the shallots and vinegar into a small heavy-based saucepan and boil over a medium heat until the liquid has reduced to about 1 tablespoon. Take off the heat to cool a little. Add the crème fraîche and mix well with a wooden spoon. Put the pan over a very low heat and gradually beat in the butter, a piece at a time and, as the sauce begins to thicken, lift the pan off the heat. When all the butter is incorporated and the sauce is creamy, it is ready.

Parsley, chervil, tarragon and chives

A seafood platter and a Breton sauce

Breton herb butter

Peasant cream sauce

Châteaubriand sauce

Warm bean salad

Leg of lamb with haricot beans

Eggs with tarragon

Stuffed mussels

Scallops with herbs

Grilled lobster

Chicken with tarragon

Mixed beetroot salad with chives

Rice and tuna salad

Glazed turnips

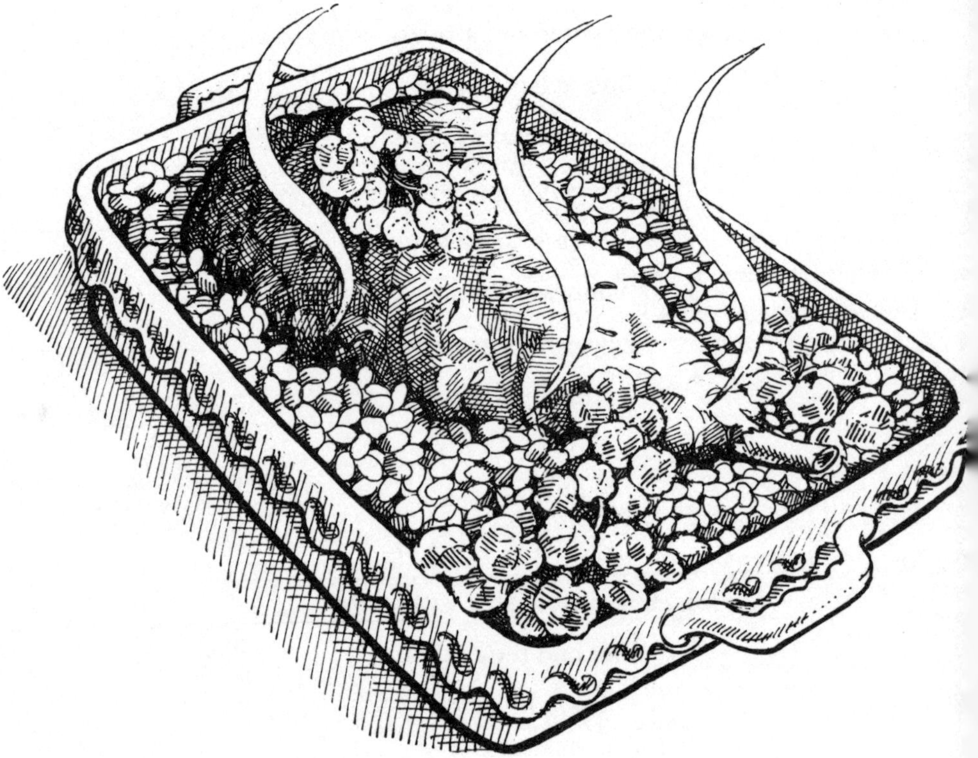

Fines herbes – finely chopped herbs such as parsley, chervil, tarragon and chives – and the bouquet garni – sprigs of herbs tied in a bunch – are at the heart of all French country cooking, and northern France is no exception.

The distinctive flavour and attractive deep green of parsley, *persil*, make it one of the most widely used and useful of herbs. The stalks can flavour soups and stews, either alone or as part of a bouquet garni, while the finely chopped leaves go into sauces and butters or as part of a mixture of *fines herbes*, or are added as a garnish right at the last moment. A simple salad, a bowl of carrots, boiled or steamed potatoes, a creamy soup, a pale omelette, a grilled fish are all transformed into something special by simply adding a dusting of parsley. We tend to grow the curly-leaved variety whereas in France they prefer a different parsley which has wide, flat leaves and even more flavour. This most popular of herbs is widely available all the year round, which is fortunate as it does not dry well. It can be successfully frozen, however, especially if you chop it first and store it in an airtight container.

Garden chervil, *cerfeuil*, with its lacy green leaves is rated by the Bretons even more highly than its cousin parsley. Until recently it was hardly ever on sale in England but now appears pre-packed in supermarkets. It is similar to but more delicate than parsley, with a slight flavour of liquorice, and is usually added right at the end of the cooking time as long cooking destroys its taste. Use it as a garnish for soups or salads, either chopped or in tiny sprigs. It is not hard to grow your own, either in the garden or windowbox, but it quickly goes to seed, so must be cut almost to ground level once it reaches 5–6 cm (2–3 in) in height. To maintain a constant supply throughout the summer, sow it at intervals during the season. Like parsley, chervil freezes well.

French tarragon, *estragon*, is a subtle herb much prized by the Bretons. Its elusive smell gives no hint of its strong flavour, so use this herb with discretion. It can be grown from cuttings, root division or seed (but make sure you are not being palmed off with the related Russian variety, which is inferior and coarser). Put one or two sprigs just before they flower into a bottle of wine vinegar and leave for a fortnight to infuse. It will give a lift to the plainest of salads. Many supermarkets now sell tarragon pre-packed and it is worth snapping up because it freezes well or can be stored in an airtight jar.

Chives, *ciboulettes*, with their thin green stalks, are a favourite herb of Normandy. Easy to grow from seed or by division, they have pretty, purple flowers but if you allow them to reach this state, the stalks themselves will lose their flavour. This herb thrives by constantly being cut and keeps bringing up new shoots throughout the summer. It is useful for adding a delicate, oniony flavour to all sorts of dishes, from soups and sauces to egg dishes and salads. Chives don't dry well but freeze easily. They are most easily chopped by snipping with scissors.

A seafood platter and a Breton sauce
Assiette du pêcheur et la sauce bretonne froide

The seafood platter lives in the memories of those who have sampled it as the epitome of the taste of northern France. The first one I had was at the *Armada* in Cancale, sitting at a window table watching the sun going down behind the harbour, the sky flaming with pink clouds which gradually faded and darkened as the night crept over the oyster beds. We turned our minds to the serious business of demolishing an enormous platter of oysters, winkles, shrimps, crab, clams, whelks, mussels and cockles, prawns and *langoustines* served on a bed of fresh seaweed and ice with a bowl of *sauce bretonne froide* pungent with herbs and another of shallot-flavoured vinegar.

It costs the earth to reproduce such a profusion here, but you might like to try the Breton sauce, flavoured with parsley, chives and chervil, which can be eaten hot or cold not only to accompany seafood but with vegetables like asparagus or artichokes or with poached fish or salads. If you baulk at a sauce made with so much butter you could copy the Breton custom of lightening an ordinary mayonnaise with a whisked egg white.

1 egg yolk
1 teaspoon mustard
1 teaspoon white wine or cider vinegar
salt
freshly milled black pepper
100 g (4 oz) slightly salted butter, melted
1 tablespoon finely chopped parsley, chives and chervil
1 tablespoon chopped capers or gherkins

Put the egg yolk with the mustard and wine or vinegar into a wide bowl. Season with salt and pepper. Beat well and gradually beat in the melted butter, first a few drops at a time, then gradually increasing the amount, beating all the time. When mixture is thick and creamy, add the chopped herbs and capers or gherkins.

Breton herb butter
Beurre aux herbes de Bretagne

This butter flavoured with parsley, chervil and chives is used as a garnish for fish or vegetable dishes or spread on *galettes*. Use it to stuff snails or shellfish such as oysters, mussels, clams or baby scallops (the filled shells are then topped with breadcrumbs and put into a hot oven until sizzling and bubbling – about 10 minutes).

Mash 225 g (8 oz) slightly salted, good quality butter with a generous mixture of chopped herbs such as parsley, chervil, chives, mustard and cress, together with a chopped shallot, a clove of garlic and a seasoning of pepper. The mixture should be very green.

Peasant cream sauce
Sauce paysanne normande

In Normandy they serve this easy-to-make chive and parsley sauce with poached fish. It uses lashings of butter and cream but is so light and delicious that we can be forgiven for eating it sometimes.

100 g (4 oz) butter
300 ml (½ pint) crème fraîche
1–2 tablespoons snipped chives
handful parsley, chopped
juice of ½ lemon

Melt the butter in a heavy-based pan. Whisk in the crème fraîche, chives, parsley and lemon juice. Let the sauce bubble, stirring all the time.

Châteaubriand sauce

This winey, buttery sauce flavoured with tarragon and shallot is good with roast or grilled meats. Traditionally it accompanies a châteaubriand which is a piece of fillet steak, cut from the thickest part, and served very rare. Reputedly the recipe is called after the St-Malo writer, François-René de Châteaubriand. The story goes that, fond though he was of rare steak, he would only eat the juicy middle and leave the rest. Perhaps he had bad teeth! His cook, a man called Montmireil, had the brilliant idea of cooking a piece of fillet between two thin slices of rump steak which were discarded before the writer was served. Professional chefs make this sauce with *demi-glace*, which is a much reduced beef stock and not often found in a domestic kitchen, so I suggest using canned beef consommé.

100 ml (4 fl oz) Muscadet or other dry white wine
1 shallot, finely chopped
100 ml (4 fl oz) canned beef consommé
100 g (4 oz) butter, cut in small pieces
1 tablespoon chopped tarragon
pinch of cayenne pepper
juice of 1 lemon

Put the wine and shallot into a saucepan and boil hard until only 1 tablespoon of liquid remains. Add the beef consommé and reduce by half. Gradually beat in the butter. Add the tarragon, cayenne pepper and the lemon juice. Pour over freshly grilled steaks.

Warm bean salad
Salade bretonne

Make this warm salad, flavoured with parsley, with either freshly cooked beans (see Etceteras), or a can of haricot beans gently heated through. Serve it with pork chops or a lamb roast, but only add the beetroot right at the last minute – added too soon it stains the beans an unappetizing pink. Use the cooked beetroot sold at the greengrocer, not the pickled kind found in jars. Lamb's lettuce, *mâche*, which once only grew wild, is now being marketed and is sold in some supermarkets. It is also easily grown from seed. If unavailable, use watercress instead.

450 g (1 lb) haricot beans, canned or freshly cooked
handful parsley, chopped
3 tablespoons oil
½ tablespoon cider vinegar
salt
freshly milled black pepper
1 pkt or 2 handfuls lamb's lettuce
100 g (4 oz) fresh cooked beetroot, cut in small cubes

If necessary, warm the beans through, drain and empty them into a salad bowl. Stir in the parsley, oil and vinegar and season with salt and pepper. Just before serving mix with the lamb's lettuce and top with the cubed beetroot.

Leg of lamb with haricot beans
Gigot de pré-salé aux pois

The *pré-salé* lambs raised in the coastal meadows of northern France are highly prized by the French, who have the knack of appreciating and exploiting such subtleties. You won't get this special lamb here but buy the best quality you can afford. (You might after all be lucky and come across lamb reared in British pastures salted by the sea.)

Roast leg of lamb, studded with garlic and flavoured with herbs, is traditionally served with a dish of haricot beans which in Normandy they call *pois à gigot*. In Brittany the beans will be flavoured with tomatoes, (see Tomatoes section). The French like their lamb pink, the British tend to think this undercooked, so gauge your cooking time accordingly.

225 g (8 oz) dried haricot beans, soaked (see Etceteras)
1 onion, quartered
2 carrots, quartered
sprigs of parsley, thyme and tarragon, tied in a bunch
1 bay leaf
1 leg of lamb
2–4 cloves garlic, cut in slivers
2–3 tablespoons oil
25 g (1 oz) butter
handful parsley, chopped

Put the soaked beans, the onion, carrots, bunch of herbs and bay leaf into a saucepan. Cover with cold water and bring to the boil and simmer, covered, for 1–1½ hours.

Heat the oven to Gas 8/450°F/230°C. Make incisions in the lamb and insert the slivers of garlic. Put it into a roasting tin and pour over the oil. Roast for 15 minutes, then lower the heat to Gas 6/400°F/200°C. Allow 15–20 minutes per 450 g (1 lb) depending on the degree of pinkness you prefer. Baste every 15 minutes. Test with a skewer: if the juices run pale pink, the lamb is rare, if yellow the lamb is well cooked. Put the cooked meat on a serving dish and leave it to rest in a cool oven for at least 15 minutes (this allows the meat to compact and makes it much easier to carve).

Make a gravy by putting the roasting tin on the heat and stirring in some water; let it bubble fiercely and reduce. Drain the beans, discard the herbs, add the butter and moisten with some of the gravy. Serve the lamb surrounded by the beans, sprinkle with the parsley and pour the remaining gravy into a sauceboat.

Eggs with tarragon
Oeufs en cocotte à l'estragon

For a simple starter, lunch or supper dish, try these little eggs *en cocotte* flavoured with tarragon.

butter
salt
freshly milled black pepper
4 teaspoons chopped fresh tarragon
4 eggs
2 tablespoons crème fraîche

Generously grease four cocottes or ramekins with butter and sprinkle a little salt and pepper into each, together with a teaspoonful of chopped tarragon. Carefully break an egg into each. Stand the pots in a frying pan and add sufficient water to reach half way up their sides. Bring to the boil, cover the pan with a lid or a piece of foil, and let the water simmer until the whites of the eggs are almost set. Meanwhile, gently heat the crème fraîche, season it with pepper and as soon as the eggs are done, pour a circle of crème fraîche around each yolk.

Stuffed mussels
Moules farcies à la dinardaise

From Dinard – once the favourite resort of the smart English set, and still popular for its sandy beaches and air of grandeur – comes this delightfully easy way with mussels. They can either be stuffed in the half shell, or removed completely and put into snail dishes.

450 g (1 lb) mussels
200 ml (7 fl oz) crème fraîche
2–3 tablespoons chopped chives, chervil and parsley
1 teaspoon apple brandy or calvados
salt
freshly milled black pepper
pinch of cayenne
2 cloves garlic, chopped
2–3 tablespoons breadcrumbs

Scrub the mussels well and wash them in several changes of water. Put them into a large saucepan and stand them over a high heat. As soon as they open remove them to a colander. Heat the oven to Gas 6/400°F/200°C. Mix the crème fraîche with the herbs, apple brandy or calvados, salt, pepper and cayenne. Discard the top shells and lay the lower shells containing the mussels on a baking sheet. Fill each of these with the cream mixture. Mix the garlic with the breadcrumbs and sprinkle over the top. Put into the oven for 10–15 minutes until hot and bubbling.

Scallops with herbs
Saint-Jacques gratinées

Scallops are delicious but in Britain they are expensive, so this Breton recipe is perhaps one to try when on that side of the Channel. For optimum freshness, try and buy scallops in their closed shells and ask the fishmonger to open them for you and preserve the water inside them, which can be used as part of the poaching liquid. Also get him to clean them for you by removing the membrane, grey-brown frill and the thin thread of the intestine, leaving just the nut of white flesh and the orange coral. Ask for four of the deep shells.

75 g (3 oz) butter
2–3 shallots, chopped
8 scallops
150 ml ($\frac{1}{4}$ pint) Muscadet or other dry white wine
75 g (3 oz) fresh breadcrumbs
2 tablespoons chopped mixed herbs: chives, tarragon, parsley and chervil
1 clove garlic, chopped
salt
freshly milled black pepper
1 tablespoon dried breadcrumbs

Heat the oven to Gas 6/400°F/200°C. Melt half the butter and fry the shallots for 5–10 minutes, until golden. While they are cooking, put the scallop flesh, their corals, the wine and any scallop liquid (or 2–3 tablespoons water) into a saucepan. Bring just to the boil, remove immediately from the heat, cover them and set aside for 3–4 minutes. Remove from the liquid and cut into bite-sized pieces. Set aside.

Mix the fresh breadcrumbs with the herbs and garlic, season with a little salt and pepper, and moisten with a little of the liquid in which the scallops were poached.

Divide the scallops between the four deep scallop shells, top with the herby breadcrumb mixture, sprinkle with dried breadcrumbs and dot with the remaining butter. Bake for 5–10 minutes until hot and bubbling.

Grilled lobster
Homards grillés à la bretonne

On either side of the Channel, lobsters tend to find their way to hotels and restaurants, and when you do see them on sale, usually already boiled, they are likely to be expensive. So as they are a rare treat, it is better to get the fishmonger to split each lobster down the middle and to eat them simply, either cold with mayonnaise or a sauce made with oil and lemon juice, or hot as in this recipe in which they are grilled in melted butter before being dusted with plenty of freshly chopped parsley.

If the fishmonger hasn't already done so, remove the long black intestine and the small sac in the head, which contains gritty bits. Everything else is edible, including all the green and creamy bits.

2 lobsters, split down the middle
100 g (4 oz) melted butter
salt
freshly milled black pepper
handful parsley, chopped
2 lemons, quartered

Either heat the grill until very hot or the oven to Gas 7/425°F/220°C. Brush the lobsters with melted butter and put under the grill or into the oven for 5–10 minutes, until hot and bubbling. Season with salt and pepper, sprinkle with the parsley and serve with the rest of the butter, and the lemon quarters.

Chicken with tarragon
Poulet à l'estragon

French tarragon has a great affinity with chicken and in this recipe they combine to make a dish that is quick and simple to prepare. The bird is stuffed with the herb, wrapped in bacon and then pot-roasted with more tarragon and white wine. In winter, when tarragon is not available, use the evergreen rosemary instead. Eat the chicken with roast potatoes or, more delicious still, potatoes fried with onions (see Potatoes and Leeks section).

- 25 g (1 oz) butter
- 3–4 sprigs of French tarragon
- 1 corn-fed or free range chicken
- 4 rashers streaky bacon
- 150 ml (¼ pint) Muscadet or other dry white wine
- salt
- freshly milled black pepper

Heat the oven to Gas 6/400°F/200°C. Put the butter and one sprig of tarragon inside the chicken. Wrap the bacon rashers widthwise over the breast and secure them with string. Put the bird into a heavy-based casserole with a close-fitting lid. Pour over the wine, season with salt and pepper and add the remaining sprigs of tarragon. Cover, bring to the boil and transfer to the oven for 1¼ hours, or until the juices run clear when the chicken is pierced in the thickest part with a skewer. Remove the chicken to a warm serving dish and cut away the string. Stir the winey juices over a high heat until they reduce by half; serve separately.

Mixed beetroot salad with chives
Salade normande au betterave rouge

Beetroot instantly stains anything it touches and for this reason this salad is assembled at the last minute and not mixed until it is brought to the table.

- 125 ml (5 fl oz) double cream
- juice of 1 lemon
- salt
- freshly milled black pepper
- 1 lettuce
- 225 g (8 oz) cooked beetroot, cut in small cubes
- 75 g (3 oz) walnuts, chopped
- 1–2 tablespoons snipped chives

Mix the cream in a salad bowl with the lemon juice and season it with salt and pepper. Just before serving, tear up the lettuce leaves, add to the bowl, and top with the beetroot, walnuts and chives. Mix at the table.

Rice and tuna salad
Salade nantaise

Next time you are serving rice, cook an extra 100 g (4 oz). Mix this amount, while it is still warm, with the dressing – so that the rice absorbs all the flavours – and set aside for the following day.

225 g (8 oz) cooked rice
salt
freshly milled black pepper
1 tablespoon vinegar
6 tablespoons oil
2 tablespoons chopped chervil
2 tablespoons chopped tarragon
2 tablespoons chopped chives
1 × 225 g (8 oz) can tuna in oil
225 g (8 oz) tomatoes, chopped small

Put the cooked rice into a salad bowl and season well with salt and pepper. Mix the vinegar and oil with the chervil, tarragon and chives. Pour over the rice, mix well and set aside to cool. If not eating until the next day, put the rice into the fridge. An hour or so before eating, break up the tuna with a fork and mix with the rice, then add the chopped tomatoes.

Glazed turnips
Navets aux fines herbes

Turnips are an underrated vegetable. I love their peppery flavour when simply boiled and mashed with butter and seasoned with plenty of salt, pepper and fresh parsley. Or better still in this Normandy recipe, when they are glazed in butter and served sprinkled with a mixture of chives and parsley. Delicious with rabbit or other game.

700 g (1½ lb) young turnips, quartered
salt
1 sugar lump
25 g (1 oz) butter
handful parsley, chopped
handful chives, chopped
freshly milled black pepper

Boil 150 ml (¼ pint) of water and add the turnips, salt and sugar. Simmer, covered, for 15–20 minutes until soft. Drain well. Melt the butter in the wiped-out pan, add the turnips and fry over a medium heat, shaking the pan from time to time, until they are glazed and golden. Sprinkle with the chopped parsley and chives. Season with salt and pepper and serve.

Thyme, sorrel and angelica

Roman fish sauce

Mussel soup

Herb soup

Cold consommé with herbs

Green eels

Snails with cream

Sardines with thyme

Mackerel parcels

Trout with thyme

Chicken with herbs and vegetables

Rhubarb tart

Butter cake and Breton cake

The murderess's cake

Angelica liqueur

Spice liqueur

Thyme, *thym*, is a herb I associate with the sun-baked hills of southern France and the Mediterranean, but it thrives in northern France just as it does here in any warm and sunny spot, whether in bed, pot or window box. It is a summer herb which dries well and gives its evocative, aromatic flavour to winter dishes of meat and game, but use it with care because it can overpower delicate ingredients.

Sorrel, *oseille*, cousin of the friendly dock leaf which children use to soothe nettle stings, has a flavour a little like spinach but infinitely more bitter. Used in small quantities it adds interest to soups or stuffings for fish and the young leaves are delicious as part of a mixed green salad. Cook a few leaves in a little salted water, drain well and mash to a purée before adding to an omelette.

As well as being cultivated, angelica, *angélique*, also grows wild in northern France; it is a giant member of the parsley family with a strong, somewhat musky smell and flavour. Some nurseries in England sell the plants, which can be grown in a corner of the garden. But beware, it can grow over 2 m (up to 7 feet) tall, so allow plenty of space. It is a bienniel and it is in the second year that it produces its many branched, leafy green stems which when candied are used to decorate and flavour cakes, trifles and confectionery. However, the fresh leaves and stems can be used with discretion to flavour rhubarb tarts or fools, milk puddings, salads and fish stocks.

Roman fish sauce
Sauce garum

Ever since the Romans came to France *garum* has been made all along the coasts of Brittany. Made by fermenting the entrails of small fish in brine, it was probably invented by the Greeks for use as a condiment. Oriental fish sauces such as *nam pla* and *ngnoc-nam*, which can be bought in ethnic shops, are made by a similar process and used with discretion – they are very fishy – are extremely useful for adding flavour to stocks and sauces. This buttery sauce flavoured with fresh thyme flowers and the seeds of fennel is eaten with fish.

1 teaspoon oriental fish sauce
1 teaspoon thyme flowers
1 teaspoon fennel
2 tablespoons water
150 g (6 oz) butter
freshly milled black pepper

Put the fish sauce into a saucepan, add the thyme flowers, fennel seeds and water. Put over a low heat and gradually beat in the butter, adding small pieces at a time as if making mayonnaise. When the sauce is thick, season with pepper.

Mussel soup
Soupe aux moules

There are recipes for mussel soups all along the coasts of northern France. This one, flavoured and coloured with sorrel, lettuce and herbs comes from Brittany. (If you have no sorrel, use spinach leaves instead.) Wash and scrub the mussels well.

1 kg ($2\frac{1}{4}$ lb) small mussels
150 ml ($\frac{1}{4}$ pint) white wine or strong dry cider
2 potatoes, chopped
2 shallots, chopped
1 clove garlic, chopped
1 leek, chopped
handful sorrel leaves
2–3 lettuce leaves
sprigs of parsley and chervil
2 tablespoons tomato purée
freshly milled black pepper
salt
1 tablespoon butter
fried bread croûtons

Put the washed mussels with the wine into a large saucepan and put over a strong heat. As soon as the shells open, remove the mussels with a slotted spoon. Strain the cooking liquid to remove any particles of sand and return to the pot. Add the potatoes, shallots, garlic, leek, sorrel, lettuce leaves, sprigs of parsley and chervil and the tomato purée. Add 1 litre ($1\frac{3}{4}$ pints) of water. Bring to the boil, season with pepper and simmer for 30 minutes. Meanwhile shell the mussels and set them aside. Purée the soup. Add the mussels and heat through. Check the seasoning, adding salt if necessary and stir in the butter. Serve the croûtons separately.

Herb soup
Soupe aux herbes

Leeks, shallots and onions form the base for this speckled green soup which is flavoured with whatever kinds of herbs the Breton cook finds easily to hand. It is delicious just as it is, but if you wish you can stir in a tablespoon or two of crème fraîche just before serving. Either way serve the soup with garlic bread or croûtons.

25 g (1 oz) butter
1 tablespoon oil
2 leeks, sliced
1 onion, chopped
1 shallot, chopped
1 clove garlic, chopped
3–4 tablespoons mixed chopped herbs: parsley, chervil, chives etc.
3–4 sprigs of watercress
3–4 sorrel or spinach leaves, chopped
1 tablespoon flour
salt
freshly milled black pepper
1 bay leaf
sprigs of fresh thyme or 1 teaspoon dried

Heat the butter and oil in a large pan, add the leeks, onion and shallot, cover and leave to sweat for 5 minutes. Add the garlic, herbs, watercress and sorrel or spinach. Mix well and stir in the flour followed by 1 litre ($1\frac{3}{4}$ pints) water. Season with salt and pepper and add the bay leaf and thyme. Bring to the boil and simmer uncovered, to preserve the fresh green of the herbs, for 20–30 minutes. Purée and serve.

Cold consommé with herbs
Consommé froid aux fines herbes

The puritan in us might insist that this delicious clear summer soup from Normandy must be made from a *pot au feu* from our own kitchens. But being a puritan can be hard work; much better take advantage of the modern world and use readily available canned consommé instead. It only takes a few minutes to prepare but time must be allowed for the soup to cool down before being refrigerated for an hour or two. If you have no apple brandy or calvados, use dry sherry instead.

2 cans condensed consommé
handful mixed chopped herbs: parsley, chervil, tarragon, chives, basil
1 mint leaf
4 sorrel leaves
4 tablespoons apple brandy or calvados

Heat the consommé. When it boils add all the other ingredients except the spirit. Remove from the heat and leave to cool. Strain into four small bowls, stir in the apple brandy or calvados and refrigerate for several hours. It will turn into jelly. Eat with a teaspoon.

Green eels
Anguilles au vert

As a nation we tend to be squeamish about eels but if you can overcome this aversion, you'll find them rich and tasty delicacies. Eels are kept alive until they are sold and before they are cooked they need to be skinned; this is not a pleasant task, so it's imperative to ask the fishmonger to do it for you and at the same time ask for the eel to be cut into pieces about 4 cm (1½ in) long. In this recipe from Flanders, the eel is served in a winey sauce flavoured and coloured green with a mixture of sorrel, tarragon, chervil, savory, sage, watercress and spinach.

50 g (2 oz) butter
4–5 shallots, chopped
4–5 sorrel leaves, chopped
1 tablespoon chopped tarragon
2 tablespoons chopped chervil
sprig of savory or thyme
2–3 sage leaves, chopped
1 bunch watercress, chopped
4–5 spinach leaves, chopped
900 g (2 lb) eels cut into 4 cm (1½ in) pieces
1 tablespoon flour
2–3 tablespoons oil
100 ml (4 fl oz) dry white wine
100 ml (4 fl oz) fish stock or water
juice of ½ lemon
salt
freshly milled black pepper
2 tablespoons crème fraîche

Melt the butter in a heavy-based casserole, add the shallots and let them soften before adding the sorrel, tarragon, chervil, savory or thyme, sage, watercress and spinach. Stew them over a medium heat until they soften. Roll the eel pieces in the flour. Heat the oil in a frying pan and brown the pieces of eel all over. Add the eels to the herbs, pour in the wine, stock or water and squeeze over the lemon juice. Season with salt and pepper. Simmer gently for 20 minutes. Just before serving stir in the crème fraîche and transfer to a warm, shallow dish for serving.

Snails with cream
Petits gris à la crème

I have a passion for snails and not just snails out of cans. I like to collect them in my own garden and am involved in a fairly hopeless crusade to persuade my friends to do likewise. No one wants to believe that our common garden snail is the same species as the *petit gris* which thrives in parts of France and everyone is equally reluctant to believe that whatever the variety, all snails are edible. I just think it is more civilized to collect snails to eat than to step on them or entice them to their deaths with slug pellets. If you can overcome your aversion, here is one way they deal with them in Normandy. (Of course, you could serve a can or two of tinned snails in the sauce instead.)

100 garden snails
sprigs of thyme, mint and chervil
2 cloves garlic
salt
freshly milled black pepper
25 g (1 oz) butter
3–4 tablespoons breadcrumbs
1 tablespoon parsley
150 ml ($\frac{1}{4}$ pint) crème fraîche
2 egg yolks
2 tablespoons oil

Collect large garden snails and put them into a clean bucket, cover with a piece of netting and weight it down with a stone. (Snails are surprisingly strong and will escape if not well secured.) Leave in a cool, shady place for at least one week for the snails to be purged of any toxic plants they may have eaten.

Wash them well in several changes of salted water and put them into a saucepan of boiling, salted water. Boil for 5 minutes. Drain and rinse under running water. Return to the saucepan. Cover with cold water and add the sprigs of thyme, mint and chervil, one clove of garlic, crushed, and season with salt and pepper. Bring to the boil, cover and simmer for $1\frac{1}{2}$ hours. Drain once more.

Remove the snails from the shells and put them into a pan with pepper, salt, the butter and breadcrumbs. Stir over a medium heat for a few minutes; add the parsley, the second clove of garlic, finely chopped, and the crème fraîche. Heat through for several minutes. Mix the egg yolks with the oil and stir into the sauce. Let it thicken but not boil. Serve with plenty of French bread.

Sardines with thyme
Sardines grillées

From June to September the sardine boats bring home their catch to Brittany's western ports while in winter these same boats are used for trawling or for lobster and crab fishing. This simple Breton recipe for grilled sardines, with its flavourings of oil and thyme might have come straight from Provence. If you come across fresh anchovies in a Breton market, they can be cooked in the same way. Both fish are quite delicate, so treat them with care. Split them open and remove the innards but retain the heads. Wash them under running cold water.

24 fresh sardines, cleaned
24 sprigs of thyme
salt
freshly milled black pepper
oil
2 lemons, quartered

Heat the grill. Put a sprig of thyme inside each sardine, season with salt and pepper and sprinkle with oil. Put under a hot grill for 2 or 3 minutes. Serve with the lemon quarters.

Mackerel parcels
Maquereaux à la normande

This is a pretty and tasty Normandy recipe for cooking mackerel. Choose sorrel leaves for preference but if not available, spinach will do. The same recipe can be used for other small whole fish such as trout or red mullet.

8 sorrel leaves
25 g (1 oz) butter, softened
4 mackerel
salt
freshly milled black pepper

Heat oven to Gas 5/375°F/190°C. Flatten out the sorrel (or spinach) leaves and spread them with butter. Season the interior of the fish with salt and pepper. Wrap each in two leaves, buttered side next to the fish. Put into a buttered baking dish and bake for 20–25 minutes.

Trout with thyme
Truite au thym

In this recipe from Brittany, the trout are filled with bacon and sprigs of thyme before being fried in butter and oil. They are served with a simple sauce of crème fraîche, lemon juice and parsley.

4 rashers streaky bacon, chopped
4 sprigs of thyme
4 trout
2 tablespoons flour
salt
freshly milled black pepper
1 tablespoon oil
25 g (1 oz) butter
3 tablespoons crème fraîche
juice of 1 lemon
handful parsley, chopped

Heat a frying pan, add the chopped bacon and let it sizzle and brown. Leave to cool. Insert a sprig of thyme and a little bacon into the cavity of each trout. Season the flour with salt and pepper and roll the fish in it. Heat the oil and butter in the frying pan and fry the fish over a medium heat, turning them over once, allowing 3–4 minutes on each side. Remove to a warm serving dish. Make the sauce by returning the pan to the heat, stir the crème fraîche into the cooking juices, season with salt and pepper and squeeze over the lemon juice. Let it bubble and reduce slightly, stirring all the time. Pour the sauce over the fish, sprinkle with the parsley and serve.

Chicken with herbs and vegetables
Waterzooi de poulet

This famous Flemish dish is often made with fish (there's a recipe in *Simply Fish*) but it is delicious with chicken, too. The jointed bird is gently poached on a bed of vegetables flavoured with thyme and other herbs. At the last minute the sauce is enriched with egg yolks and crème fraîche. It is generally served with croûtons (see Etceteras).

25 g (1 oz) butter
1 tablespoon oil
2 onions, chopped
2 leeks, chopped
2 sticks celery, chopped
2 carrots, chopped
3 sprigs of parsley
1 chicken, divided into 8 pieces and skinned
1 bay leaf
3–4 sprigs of fresh thyme or ½ teaspoon dried
2 cloves
300 ml (½ pint) stock or water
salt
freshly milled black pepper
3 egg yolks
3 tablespoons crème fraîche

Heat the butter and oil in a heavy-based casserole and add the chopped onions, leeks, celery, carrots and parsley. Cover and leave to sweat for 10 minutes over a low heat. Lay the chicken pieces on top, add the bay leaf, thyme and cloves, and pour over the stock or water. Season with salt and pepper. Bring to the boil, cover, lower the heat and simmer for 45 minutes. Transfer the chicken and vegetables to a warm, deep serving dish. Boil the remaining liquid hard until reduced by half. Mix the egg yolks with the crème fraîche in a bowl and stir in a ladleful of the hot cooking liquid. Mix, then tip it into the reduced liquid in the casserole, stir well and heat through but do not let it boil or it will curdle. Pour the sauce over the chicken and vegetables and serve.

Rhubarb tart
Pâte de rhubarbe

This tart from Normandy takes only minutes to assemble using bought puff pastry. The rhubarb, subtly flavoured with chopped angelica leaves, is meltingly sweet with just a hint of tartness. If you can't lay your hands on angelica, use ½ teaspoon cinnamon instead. This tart is best served warm.

450 g (1 lb) rhubarb, cut into 5 cm (2 in) lengths
100 g (4 oz) caster or vanilla sugar, plus 1 tablespoon
1 teaspoon finely chopped angelica leaf
puff pastry
egg white

Heat the oven to Gas 7/425°F/220°C. Put the rhubarb into a pie dish; sprinkle the 100 g (4 oz) sugar and the angelica over it. Roll out the pastry to fit and lay it over the top, tucking in the sides and corners.

Brush the pastry with egg white and dust with the remaining tablespoon of sugar. Bake for 30–35 minutes until puffed and golden.

Butter cake and Breton cake
Kouign Amann de Douarnenez and *Gâteau breton*

In Douarnenez, in the heart of Celtic Brittany they make a famous butter cake, *kouign amann*: *kouign* means cake and *amann* is butter. While the tourists soak up the legends of Tristan and Iseult and the drowned city of Is which is said to lie under the waters of the bay, and where the sea-witch Marie-Morgane lures sailors to their deaths, local bakers get on with the more prosaic business of making *kouign amann*.

Variations of this ultra-sweet cake are found all over Brittany. A soft bread dough is spread with nearly half its weight in butter and then copiously sprinkled with sugar. Sometimes almonds and chopped candied angelica are added too. It is set aside in a cool place for an hour and then rolled and turned like puff pastry. This operation is repeated two or three times, before it is spread into a flat disc, brushed with egg or milk and baked in a hot oven until golden. Often the finished cake is sprinkled with icing sugar.

More manageable for the home cook is the humble Breton cake, *gâteau breton*, for which there are dozens of 'the-one-and-only' recipe, but most agree it is made with equal quantities of butter, sugar and flour. In this version, it is flavoured with chopped candied angelica and orange flower water, but often it is quite plain. (The same recipe can be used as a base for an apple flan. If you are doing this, spread the dough evenly over a 25 cm (10 in) flan tin, cover with apple slices – you'll need about 900 g (2 lb) – bake at Gas 6/400°F/200°C for 35 minutes and then brush with apricot glaze, see Index.)

5 egg yolks
225 g (8 oz) flour
2 teaspoons finely chopped candied angelica (optional)
225 g (8 oz) caster sugar
225 g (8 oz) butter, softened and cut in pieces
1 teaspoon orange flower water

Butter a 25 cm (10 in) cake tin. Heat the oven to Gas 5/375°F/190°C. Beat the egg yolks lightly together and reserve a tablespoonful to glaze the finished cake. Mix the flour with the angelica in a large shallow bowl and make a hollow in the middle. Into this hollow put the sugar, egg yolks, butter and orange flower water, in that order. Using your fingers, begin by working the eggs and butter together, then gradually work in the sugar and flour until you have a smooth dough. As you work, the mixture becomes very sticky: use the blunt blade of a knife to scrape it off your fingers and finish mixing with the knife. (Or you could use a food processor!)

Flour your hands and, on a floured board, roll the mixture into a ball. Transfer to the cake tin, pressing the mixture flat with the back of your hand. Brush all over with the reserved egg yolk. Use the prongs of a fork to make a criss-cross pattern over the top. Bake for 20 minutes and then lower the heat to Gas 4/350°F/180°C and bake for a further 30 minutes until cake is golden brown. Leave to cool and then turn on to a wire tray. Serve in slices with perhaps a dollop of cream.

The murderess's cake
Gâteau d'Hélène Jegado

This delectable cake is reputed to be the one and the same with which a certain lady, who lived in Rennes, poisoned some 37 people, 25 of whom died. Once her victims were dead she made a great show of praying and watching by their bedside. She was executed on 26 February 1862. (The cake itself is harmless enough; it was the arsenic with which it was laced that finished her victims off!)

1 tablespoon raisins
1 tablespoon calvados or rum
100 g (4 oz) butter
100 g (4 oz) caster sugar
2 eggs, plus 1 yolk
225 g (8 oz) flour, sifted
1 teaspoon baking powder
1 teaspoon chopped candied angelica
75 g (3 oz) candied mixed peel, chopped
75 g (3 oz) almonds, chopped
pinch of cinnamon

Heat oven to Gas 4/350°F/180°C. Soak the raisins in the calvados or rum. Lightly butter an 18 cm (7 in) non-stick cake tin, or line an ordinary one with waxed paper. Cream the butter and sugar together until white and fluffy. Beat in, one at a time, the two eggs plus the extra yolk. Fold in the sifted flour, baking powder, angelica, mixed peel, almonds, cinnamon and the raisins and their calvados or rum. Turn the mixture into the cake tin, smooth the top, making a slight hollow in the centre, and bake for 1–1¼ hours, until a skewer inserted in the middle comes out clean. Leave in the tin for 5–10 minutes before turning on to a wire tray to cool.

Angelica liqueur
Ratafia d'angélique

Around Dinard in Brittany, the young leaf stalks of angelica are used to make a liqueur. These can either be chopped and used right away or left to dry until they become hard as wood. The dried stalks give a more intense flavour. Look out for them on market stalls in France specializing in herbs and spices. The French make the liqueur with *eau-de-vie*, but in Britain you could use vodka. Remember, although it will be ready to drink after three months, like most home produced liqueurs, it will improve noticeably if kept for at least a year.

Fill a preserving jar with 225 g (8 oz) chopped angelica stalks, add a handful of cloves, a vanilla pod or cinnamon stick and a grating of nutmeg. Completely cover with the *eau-de-vie* or vodka and leave for two months if the angelica is fresh, three if it has been dried. After this time, melt 225 g (8 oz) sugar in a little water, let it bubble for 5 minutes and leave to cool. Strain the liqueur, mix with the syrup and taste; if necessary add more sugar syrup. Bottle and leave at least one more month before drinking in tiny glasses as a digestif at the end of a meal.

Spice liqueur
Liqueur flamande

In Flanders they make a spicy liqueur which combines angelica seeds with coriander, star anise, cloves, cinnamon and orange peel.

1 teaspoon angelica seeds
1 teaspoon coriander seeds
2 star anise
2 cloves
1 cinnamon stick
1 piece of orange peel
1 litre *eau-de-vie* or vodka
450 g (1 lb) sugar

Put the angelica and coriander seeds, the star anise, cloves, cinnamon and orange peel into a litre bottle of spirit and leave for two weeks.

When the fortnight is up, put the sugar into a saucepan with 150 ml ($\frac{1}{4}$ pint) water, bring slowly to the boil and simmer for 5 minutes.

Allow to cool and add to the liqueur. Seal and leave for four days. Strain into bottles and leave at least a further ten days before sampling. But the longer you leave it the better!

Mustard, capers and salt

Mustard sauce

Dandelion salad

Trawlermen's salad

Normandy salad

Prawn and apple salad

Herrings with mustard

Mackerel with fennel

Salt cod tongues and cheeks

Pork chops with mustard sauce

Roast loin of pork with mustard

Roast rack of lamb

Rabbit with turnips

Beetroot with Breton vinaigrette

Salmon parcels with capers

Nasturtium flower vinegar

Salmon with herbs in salt

Chicken in salt

Soused sprats

Pickled samphire

Eggs *en cocotte*

It may be Dijon and Bordeaux which are most famous for their mustards, *moutardes*, but it is also produced, though on a much smaller scale, in Yvetot, a market town in the chalky farmland of Normandy's Caux plateau. The name of the town has Viking origins, stemming from Yvetofta on Lake Ivo in Sweden. It was heavily bombed in 1940 and nowadays, apart from the yellow expanses of the mustard fields, its greatest attraction is the modern church of St-Pierre with dazzling stained-glass windows by Max Ingrand. Brittany also produced mustard in the last century, where it was known as *moutarde celtique*. Until fairly recently mustard in England was only sold in powdered form, to be mixed with water and left to infuse for 5–10 minutes before using. In France, mixed mustard has been the norm, either pale or dark, depending upon whether it is mixed with herbs such as tarragon. For cooking purposes, the best kind to use is pale, Dijon-type mustard, which has a clean, sharp and salty flavour with a strong hot taste. If you want to use Normandy mustard look out for Olida which is the kind produced in Yvetot.

Although capers, *câpres*, do not naturally grow in northern climates, they have been used in Breton cooking for centuries, obviously brought in by the fishermen trading between Brittany and southern France. They are the flower bud of a small bush which grows wild in the Mediterranean; picked in the morning, they are left to dry for a day then pickled in salted vinegar. The Bretons use them, along with gherkins, to flavour sauces and salads. Nasturtium buds and seeds can be preserved in vinegar and used in place of capers, as *faux câpres*. You need a good summer and plenty of plants. Gather them each day when they are still small and green. Wash and dry them in kitchen paper, put them into a screw-topped jar with a spoonful of sea salt and cover with wine vinegar.

Sea salt, *sel marin*, one of Brittany's most flourishing products, is still produced in the old way in the salt marshes chequered with tidal reservoirs beneath Guérande. Here, between June and September, the *paludiers*, salt workers, rake up the grey salt, *sel gris*, which forms as the shallow water of the *oeillets* evaporates, while the women skim the white salt off the surface. The grey, moist crystals of salt from Guérande are sold in supermarkets all over France and are ideal for cooking and flavouring. Not so good for a salt mill, however, as their dampness clogs up the mechanism! Fish or meat, usually flavoured with herbs, can be cooked in a casing of salt, ideally using this Breton *sel gris*.

Mustard sauce
Sauce St-Malo

This mustardy sauce is extravagant on the wine but does give a delicious oomph to plainly grilled, poached or fried fish. You could always use cider instead and if you have no fish stock, add the equivalent amount of water and give it the fishy flavour by either breaking up an anchovy fillet and frying it with the onion, or add a dash of concentrated oriental fish sauce sold in many ethnic shops under names such as *nam pla*.

50 g (2 oz) butter
1 onion, chopped
300 ml (½ pint) dry white wine
sprigs of parsley and thyme
1 bay leaf
150 ml (¼ pint) fish stock
1 tablespoon made mustard

Melt half the butter in a saucepan and fry the chopped onion until soft. Add the wine, sprigs of parsley and thyme and the bay leaf. Boil hard until reduced by two-thirds. Strain and return to the pan, stir in the fish stock and reduce again by one-third. Dilute the mustard in a little of the sauce and stir it into the mixture. Beat in the remaining butter in small pieces.

Dandelion salad
Salade de pissenlits

I remember as a child in Devon being told that if you eat dandelions you'll wet the bed. The French agree, as their name for dandelion, *pissenlit*, means just that. In spring few lawns are free of these tender-leaves plants and when you dig them up (but before you treat them with weedkiller), consider making this salad which is dressed with a mustardy vinaigrette. It's important to use fresh, young plants. Of course instead of dandelions you could use rocket, lamb's lettuce or any other sort of green salad.

8 dandelion plants
4 hard-boiled eggs
2 cloves garlic, chopped
1 teaspoon mustard
3 tablespoons oil
½ tablespoon vinegar
salt
freshly milled black pepper
50 g (2 oz) streaky bacon, chopped
1 tablespoon butter

Wash the dandelion leaves, dry them and put into a salad bowl. Peel and halve the eggs. Put the garlic, mustard, oil, vinegar, salt and pepper into a screw-topped jar and shake it well. Fry the bacon in the butter until crisp and tip on to the dandelion leaves. Top with the eggs and pour over the sauce. Mix at table.

Trawlermen's salad
Salade des chalutiers

The fishing port of Fécamp was once the home of Normandy's huge fleet of trawlers which fished as far as Newfoundland for cod, herring and mackerel. Nowadays the outer basin houses a large yachting marina but fresh and frozen fish is still unloaded in the Bassin Freycinet and herring-curing continues to be one of the town's industries. This recipe uses fillets which are sold, ready-packed, all over France. Here you could use kipper fillets. In the original recipe, the salad is made with dandelion leaves, but in the absence of these you could use lamb's lettuce, rocket or watercress – or just plain lettuce.

1 tablespoon made mustard
3 tablespoons oil
1 tablespoon vinegar
salt
freshly milled black pepper
1–2 tablespoons chopped mixed herbs: parsley, chervil, chives and tarragon
4 fillets smoked herring
225 g (8 oz) young dandelion leaves
garlic croûtons

Mix the mustard, oil and vinegar and season with salt and pepper. Stir in the herbs. Cut the herring fillets in thick slices, lay in a dish and pour over the dressing. Leave to marinate for at least an hour. To serve, top with the dandelion leaves and sprinkle the croûtons over the salad. (To make garlic croûtons: Rub stale French bread with a cut clove of garlic, cut into small cubes and fry in hot oil until crisp and golden, turning once.)

Normandy salad
Salade normande à la moutarde

This mixed salad of chicory, apples and walnuts looks pretty if you use red-skinned apples such as English Spartans. The mustard-flavoured dressing can be used for other crisp salads too. In Normandy use Yvetot mustard, otherwise Dijon will do just as well.

2–3 tablespoons crème fraîche
½ teaspoon made mustard
juice of 1 lemon
salt
freshly milled black pepper
450 g (1 lb) chicory, sliced
2 firm red-skinned apples, quartered, cored and finely sliced
50 g (2 oz) shelled walnuts, chopped

Mix the crème fraîche with the mustard and lemon juice and season with salt and pepper. Put the sliced chicory, apples and walnuts into a salad bowl and stir in the dressing.

Prawn and apple salad
Salade normande au cidre sec

This is a light and crisp salad which can be served as a starter or as part of a summer lunch or supper. The dressing is made with crème fraîche, mustard and cider but if you feel this is too rich use a thick yoghurt instead.

2 tablespoons crème fraîche
½ teaspoon made mustard
2 tablespoons strong dry cider
salt
freshly milled black pepper
1 small frizzy or other lettuce
3 crisp eating apples, peeled, cored and finely sliced
225 g (8 oz) peeled prawns

Mix the crème fraîche with the mustard and cider and season with salt and pepper. Wash and dry the lettuce and break it into pieces and put into a shallow bowl. Add the sliced apples and the prawns and mix gently. Pour over the dressing, mix again and serve.

Herrings with mustard
Harengs à la tréportaise

This recipe comes from Tréport, which is a very attractive and popular old fishing port with a string of fish restaurants along its quay, right on the border between Normandy and Picardy.

Herring are cheap but they are also bony, so beg the fishmonger to bone them for you, but if you daren't, it's not too difficult to do yourself. Slit the fish along the belly to the tail. Lay it bellyside down on a table and press with your thumb along the back bone; you will feel the bone begin to separate. Turn the fish over and, using a knife and your fingers, ease out the spine and all the little bones attached. Cut it free at the head and tail and lift out. Any tiny bones left in can be removed with tweezers.

4 herrings
4 tablespoons oil
2 tablespoons wine vinegar
1 lemon, sliced
2 onions, finely chopped
2–3 sprigs of thyme
2–3 sprigs of parsley
1 bay leaf
salt
freshly milled black pepper
50 g (2 oz) butter
1 tablespoon made mustard

Put the herrings into a shallow, non-metallic dish with the oil, vinegar, sliced lemon, onions, thyme, parsley and bay leaf and season with salt and pepper. Leave for 2 hours. Melt the butter in a frying pan. Wipe the herrings with kitchen paper and fry them for 3–4 minutes on each side. Put them on to a warm serving dish. Strain the juices from the marinade into the frying pan and let them bubble. Remove from heat, stir in the mustard and pour the sauce over the fish.

Mackerel with fennel
Maquereaux au fenouil

Mackerel are delicious grilled or baked, the cavities spread with mustard and stuffed with fennel.

1–2 teaspoons made mustard
4 mackerel
4 sprigs of fennel
freshly milled black pepper
oil

Heat grill. Spread a little mustard inside the cavity of each fish and add a sprig of fennel. Brush the grill pan with oil, add the fish, season lightly with pepper and grill for 3–5 minutes on each side. Or sprinkle with a little oil and bake in a pre-heated oven, Gas 6/400°F/200°C, for 15–20 minutes.

Salt cod tongues and cheeks
Langues et joues de morue

Tongues and cheeks of salt cod are sold in fish shops and on market stalls along the northern coast of France and are considered a delicacy. Salt cod, along with other poor man's food such as truffles, frogs' legs and snails, has become an expensive luxury and few peasants now eat it on a Friday, but if you want to try the tongues and cheeks here is what you do.

To rid them of their saltiness soak them under running cold water for at least 6 hours – the village fountain perhaps? – drain and simmer them in water for 5 minutes. Serve them hot with a sharp vinaigrette made by mixing 2 tablespoons of wine vinegar with 1 teaspoon of mustard, pepper and 4 tablespoons of oil flavoured with chopped parsley, thyme and tarragon. This vinaigrette should be made at least an hour ahead to allow the flavour of the herbs to impregnate the sauce.

Pork chops with mustard sauce
Côtes de porc normandes

This is an adaptation of a Normandy dish which sometimes includes grated cheese and crème fraîche; this version is less rich. The chops (the same recipe can be used for escalopes) are gently cooked in a sauce of wine or cider, mustard and onions and emerge from the pan moist, tender and full of flavour. Serve them with apple slices gently fried in butter or perhaps a *purée bretonne*, which is a mixture of mashed potatoes and carrots (see Index).

50 g (2 oz) butter
2 onions, chopped
4 lean pork chops
2 tablespoons cider vinegar or white wine vinegar
100 ml (4 fl oz) dry white wine or cider
1 tablespoon made mustard
3 gherkins, chopped
salt
freshly milled black pepper

Melt half the butter in a frying pan and fry the chopped onions until golden. Remove to a bowl. Add the remaining butter to the pan and fry the chops for 3 or 4 minutes on each side over a medium heat. Mix the vinegar, wine or cider, mustard and chopped gherkins with the onions and pour over the chops. Season with salt and pepper, bring just to boiling point, cover (either with a lid or sheet of foil) and simmer over a low heat for 10 minutes. Remove the chops to a warm serving dish and boil the sauce hard until reduced by half. Pour over the chops and serve immediately.

Roast loin of pork with mustard
Larblez au four

Larblez is the Breton name for pork loin which the French sometimes call *un train de côtes de porc*. Here it is spiked with garlic and spread with mustard before being roasted with onions and potatoes flavoured with sprigs of rosemary. Accompany it with a green salad or red cabbage with apples.

1 kg ($2\frac{1}{4}$ lb) loin of pork
2 cloves garlic, cut in slivers
1–2 teaspoons made mustard
freshly milled black pepper
3 tablespoons oil
700 g ($1\frac{1}{2}$ lb) potatoes, cut in even-sized pieces
350 g (12 oz) onions, roughly chopped
salt
sprigs of rosemary
1 tablespoon chopped parsley

Heat the oven to Gas 7/425°F/220°C. Put the pork into a roasting tin and cut slits in it with a pointed knife into which you slip the slivers of garlic. Spread the meat with mustard and season with pepper. Sprinkle with 2 tablespoons of the oil and put into the oven for 15 minutes. Meanwhile blanch the potatoes by putting them into a pan of boiling, salted water for 2–3 minutes. Drain well. At the end of the 15 minutes, lower the oven to Gas 6/400°F/200°C. Surround the meat with the onions and potatoes, season them with salt and pepper and sprinkle over the remaining oil. Tuck the sprigs of rosemary among them. Roast for 1¼ hours, basting 2 or 3 times. To serve, divide the meat into chops, put them on a warm serving dish surrounded by the vegetables. Sprinkle with the parsley.

Roast rack of lamb
Carré d'agneau à la sauce moutarde

In this recipe from Normandy, the lamb is roasted in a coating of parsley and breadcrumbs and served with a sauce made by beating melted butter into a tablespoon of mustard. It appealed to me originally because it breaks away from the idea that somehow mustard only goes with certain meats. It was pleasant to discover how good it is with lamb.

- 2 best end of neck joints, each with 6 chops
- 100 g (4 oz) butter
- 3–4 tablespoons breadcrumbs
- 3–4 tablespoons chopped parsley
- salt
- freshly milled black pepper
- 1 tablespoon made mustard

Heat the oven to Gas 7/425°F/220°C. Put the joints into a roasting tin, fat side up. Melt 25 g (1 oz) of the butter and brush it over the meat. Mix the breadcrumbs with the parsley and sprinkle evenly over the lamb. Roast for 30 minutes. Divide into chops, put on to a hot dish and season with salt and pepper. Melt the remaining butter. Put the mustard into a bowl and gradually beat in the butter as if making mayonnaise. Serve separately.

Rabbit with turnips
Lapin aux navets

In this Flemish recipe, a rabbit is marinated with herbs, onions, shallots and garlic in cider for several hours before being gently simmered in a mustard-flavoured sauce. The turnips are added towards the end of the cooking time and their slightly bitter, peppery taste is a delicious contrast to the sweet flavour of the rabbit.

1 rabbit, divided into 8 pieces
300 ml (½ pint) dry cider
2 onions, chopped
2 shallots, chopped
2 cloves garlic, chopped
sprigs of thyme and parsley
1 bay leaf
8 black peppercorns
1 oz (25 g) butter or 2 tablespoons oil
2 teaspoons flour
salt
freshly milled black pepper
1 tablespoon made mustard
450 g (1 lb) young turnips
handful parsley, chopped

Put the pieces of rabbit into a non-metallic bowl with the cider, onions, shallots, garlic, thyme, parsley, bay leaf and peppercorns, and leave to marinate for several hours. Drain in a colander over a bowl. Remove the meat and dry it with kitchen paper. Heat the butter or oil in a flameproof casserole and brown the pieces of meat all over, in two batches if necessary. Remove to a plate. Add the drained onions, shallots and garlic from the marinade and fry until golden, but not brown, over a medium heat, stirring from time to time. Mix in the flour and stir over a low heat for 2 minutes. Gradually mix in the liquid from the marinade and stir until the mixture thickens and reaches boiling point. Return the rabbit pieces, season with salt and pepper and stir in the mustard. Cover, lower heat and simmer for 1 hour.

After 45 minutes, peel and quarter the turnips and simmer them for 10 minutes in salted water. Drain, add them to the rabbit and continue cooking for a further 10 minutes. Using a slotted spoon, remove the rabbit pieces and turnips to a warm serving dish. Rapidly boil the sauce until it is reduced by half, pour over the rabbit and turnips, dust with parsley and serve.

Beetroot with Breton vinaigrette
Betterave en salade

The sweetness of beetroot needs the complement of a sharpish sauce and Brittany's shallot and herb vinaigrette is ideal. This sauce is not just restricted to beetroot but can be used with all sorts of other salads as well. If you are watching your cholesterol use yoghurt instead of the crème fraîche.

- 350 g (12 oz) cooked beetroot, sliced
- 1 tablespoon vinegar
- salt
- freshly milled black pepper
- 6 tablespoons oil
- 1 shallot, chopped
- 1–2 tablespoons chopped mixed herbs (such as parsley, chervil and chives)
- 1 tablespoon chopped capers or gherkins
- 1–2 tablespoons crème fraîche

Arrange the sliced beetroot in a shallow dish. Shake all the remaining ingredients together in a screw-topped jar and pour over the beetroot.

Salmon parcels with capers
Saumon en papillote aux câpres

The peppery flavour of capers provides a sharp contrast to the mildness of salmon. In this recipe they are added as a garnish although sometimes the Bretons use a tablespoon or two to flavour a béchamel sauce to be served with grilled fish. Serve these salmon steaks with steamed or boiled potatoes.

- 4 salmon steaks
- salt
- freshly milled black pepper
- juice of ½ lemon
- 50 g (2 oz) butter
- 1–2 tablespoons capers

Heat oven to Gas 6/400°F/200°C. Cut 4 squares of foil large enough to encase each steak and lay one on each. Season with salt and pepper and lemon juice. Dot with the butter. Fold into secure but loose parcels. Bake for 15–20 minutes. To serve, open the parcels and sprinkle with the capers.

Nasturtium flower vinegar
Vinaigre aux capucines

Nasturtium leaves and flowers picked at their prime give a peppery flavour to salads. The flowers can also be used to flavour and colour vinegar a deep orange-pink. Left to steep for a month the vinegar can be used to give a sweet pungency to salad dressings.

Handful nasturtium flowers
2 cloves garlic, peeled but left whole
2 shallots, chopped
salt
freshly milled black pepper
1 bottle white wine vinegar or cider vinegar

Put the flower heads into a clean bottle with the garlic, chopped shallots, salt and pepper. Fill to the top with the vinegar. Leave to infuse for a month before straining and re-bottling.

Salmon with herbs in salt
Saumon au sel marin

In Brittany you might be lucky and come across bass, bar, or tuna, *thon*, cooked in this way, but I am suggesting salmon because it is relatively cheap and easy to find in Britain. The fish emerges perfectly cooked, juicy and full of flavour and without a hint of over-salting. Dover sole can be treated in the same way but reduce the cooking time by half. Ideally, use the moist grey salt from Guérande, otherwise use coarse white salt crystals and moisten them with egg white.

900 g (2 lb) salmon
50 g (2 oz) Breton herb butter (see Index)
1–2 kg (2¼–4½ lb) coarse sea salt

Heat the oven to Gas 7/425°F/220°C. Fill the cavity of the fish with herb butter. Put a layer of salt about 2 cm (1 in) thick on the base of an oven dish. Place the fish on it and completely cover with another layer of salt to the same thickness as the first. Bake for 25–30 minutes. Remove from the oven and allow to cool for 5 minutes. Carefully turn out on to a board, knocking the base to dislodge the now solid salt. Carefully break away the salt crust using a wooden mallet or pestle.

Chicken in salt
Poularde au sel

A chicken roasted this way needs no attention while it is in the oven; it will emerge moist and golden and does not taste over-salted. But you may on reflection decide to wrap it in foil instead!

1 chicken
2–3 kg (4½–6½ lb) coarse sea salt

Heat the oven to Gas 7/425°F/220°C. Put a layer of salt about 3 cm (1½ in) thick into a very deep roasting tin. Put the chicken on top. Completely cover it with salt. Put it into the oven for 1½ hours. To serve, break away the salt using a wooden mallet or pestle.

Soused sprats
Sprats en potiche

From Douarnenez, with its Celtic legends of King Mark and Tristan and Iseult, comes this very down-to-earth recipe for soused or potted sprats. Occasionally in the winter months you may come across these little fish, which are so tender they don't need to be gutted. After sousing them, keep them for at least a week – I've eaten them after two months – and then eat them with hot jacket potatoes filled with plenty of butter.

900 g (2 lb) sprats
2 tablespoons sea salt
300 ml (½ pint) cider vinegar or white wine vinegar
600 ml (1 pint) water
1 tablespoon caster sugar
1 carrot, finely chopped
1 bay leaf
2 sprigs of thyme
2 cloves
1 teaspoon mustard seeds
1 teaspoon peppercorns
6 shallots, finely chopped
oil

Wipe the sprats dry with kitchen paper. Lay them in a deep dish and cover them with a layer of coarse sea salt. Leave overnight. The following day, put the vinegar, water, sugar, carrot, bay leaf, thyme, cloves, mustard seeds and peppercorns into a large saucepan, bring to the boil and boil uncovered for 30 minutes. Wipe the fish, cut off and discard the heads. Pack the fish interspersed with the finely chopped shallot, into a 1 litre (1¾ pint) preserving jar. Remove the flavoured vinegar from the heat and set aside to cool. When cold, pour it over the fish. Top with oil, cover and leave for at least one week before eating.

Pickled samphire
Salicornes confites

Salicorne, our glasswort or marsh samphire, is sometimes sold in this country in upmarket fishmongers or in local markets. It grows wild in the salt marshes of Brittany, Normandy and Flanders as well as in places like our own East Anglia. It has brilliant green fleshy stems and can be pickled, or boiled or steamed until tender and eaten with melted butter like asparagus. Rock samphire, which grows in the gaps between rocks, has many aliases, including St Peter's cress and sea fennel (in French *criste-marine*, *perce-pierre* and *casse-pierre*). It is unrelated to marsh samphire but can be similarly prepared. In Brittany the most renowned pickled samphire comes from around the Guérandais, and I've even managed to buy jars of it produced from there in a large hypermarket in the south of France. Use it just as you would gherkins, to garnish salads or with cold meats.

450 g (1 lb) samphire
100 g (4 oz) coarse sea salt
1 bottle wine vinegar
sprigs of tarragon
18 peppercorns

Put the samphire in a large bowl, add the salt and leave to macerate for 24 hours. Drain well, return to the bowl, completely cover with wine vinegar and leave for a further 24 hours. Lift out the samphire using a slotted spoon, and put it into preserving jars with the tarragon and peppercorns. Boil the vinegar from the bowl for 5 minutes and set aside to cool. Strain, half-fill each jar and top up with fresh vinegar. Seal and leave for at least two weeks before eating.

Eggs *en cocotte*

Oeufs en cocotte aux salicornes confites

The original recipe from Flanders used pickled rock samphire, *perce-pierre*, but you can of course use any kind of pickled samphire (see the previous recipe).

50 g (2 oz) butter
salt
freshly milled black pepper
2 tablespoons pickled samphire
8 eggs
4 tablespoons double cream
white wine vinegar

Butter four cocotte pots generously and season with salt and pepper. Divide the pickled samphire between them and break two eggs into each. Coat with the cream. Stand the pots in a frying pan half-filled with water and bring it to the boil on top of the stove. Cover the pan and cook gently until the eggs are set. Serve sprinkled with a little vinegar.

Spring and Summer Vegetables

It is late April, and as I gaze out of my window in Wandsworth at the fruit trees in the neighbouring gardens, I dream of the orchards in Brittany and wonder if, like here, the white pear blossom will already have fallen and if the apple trees, which only recently were covered in tight rose-pink buds, are now in full bloom. Does everyone there, like everyone here, have a lift in their hearts knowing that winter is over?

In a few days we will arrive in Calais to an early morning mist through which the sun is beginning to break and we will drive between the wide, open fields of the Nord already tilled and planted with the summer crops. At this time of year, despite the leafless trees, the evidence of burgeoning life is everywhere in a profusion of green, yellow and white. The dun-coloured earth is lined with tender sprouting corn guarded by scarecrows and the grass verges are bright with the first of the wild flowers, from dandelions to daisies. A windmill stands, its four sails skeletal against the grey sky, surrounded by fields carpeted with citrus-yellow rape and all along the edge of the road and bordering the trees is the deeper gold of gorse and the snow white of may blossom just beginning to open.

In no time at all the first early vegetables, artichokes, carrots and peas will be on sale in the markets from Brittany's golden belt, *la ceinture dorée* between St-Malo and the Loire, from the Manche, the 'sleeve' of Normandy and the *hortillonages*, the market gardens of Picardy. Soon the first of the asparagus will arrive and as the season progresses will come the tender broad beans, spring onions, succulent French beans and sun-ripened tomatoes.

All over France the markets thrive and it is there that you will find the best of the crop. Stallholders come from far and wide. Many are professionals who make their living going from market to market during the week, but others are local producers, who take a stand to sell what they grow and may or may not be there another time. French cooks shop without inhibition, selecting exactly what they want and a stallholder wouldn't dream of telling them not to touch. This is a custom that has been adopted by many of our supermarkets and let's hope the idea spreads to our own market traders who mostly get very cross if you dare to prod or touch any of their wares.

Artichokes

Artichokes – along with cauliflowers – have become the emblem of the Breton farmers. Never very cheap in Britain, it is hard to imagine ever growing tired of them, but in Brittany they produce so many that the farmers, protesting at low profits, frequently dump whole lorry-loads, hoping that by blocking the roads they will draw attention to their plight.

Related to the thistle, artichokes have been enjoyed in the Mediterranean region for thousands of years, and came to France via Italy in the sixteenth century. Their name probably derives from the arabic *d'al karchouf*, which the Italians turned into *articioco*, and the French *artichaut*. They are grown all over France but principally in the north in Brittany and in southern France in Roussillon and Provence.

In the golden belt between St-Pol-de-Léon, Paimpol and St-Malo you come across field after field of this flavoursome vegetable which the Bretons call the *gros vert de Laon*, the *gros camus* or sometimes simply *le breton*, the row upon row of swollen, top-heavy heads as typical of the region as the sunflowers of the Midi. Here, from January to September, lorry-loads of Breton vegetables are auctioned before being sent on their way all over France and to Roscoff for shipment to Plymouth.

Whether you select your artichokes from the huge piles on French market stalls or from the more meagre display in an English greengrocer or supermarket, choose firm, fresh-looking heads. Avoid ones which look dry, with leaves that are beginning to brown and curl with age. If not to be cooked right away, keep them in the fridge or stand their stems in a bowl of cold water. Once cooked, eat within a day, as they don't keep well and develop unpleasant toxins.

Very small, very young, newly formed artichokes can be eaten raw with coarse salt and plenty of butter. When they get a bit bigger they can be cooked whole in butter or oil with garlic and herbs, and perhaps a bit of bacon, and served as an accompaniment to a roast. Sliced thinly, with the choke removed, small artichokes can be dipped in batter and fried like fritters, which the Bretons call *biguezennou*. Sadly, unless you grow your own or are lucky to be in Brittany at the right moment, you are unlikely to come across such tender examples.

In some of the recipes when just the bottoms are used, frozen or canned bottoms can be used instead if fresh artichokes are not available or they are just too expensive, although they are not as sweet and succulent as fresh. And in some of the recipes you could substitute Italian baby artichokes sold in jars or canned artichoke hearts.

Preparing and cooking artichokes

Half fill a large bowl with cold water and add a tablespoon of salt and one of vinegar or lemon juice. Don't cut off the stems, but break them away, which will help to pull out any coarse fibres piercing the heart. Trim the bases evenly so that the artichokes can stand upright. Fancy cooks and restaurants believe in trimming the points of the leaves, but it makes no difference to the enjoyment of eating and causes extra work. As you prepare them, drop each artichoke, upside down, into the bowl of acidulated water – this prevents them turning black and evacuates any insects. Leave to soak for half an hour or so.

Cook them in boiling, salted water, with a dash of lemon juice or vinegar, for 25–45 minutes. They are ready when the base leaves can easily be detached. They must be well drained and then can be served either hot, warm or cold with a sauce. (If to be served cold, cool them quickly in a bowl of cold water before draining well.)

How to eat a whole artichoke

The simplest and arguably most delicious way of eating mature artichokes is to serve them whole, one for each person. Prepare and cook them as above and have a bowl of sauce on the table (which can simply be a bowl of melted butter, mayonnaise or vinaigrette or something a little more complicated like béchamel, tartare, or *sauce bretonne froide* (see Index). Using their fingers, everyone detaches the leaves one by one, dipping the bases into the sauce. This fleshy, edible bit is then scraped off between the teeth and the rest of the leaves discarded on to the plate. Finally the choke, a cluster of fibres protecting the succulent saucer-shaped base of the artichoke, is reached. This hairy choke must be carefully cut and eased away so that the base can be divided into three or four delectable mouthfuls.

Artichokes braised in cider
Les bretons braisés

In this recipe, in which they are served as a vegetable to accompany a roast or a chicken, the artichokes are cut into quarters and the chokes removed. They make a most attractive garnish.

3–4 medium-sized artichokes
salt
1–2 tablespoons lemon juice
2 tablespoons oil
100 g (4 oz) lean bacon, chopped
2 onions, chopped
4 cloves garlic, chopped or crushed
1 clove
few sprigs of thyme
freshly milled black pepper
300 ml (½ pint) stock or water
300 ml (½ pint) strong dry cider
handful parsley, chopped

Trim the artichokes by slicing off and discarding the top third of each leaf. Cut them into quarters and with a sharp, pointed knife cut out the inedible choke from each quarter. Soak the quartered artichokes in a bowl of salted water with the lemon juice as you go. Heat the oil in a pan and fry the bacon and onion for a few minutes. Add the garlic, clove, sprigs of thyme and the quartered artichokes. Season with salt and pepper and pour over the stock or water and the cider. Bring to the boil and simmer for 20–30 minutes until tender. Put into a warm serving dish, strain over a little of the sauce and garnish with the parsley.

Preparing artichoke bottoms

Eating artichokes whole is a pleasant, but time-consuming process, and if you eat them often, as the Bretons do, I suppose eventually you could become tired of the ritual. So there are recipes which call for the leaves to be discarded and just the *fond*, the base or bottom, to be used (sometimes more crudely called the *cul*, or bum!).

Prepare and cook the artichokes, as described at the beginning of this section. Drain and put them into a bowl of cold water until cool enough to handle. Pull off all the leaves until you reach the choke. Carefully prise this away with a teaspoon and discard. If the bottoms are not to be used right away, squeeze lemon juice over them to prevent them going black.

Artichoke leaves

The puritan in me can't bear the thought of not using every part of the artichoke, but this is overcome by serving the leaves as a starter at another meal by arranging them attractively on a dish with a bowl of vinaigrette or other sauce in the centre.

Artichoke bottoms with butter
Fonds d'artichauts manchais

In Normandy they serve artichoke bottoms with hot melted butter and tarragon. Allow two artichokes per person. Cook them, divest them of their leaves, cut away the choke and press a hollow in each fond with the back of a spoon. Put them into a bowl of hot water to keep warm, while you melt the butter. Drain the bottoms well and pour a tablespoon of butter into each hollow, garnishing each with a leaf or two of tarragon.

Artichoke bottoms with prawns and Breton sauce
Fonds d'artichauts aux crevettes à la sauce bretonne

For this pretty, cold starter from Brittany, the whole artichoke is used, but the leaves are removed and the pulp is scraped from their bases to be mixed with the prawns to make a filling for the bottoms.

4 whole cooked artichokes
1 tablespoon vinegar
salt
freshly milled black pepper
generous pinch of nutmeg
parsley, chervil and chives, chopped
1 tablespoon finely chopped gherkins or capers
6 tablespoons oil
150 g (6 oz) cooked prawns
2–3 tablespoons crème fraîche
lettuce leaves

Remove the leaves from the artichokes and, holding a few in one hand at a time, use a teaspoon to scrape the fleshy bases into a bowl. With the teaspoon, scrape away and discard the choke, and set aside the artichoke bottoms in a bowl of cold water. Mix the vinegar in a large bowl with the salt, pepper, nutmeg, parsley, chervil, chives and chopped gherkins or capers. Gradually beat in the oil. Add the prawns and the pulp scraped from the leaves and mix carefully. Set aside. Just before serving, mix in the crème fraîche and pile the mixture into the drained artichoke bottoms. Serve on a platter garnished with the lettuce leaves.

Artichoke bottoms stuffed with mushrooms
Fonds d'artichauts aux champignons

Artichokes, mushrooms and lemon juice have an affinity and there are many variations on this theme. In Normandy they serve flat field mushrooms stuffed with a mixture of mashed artichoke bottoms, ham and a lemon-flavoured mayonnaise. This Brittany recipe turns that idea on its head. It's the bottoms which are stuffed with an attractive mixture of dark mushrooms in a lemony cream sauce. Serve as a starter.

1 clove garlic, chopped
juice of ½ lemon
salt
freshly milled black pepper
4 tablespoons crème fraîche
100 g (4 oz) mushrooms, thinly sliced
4–5 lettuce leaves
4 artichoke bottoms
handful parsley, chopped

Mix the garlic and lemon juice with the salt and pepper and beat in the crème fraîche. Add the sliced mushrooms, cover and leave for an hour or two. Arrange the lettuce leaves on a dish and lay the artichoke bottoms on top. Spoon the mushroom mixture into the centre of each and pile any remainder into the middle of the dish. Sprinkle with parsley.

Artichoke omelette
Omelette aux culs d'artichauts

Serve this Breton omelette on its own or with a tomato or Beaumanoir sauce (see Tomato section).

50 g (2 oz) butter
4 cooked artichoke bottoms, finely sliced
8 eggs, beaten
salt
freshly milled black pepper
1 tablespoon chopped parsley or snipped chives

Melt the butter in a frying pan and gently fry the sliced artichoke bottoms. When they are hot through and soft, raise the heat and pour over the beaten eggs, season with salt and pepper. Cook over a high heat, lifting the edges as they set and tipping the pan to allow the uncooked egg to flow under. When the omelette is set, sprinkle it with the parsley or chives, divide it into portions and slide straight on to hot plates.

Artichokes with mushrooms
Fonds d'artichauts Brocéliande

Once almost all inland Brittany was covered by a forest called Brocéliande, and this name in recipes usually means they contain mushrooms. This one, which is no exception, makes a very attractive and tasty starter. Sometimes I fry some finely chopped rashers of bacon in the oil before adding the mushrooms.

3–4 tablespoons oil
350 g (12 oz) field mushrooms, sliced
50 g (2 oz) butter
1 teaspoon flour
100 ml (4 fl oz) Muscadet or dry white wine
100 ml (4 fl oz) water
4 artichoke bottoms
salt
freshly milled black pepper
handful parsley, chopped
1 clove garlic, chopped

Heat the oil in a frying pan and add the mushrooms. Fry over a medium heat until they release all their water. Remove to a plate and wipe out the pan with kitchen paper. Melt the butter in the pan, stir in the flour and gradually mix in the wine and water. Add the artichoke bottoms and pile the mushrooms on top. Simmer gently for a few minutes until heated through, season with salt and pepper and dust with the parsley and garlic.

Artichoke soufflé
Soufflé de St-Pol-de-Léon

This recipe comes from the very centre of artichoke-growing country. It needs a lot of artichokes, which is fine if you happen to be in Brittany, but you can cheat and use canned or frozen ones instead.

50 g (2 oz) butter
8 artichoke bottoms
50 g (2 oz) flour
300 ml (½ pint) single cream
4 eggs, separated
salt
freshly milled black pepper
pinch of nutmeg
handful chives, snipped
2 tablespoons grated mature Cheddar or Gruyère cheese

Heat the oven to Gas 6/400°F/200°C. Melt the butter and fry the artichoke bottoms until tender. Mash them well and mix them in a bowl with the flour and cream. Beat in the egg yolks one by one and season well with salt, pepper, nutmeg and chives. Beat the egg whites until stiff and fold into the artichoke mixture. Generously butter a 1½ litre (2½ pint) soufflé dish – approx. 9 cm deep and 14 cm in diameter (3½ × 5½ in) – and turn the mixture into it. Sprinkle with grated cheese and put into the oven for 30 minutes until puffed and golden.

Lamb with spring vegetables and artichokes
Sauté d'agneau aux petits légumes et artichauts

This recipe comes from Dol in Brittany. Instead of fresh peas, you could use frozen or canned *petits pois*, in which case add them right at the end, with the artichoke hearts. Serve the lamb with steamed new potatoes or rice.

50 g (2 oz) butter or 4 tablespoons oil
700 g (1½ lb) braising lamb, cut in cubes
2 onions, chopped
1 level tablespoon flour
150 ml (¼ pint) stock or water
150 ml (¼ pint) dry white wine or strong dry cider
1 clove garlic, chopped
sprigs of thyme and parsley, tied in a bunch
1 bay leaf
salt
freshly milled black pepper
350 g (12 oz) young carrots, quartered
350 g (12 oz) peas, shelled
150 g (6 oz) young turnips, left whole
1 can artichoke bottoms, sliced
handful chervil, chopped

Melt the butter or oil in a heavy-based casserole and fry the meat on all sides, in two or three batches. Remove to a plate when browned. Add the onions to the casserole and fry until golden. Return the meat to the casserole, stir in the flour and gradually mix in the stock or water and the wine or cider. Bring to the boil and add the garlic, thyme, parsley and the bay leaf and season with salt and pepper. Cover and simmer for 30 minutes. Add the carrots, peas and turnips and simmer for a further hour or until the meat is tender. Add the sliced artichoke bottoms and simmer a few minutes longer until heated through. Remove the bunch of herbs, sprinkle with the chervil and serve.

Chicken with artichokes
Poulet à la Monselet

Charles Monselet was a nineteenth-century gastronome and author from Nantes, and one of his books was romantically titled *La Cuisine poétique*. Dishes garnished with artichoke hearts, potatoes or truffles often bear his name. This one is a complete meal in a pot; all that it needs to accompany it is a simple green salad. Small onions can be difficult to peel, but this is overcome by steeping them for a few minutes in boiling water. For best results choose a maize-fed or free range chicken.

2–3 tablespoons oil or butter
1 chicken, divided into 8 pieces
6–8 small onions
12 small new potatoes
8 artichoke bottoms
150 ml (¼ pint) dry white wine
150 ml (¼ pint) water
sprigs of parsley and thyme, tied in a bunch
1 bay leaf
salt
freshly milled black pepper
handful parsley, chopped

Heat the oil or butter in a flameproof casserole and brown the chicken pieces all over, in two batches if necessary. Set them aside on a plate. Brown the onions lightly. Remove, throw away the fat and wipe out the pan with kitchen paper. Return the onions to the casserole and put the chicken pieces on top. Add the potatoes and artichoke bottoms, and pour over the wine and water. Top with the sprigs of parsley and thyme and the bay leaf. Season with salt and pepper. Bring to the boil, cover and simmer for 1 hour until the potatoes are tender. Serve in the pot sprinkled with chopped parsley.

Asparagus

To prepare and cook asparagus

Asparagus with orange sauce

Asparagus soldiers with eggs

Asparagus with eggs

Asparagus with butter and cream

Asparagus with truffle peelings

Asparagus salad

Asparagus gratin

Asparagus roulades

Asparagus has been cultivated in Europe since Roman times and in France since the sixteenth century. The best is said to come from Argenteuil in the Ile-de-France, but it is produced in many other areas, including Brittany, Normandy and Picardy. Marchienne in the Nord used to be a big production area and is the name of a variety with fat, thick stems tipped with pink.

French asparagus is usually harvested before the shoots push through the earth's surface, so because of the lack of light, the crop is white and tender with a delicate flavour. Green and purple asparagus, favoured in Britain, is cut when the shoots stand above the ground, and many people consider these varieties superior, both nutritionally and with regard to taste. All asparagus can be cooked in the same way.

Asparagus is never cheap because each shoot is harvested by hand. Allow at least 100 g (4 oz) per head, but if you can afford it, twice as much is better! It is usually sold tied in bunches, though often French market stalls sell it loose and the shoppers can help themselves to exactly what they want. Either way it is worth checking that the stalks are of a uniform thickness so that they cook evenly. They should be firm and fresh-looking; avoid any which look tired and wrinkled.

Asparagus is delicious hot, warm or cold. If eating with your fingers, serve it warm and dip the spears into a sauce which can vary from a simple lemon-flavoured vinaigrette, or melted butter with a squeeze of lemon or orange juice to the more elaborate offerings of restaurants, which often serve it with a classic hollandaise or maltaise sauce (a variation on the theme flavoured with the juice of a blood orange). The cold Breton sauce, *sauce bretonne froide* (see Index) is easier to make and so is the orange sauce further on in this section. In Normandy don't be surprised to come across it served in a gratin with cream, *asperges à la crème*! Cold asparagus is good with either a vinaigrette, mayonnaise or tartare sauce.

To prepare and cook asparagus

Wash the asparagus and, using a swivel-bladed peeler, peel away the skin from just below the head to the cut end. Trim the stalks to an even length; they are tougher and take longer to cook than the tender heads, so the best way to cook them is to stand them upright in a tall pan half-filled with boiling water. The boiling water softens the stalks, while the heads themselves are gently steamed. You can buy a special asparagus kettle with a wire basket from a kitchen shop, or improvise by standing a cutlery drainer in a tallish saucepan and making a domed lid of foil. (You can cook asparagus flat in a roasting tin covered with boiling water, but it is not so satisfactory because by the time the stalks are tender, the heads can be over-cooked and falling to pieces.)

Half-fill the asparagus kettle with water, bring to the boil and add a teaspoon of salt. It is a good idea to tie the prepared stalks into bundles by binding them with fine string in a criss-cross spiral. This prevents them collapsing and breaking when they are cooked. Stand the bundles of asparagus in the wire basket and lower them into the water. (The trimmings can be added to give more flavour.) Cover and boil until tender, usually 15–45 minutes depending on the quality of the stalks, but don't overcook as they will be mushy. Test by piercing a stalk with a pointed knife. When it yields, lift out the basket, covering your hand with a cloth, and allow the asparagus to drain for a few minutes. Put on to a warm serving dish and remove the string. (The water makes a wonderful stock for soup.)

Asparagus with orange sauce
Asperges à la sauce orange

This is one of those light summery sauces now popular in France and made there with fromage blanc, which is a fresh cream cheese not easy to find here. It works well, too, with fromage frais, a low-fat cheese, with a consistency like yoghurt, now widely sold in British super-markets. If you can't find any, use a thick-set yoghurt instead.

450–700 g (1–1½ lb) asparagus
4 tablespoons fromage frais
1 egg, separated
salt
juice of 1 orange
pinch of paprika

Boil the asparagus in bundles as explained at the beginning of this section. Drain well and set aside to cool a little. Put the fromage frais into a bowl and stir in the egg yolk and salt, followed by the orange juice and paprika. Beat the egg white until stiff and fold into the sauce.

Serve the asparagus, string removed, on a warm dish with the sauce in the centre.

Asparagus soldiers with eggs
Asperges à la Fontenelle

It is said that this dish was invented to please the Normandy philosopher and author Bernard le Bovier de Fontenelle who was born in Rouen in 1657 and lived until 1757, which, with our present-day concern about cholesterol could be taken as rather reassuring! It's a childishly pleasant way of eating asparagus, dipping it first into melted butter, then into a soft-boiled egg. Eat with crusty bread for a light supper or lunch.

450–700 g (1–1½ lb) asparagus
4 eggs
100 g (4 oz) butter
salt and pepper

Boil the asparagus in bundles as explained at the beginning of this section. Drain well and set aside to cool a little. Boil the eggs for 4 minutes. Melt the butter and pour into a bowl. Arrange the asparagus on a large dish, removing the string, with the bowl of melted butter in the centre. Serve the eggs in egg cups with a spoon. Eat the asparagus with the fingers, dipping the spears first into the butter then into the soft egg, seasoning as you go with salt and pepper. Finish off the egg with the spoon.

Asparagus with eggs
Asperges à la flamande

In Flanders they also eat asparagus with eggs but this time they are hard-boiled, finely chopped and crushed, and combined with butter and lemon juice to make a sauce. The sauce can be poured over the asparagus, in which case eat it with knives and forks, or serve it separately, when fingers can be used.

450–700 g (1–1½ lb) asparagus
4 eggs
100 g (4 oz) melted butter
juice of ½ lemon
salt
freshly milled black pepper
handful parsley, chopped

Boil the asparagus in bundles as explained at the beginning of this section. Drain well and set aside to cool a little. Meanwhile hard-boil the eggs for 9 minutes, drain and put them under running cold water. Shell them as soon as they are cool enough to handle. Chop and mash two of them and mix with the melted butter. Add lemon juice, season to taste with salt and pepper and stir in half the parsley. Put the asparagus on to a warm dish, remove the string, and either pour the sauce over or serve it in a separate bowl. Cut the remaining eggs in quarters, arrange around the asparagus and sprinkle with the rest of the parsley.

Asparagus with butter and cream
Asperges à la bretonne

This Breton way of serving asparagus definitely calls for knives and forks. It is first boiled until beginning to soften, then gently braised in butter and finally topped with crème fraîche. In Brittany they eat it with croûtons fried in butter, but I like it better with fresh bread to mop up the juices.

450–700 g (1–1½ lb) asparagus
75–100 g (3–4 oz) butter
salt
freshly milled black pepper
3–4 tablespoons crème fraîche

First boil the asparagus in bundles as explained at the beginning of this section until just beginning to soften. Drain. Melt the butter in a shallow flameproof gratin dish (or frying pan), and lay the asparagus in it, removing the string. Season with salt and pepper. Cover, either with a lid or foil, and cook gently for about 10–20 minutes, until tender. Spread crème fraîche over the top and simmer for a few more minutes.

Asparagus with truffle peelings
Asperges à la Caux

I haven't tried this recipe from the chalky Caux region of Normandy. It calls for a tin of truffle peelings, which are hideously expensive, but you might find yourself in possession of one at the same time as the asparagus season, in which case have a go.

All you do is cook some asparagus in bundles, drain them and make a sauce by melting 100 g (4 oz) of butter, stirring in a can of truffle peelings, the juice of half a lemon, 2–3 tablespoons meat stock and a handful of chopped parsley. Stir until boiling and pour over the asparagus. Serve very hot.

Asparagus salad
Salade d'asperges

One of the nicest ways of eating asparagus in early summer is cold as a starter, with a simple vinaigrette sauce. If money is tight, buy only a little and make it part of a mixed hors d'oeuvre of other vegetables such as sliced tomatoes and grated carrots.

Boil asparagus as described at the beginning of this section. Drain it well and dip the stalks into cold water. Drain again, arrange on a dish and pour over a Breton vinaigrette. This is an ordinary vinaigrette flavoured with chopped parsley, chervil and chives, salt, pepper, a pinch of mixed spice and a tablespoon of finely chopped capers or gherkins.

Asparagus gratin
Asperges au gratin

A gratin of asparagus makes a luxurious lunch or supper dish or perhaps a starter for a dinner party when the weather is chilly. In France, the cheese would probably be Gruyère but in Britain we can choose from one of the range of our hard cheeses which melt without being stringy.

450 g (1 lb) asparagus
300 ml (½ pint) milk
25 g (1 oz) butter
25 g (1 oz) flour
salt
freshly milled black pepper
grated nutmeg
75 g (3 oz) cheese, grated

Prepare and cook the asparagus as explained at the beginning of this section. Heat the oven to Gas 7/425°F/220°C. Make a cheese sauce by putting the milk, butter and flour into a saucepan and whisking over a medium heat until it begins to thicken. Lower heat and continue whisking until it bubbles. Season with salt, pepper and nutmeg. Stir in all but 25 g (1 oz) of the cheese. Drain the asparagus well and lay it in a buttered ovenproof dish. Pour over the sauce, sprinkle with remaining cheese and put into the oven for 5–10 minutes, until it bubbles and browns.

Asparagus roulades
Roulades d'asperges à la flamande

This simple Flemish salad is a delicious way of making just a little asparagus go a long way. Serve it as a starter for four or as a light lunch or supper dish for two.

lettuce leaves
8 stalks cooked asparagus
4 slices lean ham
6 tablespoons mayonnaise
2 tomatoes, sliced
3 hard-boiled eggs, quartered
handful parsley, chopped

Line a serving dish with lettuce leaves. Lay two stalks of asparagus in the centre of each piece of ham, and spread with a tablespoon of mayonnaise. Roll up and arrange, flap-side down, on top of the lettuce. Spread each roll thinly with the remaining mayonnaise. Garnish with the sliced tomatoes, quartered eggs and chopped parsley.

Tomatoes

Tomato soup

Privateers' soup

Salad tartare

Tomato, shallot and onion sauce

Haricot beans with tomatoes

Tuna with tomatoes and onions

Stuffed squid

Grilled salmon with tomatoes

Breton bouillabaisse

Mussel kebabs

Bream with tomatoes

Beaumanoir sauce

Chicken liver *galettes*

Beef stewed with tomatoes

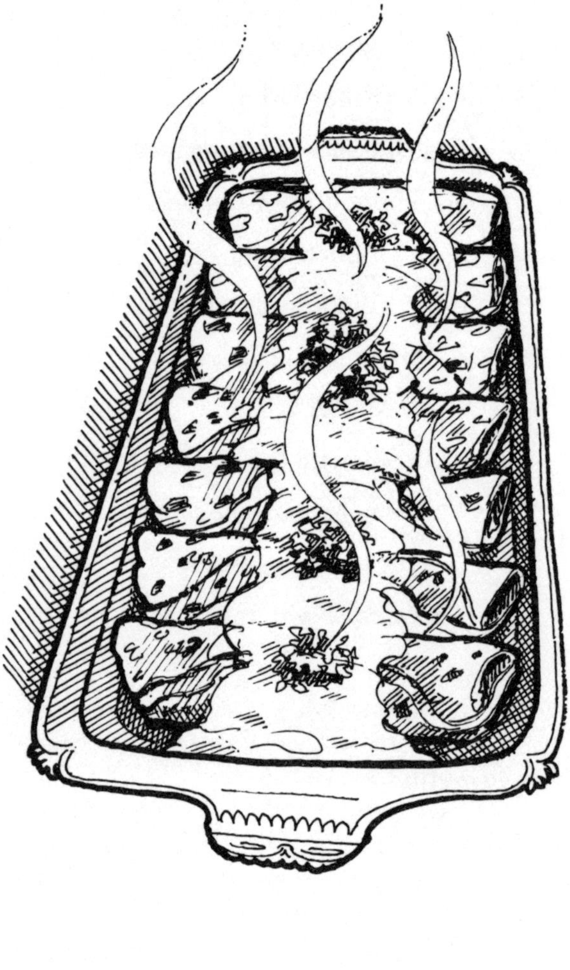

A yellow fruit, known by the Aztecs as *tomatl*, was brought back to Europe by the Spanish in the sixteenth century and in Italy it became known as *pomodoro*, or golden apple. This name was perhaps misunderstood by the southern French, who call it their apple of love, *pomme d'amour*. Although the Spanish relished it right from the start, it seems as if everyone else regarded it with great suspicion and thought it caused all sorts of ills until a red variety reached Europe from South America, brought back by Italian Jesuits two hundred years later. The Italians adopted it enthusiastically as did the southern French but it was not until the late nineteenth century that it was grown to any great extent in market gardens in the north of France.

Nowadays it is produced, especially in Brittany, in huge numbers in forcing houses and since early this century has become an indispensable part of the cooking of the region. Many of the recipes, especially the fishy ones, have a distinct similarity to the cooking of the Midi and it seems likely that both the tomato and how to cook it were transported from there by Breton fishermen.

French markets are a constant source of locally grown produce and when in France you will have no difficulty in buying splendid tomatoes. They may be somewhat rough and misshapen compared to many on sale in this country but they will be juicy and full of flavour. Fortunately, in Britain, certainly in and around London, there does seem to be a minor revolution going on and it is at last possible to buy tomatoes which actually taste like tomatoes. They are more expensive than some but well worth the extra money. Look out for interesting varieties in supermarkets and enterprising greengrocers. They are often sold rather unripe so it's a good idea to set them aside for a few days before using them (green tomatoes should be ripened by storing in the dark – a drawer or airing cupboard is ideal).

In recipes which call for peeled, de-seeded tomatoes, I tend to go for the Italian ones in cans. It is not just to save time. The variety used is the plum tomato which is full of flavour, has few seeds and is ideal for cooking. If you are peeling tomatoes, remember it is easy to do if you cover them with boiling water, leave them for a few seconds, lift them out and drain them. The paper-thin skin comes away easily.

Tomato soup
Les trois soupes aux tomates

Three places in Brittany take special pride in their tomato soup: Rennes, Nantes and Lower Brittany, *Basse-Bretagne*. The basic ingredients are similar but each has its own character. In the version below, which comes from Rennes, onions are first softened in butter before garlic, tomatoes, herbs, seasoning and water are added. *La nantaise* is made the same way but without any celery and it is thickened at the last minute with a large cup of cream and then reheated until just barely boiling. *La basse-bretonne* is made without any initial frying; all the ingredients, except the butter, are thrown into the pot using only half the amount of tomatoes, but including 225 g (8 oz) of diced potatoes, with butter or a tablespoon or two of cream added just before serving. All three soups are usually served with croûtons of bread either grilled at the top of a hot oven or fried in a little oil or butter.

25 g (1 oz) butter
2–3 onions, roughly chopped
1–2 cloves garlic, roughly chopped
700 g (1½ lb) tomatoes, peeled and roughly chopped, or the equivalent Italian canned
sprig of celery
sprig of fresh thyme or ½ teaspoon dried
1 bay leaf
1 sugar lump
1 litre (1¾ pints) water
salt
freshly milled black pepper

Melt the butter in a saucepan and fry the onions for about 5 minutes, until golden. Add the garlic, tomatoes, celery, thyme, bay leaf, sugar and water. Season to taste with salt and pepper. Bring to the boil and simmer for 20–30 minutes. Purée the soup either in a food processor, liquidizer or *mouli-légumes*.

Privateers' soup
Soupe des corsaires

Wherever Frenchmen sail the seas, they make fish soup. This one, ascribed to Breton *corsaires*, or privateers, is flavoured with tomatoes and white wine and it is tempting to think they picked up the recipe when calling at some Provençal port, changing the spices from saffron and orange to cloves and nutmeg. Meanwhile, another version was being made by the pirates using red wine and without the tomatoes.

This soup calls for fish pieces and heads which many fishmongers obligingly sell. If not, buy a selection of the cheaper white fish such as coley, whiting or dab. Sieving fish soup is a messy job, so don't plan to make it just before guests arrive! Serve with plenty of garlic bread or croûtons.

25 g (1 oz) butter
1 onion, chopped
1 shallot, chopped
1 leek, sliced
1 carrot, sliced
1 tablespoon tomato purée
3–4 cloves garlic, peeled
450 g (1 lb) fish pieces plus 2 fish heads
450 g (1 lb) tomatoes, peeled and chopped or 1 can Italian chopped tomatoes
150 ml (¼ pint) dry white wine
600 ml (1 pint) water
1 clove
½ teaspoon grated nutmeg
1–2 tablespoons chopped parsley
cayenne pepper
salt
juice of ½ lemon

Melt the butter in a large saucepan and add the onion, shallot, leek and carrot. Cover and let them sweat over a medium heat for 10 minutes. Stir in the tomato purée. Add the garlic, all the fish, the tomatoes, wine and water. Bring to the boil and add the clove, nutmeg and parsley. Season with the cayenne pepper and salt. Cover and simmer for 25 minutes. Put through a *mouli-légumes* or sieve, discarding all the bones. Transfer the soup to a food processor or liquidizer and blend to a purée. If the soup seems too thick, add more water. Check the seasoning, adding more cayenne and salt if necessary, and squeeze in the juice of the lemon.

Salad tartare
Salade nantaise

This mixed salad of tomatoes, French beans and cucumber makes an attractive starter. It is served with a chive-flavoured sauce made like a mayonnaise but with hard-boiled egg yolks: tartare sauce. The beans need to be cooked and cooled before the salad is mixed, so allow time for this or simply cook extra for a meal the day before.

225 g (8 oz) cooked French beans
225 g (8 oz) ripe tomatoes, sliced
½ cucumber, sliced
2 hard-boiled egg yolks
150 ml (¼ pint) oil
1 teaspoon vinegar
salt
freshly milled black pepper
2–3 tablespoons snipped chives

Cut the beans into three or four pieces and mix with the tomatoes and cucumber in a salad bowl. Put the egg yolks into a mortar or bowl and crush to a paste. Gradually beat in the oil as if making a mayonnaise and mix in the vinegar. Season with salt and pepper. Stir in the snipped chives, pour the sauce over the salad and gently mix everything together.

Tomato, shallot and onion sauce
Sauce à l'armoricaine

Debate has raged for almost a century as to whether this sauce originated in Brittany or whether it was the inspired invention of a chef called Peters (Pierre Fraisse) from Sète in Languedoc, who owned a successful restaurant in Paris. The story goes that he ran the sauce up late one night to feed a party of last-minute diners using the few remaining ingredients still in the kitchen: tomatoes, garlic, shallots, olive oil, white wine and cognac and some live lobsters which he had planned to cook the next day. There was no time to boil the lobsters, so he chopped them up and threw them into the pot. As he had just made a trip to the States, he called his dish *homard à l'américaine* (note the spelling) and it soon became *très chic*.

The Bretons make *sauce à l'armoricaine* which they say was invented by the fishermen. It uses all things Breton: tomatoes, Muscadet, garlic and shallots, butter not oil, and apple brandy not cognac. Lobster, once an everyday food for people living near the sea is now almost prohibitively expensive, but the Bretons cook all sorts of other shellfish and fish in this sauce, including mussels and clams, prawns and crabs, monkfish and squid. It is delicious, too, with any kind of firm white fish such as coley, hake, haddock or cod.

25 g (1 oz) butter
1 onion, finely chopped
3 shallots, finely chopped
450 g (1 lb) tomatoes, peeled and roughly chopped or 1 can Italian chopped tomatoes
1 clove garlic, crushed
1 tablespoon chopped parsley
1 sprig of tarragon
700 g (1½ lb) of your chosen fish (skinned and cut into bite-sized pieces) or shellfish (see above)
2–3 tablespoons calvados or apple brandy
300 ml (½ pint) Muscadet or other dry white wine

Heat the butter in a wide-mouthed casserole, add the finely chopped onion and shallots and fry them over a gentle heat until golden, but don't let them brown. Add the tomatoes, garlic, parsley and tarragon and simmer gently, uncovered, for 10–15 minutes. Add the fish or shellfish. Put the calvados or apple brandy into a ladle or small pan, heat it and set it alight and pour it flaming over the sauce. When the flames die down, add the wine. Season to taste with salt and pepper and simmer gently long enough for the fish to poach. (15–20 minutes for monkfish, 5–10 minutes for softer fish like haddock or cod or for shellfish like prawns).

Haricot beans with tomatoes
Haricots blancs à la bretonne

As well as accompanying roast and stewed lamb, this dish is sometimes served with grilled meat or eggs. You can save time by using canned beans and simply adding them to the tomato sauce, however the result is less satisfactory because they lack the flavour of cloves, herbs and vegetables with which the dried beans are cooked.

450 g (1 lb) dried haricot beans, soaked (see Etceteras)
1 onion, stuck with 2 cloves plus 1 onion, chopped
1 carrot, quartered
sprigs of thyme and parsley
1 bay leaf
1 tablespoon oil
1 clove garlic
450 g (1 lb) tomatoes, peeled and chopped or 1 can Italian chopped tomatoes
salt
freshly milled black pepper

Put the soaked and drained beans into a large pan with the onion stuck with cloves, the carrot, thyme, parsley and bay leaf. Cover generously with cold water, bring to the boil, put on the lid and simmer for 1–1½ hours until tender. Discard onion, carrot and herbs.

To make the sauce: heat the oil and lightly brown the chopped onion, add the garlic and tomatoes and simmer, uncovered, for 15–20 minutes. Season quite generously with salt and add pepper to taste. Drain the beans, stir them into the sauce and simmer for a further 5–10 minutes.

Tuna with tomatoes and onions
Thon à la cocotte

Concarneau, in Brittany's Finistère, as well as being a lively tourist centre, is one of France's biggest fishing ports, and the tuna, cod, herrings and sardines caught by its fishermen are central to its thriving canning industry and huge fish auction market. In this simple recipe, a slice of tuna is cooked with tomatoes and onions and served either with mashed or steamed potatoes or boiled rice. When buying tuna it is best to avoid the tail end, which is very bony.

50 g (2 oz) butter
1 tablespoon oil
2 onions, chopped
700 g (1½ lb) tuna, in one piece
150 ml (¼ pint) Muscadet or other dry white wine
salt
freshly milled black pepper
sprigs of thyme and parsley, tied in a bunch
1 bay leaf
450 g (1 lb) tomatoes, peeled and roughly chopped or 1 can Italian chopped tomatoes, drained
sprig of fresh fennel or 1 teaspoon fennel seeds
handful fresh coriander or parsley, chopped
juice of ½ lemon

Heat the butter and oil in a heavy-based casserole and fry the onions until golden. Add the tuna and seal it quickly on both sides. Pour over the wine, season with salt and pepper and add the sprigs of thyme and parsley and the bay leaf. Cover and simmer for 30 minutes. Add the tomatoes, fennel and coriander or parsley and simmer, uncovered, for a further 10 minutes. Serve the fish on a warm platter, squeeze over the lemon juice and surround with the tomatoes and onions.

Stuffed squid
Encornets à la normande

This is a delicious Normandy recipe for stuffed squid stewed in wine or cider. In France when you buy squid on a market stall or at the fishmongers, they will ask if you would like them to prepare them for you. Here they are more likely to leave the job to you. It is not difficult but adds an extra chore.

4 squid
2 tablespoons oil
2 onions, chopped
2 tomatoes, peeled and chopped or 2 tablespoons canned chopped tomatoes
1 tablespoon tomato purée
1 tablespoon chopped parsley
1 clove garlic, chopped
2–3 tablespoons fresh breadcrumbs
2 egg yolks, lightly beaten
salt
freshly milled black pepper
150 ml (¼ pint) dry white wine or cider
25 g (1 oz) butter

Cut off the tentacles from each squid and set aside. Gently detach the head and throw away. Wash out the body sac, removing the innards and transparent quill. Chop the tentacles. Heat the oil in a frying pan and fry the onions and tentacles over a medium heat, stirring. Add the tomatoes, tomato purée, parsley and garlic, lower the heat and fry gently for 5 minutes. Heat the oven to Gas 5/375°F/190°C. Remove the frying pan from the heat and mix in the fresh breadcrumbs and egg yolks. Season with salt and pepper. Spoon the mixture into the squid sacs and secure the tops with toothpicks. Lay them side by side in a buttered oven dish. Pour the wine or cider round the squid and dot with the butter. Bake for 20–25 minutes.

Grilled salmon with tomatoes
Saumon grillé aux tomates

On a cool summer's evening nothing could be simpler than this Brittany way of serving salmon steaks. Go for really good, well-flavoured tomatoes.

3–4 tablespoons oil
sprigs of thyme
4 salmon steaks
25 g (1 oz) butter
2 onions, chopped
12 small whole tomatoes
1 clove garlic, chopped
salt
freshly milled black pepper
handful parsley, chopped

Put 2 or 3 tablespoons of the oil into a glass or china dish with some sprigs of thyme and marinate the fish steaks for an hour, turning them over half way through. When ready to start cooking, heat the grill for 5 minutes. Meanwhile, heat the remaining tablespoon of oil with the butter in a frying pan and add the chopped onions. Fry over a medium heat, turning from time to time, until golden. Add the tomatoes, garlic and more sprigs of thyme and cook gently until soft. Season with salt and pepper. Grill the steaks for 3 or 4 minutes on each side. Season them with salt and pepper and serve them surrounded by the tomatoes and onions and sprinkled with parsley.

Breton bouillabaisse
Bouillabaisse des Kermokos

To the Bretons the people from the Midi – the south of France – were known as mokos and the children who were born to the Provençal women by the *marins de la Royale* were nicknamed *kermokos*. Hence the name of this dish, which is a cross between the Breton *cotriade* and the southern *bouillabaisse*. Like the Mediterranean version, it is flavoured with oil and saffron but differs in that it contains no orange peel or fennel and is not served with the fiery *rouille* sauce.

Make it when you have at least six people to feed because it requires several different varieties of fish. The kinds you use will depend on what the fishermonger has on the counter but they should all be firm, white fish such as cod, haddock, coley, rock salmon, conger eel, gurnard, hake, monkfish, grey mullet, wrasse, sea bream and rascasse (this last is readily available in France but almost unobtainable here). Serve this dish with slices of French bread sprinkled with oil which have been toasted until golden.

4 tablespoons olive oil
2 onions, chopped
450 g (1 lb) tomatoes, peeled and chopped or 1 can Italian chopped tomatoes
3–4 cloves garlic, chopped
$1\frac{1}{2}$ kg ($3\frac{1}{2}$ lb) assorted fish steaks (4–6 varieties – see above)
2–3 sprigs of thyme
1 bay leaf
1 tablespoon salt
freshly milled black pepper
several strands of saffron
handful parsley, chopped

Use a large saucepan. Heat the oil and fry the onions until golden. Add the tomatoes and garlic, put the toughest fish (conger, monkfish, wrasse, sea bream, gurnard, rascasse) on top and add the thyme, bay leaf, salt, pepper and saffron. Just cover with boiling water. Boil hard for 5 minutes with the pan uncovered. Add the remaining fish and continue to boil for a further 5 minutes. Do not stir. Remove from the heat. Put the fish on a hot platter moistened with some of the liquid and sprinkle with the parsley. Put the remaining liquid into a warm soup tureen. Serve the fish and soup at the same time in shallow soup plates. Everyone then helps themselves to fish and soup, dunking the bread into it.

Mussel kebabs
Moules en brochettes

Wash 450 g (1 lb) mussels in several changes of water. Scrub them well. Put them in a large pan over a high heat and let them just open. Remove and shell. Choose thin skewers and thread the mussels on to them, alternating them with pieces of bacon, tomato, green pepper and onion. Brush them with oil. Heat the grill and cook the kebabs until piping hot, turning frequently. Serve dusted with cayenne pepper.

Bream with tomatoes
Daurade au four

Bream vary in quality and flavour. The best is the gilt-headed bream, known as *daurade* in French, but our red sea-bream with its goggly eyes is not to be despised and is delicious cooked in this Breton fashion. Bream needs to be cleaned, scaled, trimmed and the gills removed before cooking, and it is worth asking the fishmonger to do this job.

2 onions, sliced
1 bream, weighing about 1 kg ($2\frac{1}{4}$ lb)
salt
freshly milled black pepper
2 sprigs of thyme
2 sprigs of parsley
1 tablespoon cider or wine vinegar
450 g (1 lb) tomatoes, peeled and chopped or 1 can Italian chopped tomatoes
2–3 tablespoons breadcrumbs
50 g (2 oz) butter
100 ml (4 fl oz) Muscadet or other dry white wine
2 tablespoons apple brandy or calvados

Heat the oven to Gas 6/400°F/200°C. Butter an oven dish and lay the sliced onions in it. Put the fish on top and season it with salt and pepper. Put the sprigs of thyme and parsley in the fish's cavity and sprinkle with the vinegar. Bake for 10 minutes, then lower the heat to Gas 4/350°F/180°C and surround the fish with the canned tomatoes. Sprinkle over the breadcrumbs, dot with half the butter and pour over the wine. Bake for a further 30 minutes. Just before serving, melt the remaining butter and pour it over the fish together with the apple brandy or calvados.

Beaumanoir sauce

This winey tomato sauce bears the name of a Breton family whose most famous son was the hero of the Battle of the Thirty fought during the war of succession in the fourteenth century. Jean de Beaumanoir led the garrison of Josselin to victory against that of Poërmel, captained by an Englishman, in a sort of fighting match, a fore-runner of football or rugby perhaps. Bored with frequent skirmishes, the two sides selected 30 men apiece who battled on foot but were armed with battle axes, pikes, daggers and swords, so not surprisingly many were killed. Perhaps the sauce was invented by a peaceful descendant, but whatever its origins, it goes well with meat, egg dishes or fish, or with the chicken liver *galette* given below. The sauce should be well seasoned.

25 g (1 oz) butter or oil
1 level tablespoon flour
1–2 tablespoons tomato purée
100 ml (4 fl oz) Muscadet or other white wine
100 ml (4 fl oz) water
pinch of nutmeg
pinch of cinnamon
½ teaspoon dried thyme
1 clove garlic, chopped
salt
freshly milled black pepper

Heat the butter or oil in a small pan and stir in the flour. Cook gently for 2 minutes, stirring. Mix in the tomato purée and gradually stir in the wine and water. Bring to the boil, stirring constantly. Lower the heat, add the nutmeg, cinnamon, thyme and garlic and simmer for 3–4 minutes, stirring to prevent burning. Season generously with salt and pepper.

Chicken liver *galettes*
Galettes au foie de volaille

In Brittany you might come across savoury *galettes* coated in Beaumanoir sauce (see above). I have used chicken livers but you could use almost any kind of meat either finely chopped or minced.

1 tablespoon oil
25 g (1 oz) butter
1 onion, chopped
225 g (8 oz) chicken livers, chopped
½ teaspoon dried thyme
1 tablespoon chopped parsley
1 clove garlic, chopped
salt
freshly milled black pepper
4 *galettes* (see Etceteras)
300 ml (½ pint) Beaumanoir sauce (see above)

Heat oven to Gas 5/375°F/190°C. Heat the oil and butter in a frying pan and fry the onion until golden. Raise the heat and stir in the chicken livers. Brown them quickly, turning them over and over. Stir in the thyme, parsley and garlic and season with salt and pepper. Butter a shallow ovenproof dish. Either fill each *galette* with a portion of the chicken livers and roll up, or lay the *galettes* flat in the dish, sandwiching them with the filling. Pour the Beaumanoir sauce over the *galettes* and put into the oven for 10–15 minutes until hot and bubbling.

Beef stewed with tomatoes
Sauté de boeuf à la normande

Make this lovely, warming stew a day ahead and reheat it for 30 minutes, either on top of the stove or in the oven set at Gas 4/350°F/180°C. It needs no other accompaniment than mashed or jacket potatoes.

700–900 g (1½–2 lb) braising beef
2 tablespoons oil
3 onions, roughly chopped
1 tablespoon tomato purée
450 g (1 lb) tomatoes, peeled and chopped or 1 can Italian chopped tomatoes
100 ml (4 fl oz) water
salt
freshly milled black pepper
1 teaspoon paprika
2–3 sprigs of thyme
3 carrots, cut in thin lengths

Heat the oven to Gas 3/325°F/160°C. Cut the meat into biggish chunks. Heat the oil in an ovenproof casserole and brown the meat all over, in three or four batches if necessary. Remove the pieces to a warm plate as you go. Add the onions to the casserole and fry them until golden. Stir in the tomato purée. Return the meat to the casserole and add the chopped tomatoes and water. Bring to the boil, season with salt and pepper and add the paprika, thyme and carrots. Cover and put into the oven for about 1½ hours, until the meat is tender.

Carrots to broad beans

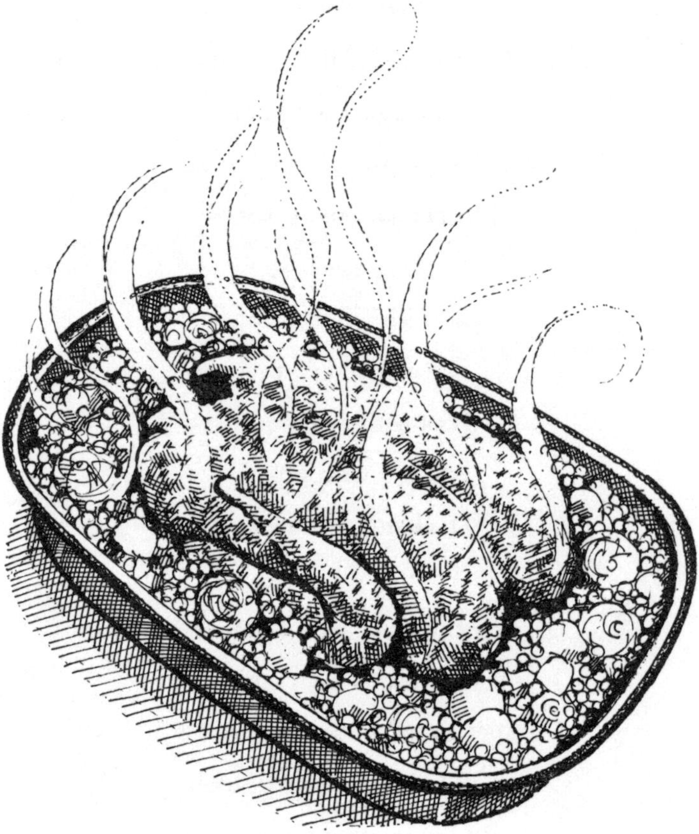

From the market gardens of the Nord right through to Brittany carrots, peas, French beans and broad beans flourish, and the Manche, the sleeve of Normandy, which stretches from Mont-St-Michel through Cherbourg to the salt marshes south of Utah beach, is famous for its early vegetables.

CARROTS

The carrot came to France and the British Isles via the Spanish who on their travels brought back so many of our now familiar vegetables. This one did not originate from South America, like the potato and tomato, but came via Asia and North Africa, and reached northern Europe through the Spanish Netherlands.

Here it is hardly possible to buy carrots which have not been pre-washed and often pre-packed, but in northern French markets earthy piles are heaped high on stalls, and like everything else are carefully selected by the cook. In Tilques, near St-Omer in the Pas de Calais, you will find long, deep orange carrots which are renowned for their keeping qualities; or go to Créance in Normandy and sample the flavour of carrots grown in soil fertilized by seaweed; and if you are in Brittany, look out for the thin, tasty carrots from Nantes, *carottes nantaises*.

Like potatoes, most of the flavour and goodness is near to the skin, so avoid peeling carrots whenever possible. Simply top and tail them and wash them under the tap. When they must be peeled, use a swivel-bladed vegetable peeler. They make delicious soups, either on their own or with other vegetables, add a sweet something to stews and are delicious grated raw and served either on their own mixed with vinaigrette or as part of a mixed salad.

For a simple vegetable accompaniment, cook new carrots whole. Slice older ones, cover in a very little water with a little salt, a lump of sugar and a small piece of butter. As soon as they are tender, remove the lid and boil away most of the liquid. Serve seasoned with freshly milled black pepper, coriander or cumin, or sprinkle with chopped parsley, chervil or fennel. Or stir in a few tablespoons of béchamel sauce.

Carrot soup
Soupe de carottes

The method of preparing this golden, sweetly flavoured soup from Flanders is unusual because the carrots are boiled before adding the remaining vegetables which have been sweating in butter.

350 g (12 oz) carrots, chopped
$1\frac{1}{2}$ litre ($2\frac{1}{2}$ pints) water
salt
225 g (8 oz) onions, chopped
225 g (8 oz) leeks, chopped
2 sticks celery, chopped
2 tablespoons oil
1 bay leaf
sprigs of thyme and parsley
freshly milled black pepper
pinch of nutmeg
150 ml ($\frac{1}{4}$ pint) milk
25 g (1 oz) butter

Put the carrots into a saucepan with the water and a little salt. Cover and bring to the boil. Reduce the heat and leave to simmer. Meanwhile prepare the onions, leeks and celery. Heat the oil in another pan, add the vegetables and let them sweat over a low heat, covered, for 15 minutes. Add these vegetables to the carrots and season with the herbs, pepper, nutmeg and sufficient salt to taste. Cover and simmer for 1 hour. Liquidize or put through a *mouli-légumes*. Return to the pan, stir in the milk, heat through, add the butter and serve.

The farmer's wife's carrots
Carottes à la fermière

Carrots and new potatoes are here braised together with bacon in a little butter, until the vegetables absorb almost all the liquid and are meltingly tender and sweet.

25 g (1 oz) butter
100 g (4 oz) streaky bacon, chopped
900 g (2 lb) carrots, sliced
450 g (1 lb) small new potatoes, sliced
salt
freshly milled black pepper
1 tablespoon crème fraîche
1 tablespoon chopped parsley

Melt the butter and fry the chopped bacon for a few minutes. Stir in the carrots and barely cover with water. Simmer, covered, for 20 minutes. Add the potatoes and simmer for a further 20 minutes. Season to taste with salt and pepper and stir in the crème fraîche. Garnish with the chopped parsley.

Carrots braised with onions
Carottes braisées aux oignons

In this Normandy recipe, carrots and onions, delicately flavoured with herbs, are gently cooked until they have soaked up all the buttery juices. It's an optional extra to stir in a little crème fraîche right at the end.

50 g (2 oz) butter
3 onions, chopped
700 g (1½ lb) carrots, thinly sliced
1 sugar lump
300 ml (½ pint) water
sprigs of thyme, parsley, chervil and tarragon, tied in a bunch
1 bay leaf
salt
freshly milled black pepper
3 tablespoons crème fraîche (optional)

Melt the butter in a heavy-based saucepan and add the onion. Let it soften and turn golden. Add the carrots and sugar and stir for a minute or two over the heat. Pour in the water, add herbs and season with salt and pepper. Cover and simmer for 45 minutes. Remove the lid and continue to cook for a further 10–15 minutes until most of the liquid has been absorbed. Just before serving, remove the bunch of herbs and stir in the crème fraîche.

Mashed potatoes with carrots
Purée bretonne

The carrots colour this Breton dish of mashed potatoes a pale orange and the addition of beaten egg white gives it a surprising lightness. Eat it with pork, lamb chops or sausages, or as a simple supper dish topped with poached eggs.

900 g (2 lb) potatoes, peeled and quartered
150 g (6 oz) carrots, sliced
1–2 tablespoons milk
25 g (1 oz) butter
1 egg, separated
salt
freshly milled black pepper

Put the potatoes into a pan of cold, salted water, bring to the boil and add the carrots. Cover and simmer for 20–30 minutes, until they are tender. Drain well and mash until smooth. Beat in the milk, butter and egg yolk. Whip egg white until stiff and carefully fold into the mixture. Season generously with salt and pepper.

PEAS

Little fresh green peas, *petits pois*, grown all over northern France, from the Pas de Calais right through to Brittany, are one of the joys of French food. Their sweet, exquisite flavour is quite unlike that of all those gross ones that we as a nation insist on buying frozen; and as for their canned variety, the tiny peas they use retain a delicacy of flavour completely lacking from our own tinned peas.

Peas have been part of the staple diet of Europe for thousands of years and yet last summer in a new greengrocers in my part of Wandsworth, the Saturday assistant nodded me towards the freezer when I asked for them and looked totally blank when I said I wanted fresh not frozen. With a worried frown, his gaze scanned the shop looking, I imagine, for a pile of loose peas, because when I explained they came in pods, he just looked disbelieving!

It made me wonder how many other people are equally unfamiliar with the real thing and, if they do know about them, avoid them because of all that bother shelling them. Of course, you don't have to shell them at all if you buy mange-tout or sugar snap peas, which simply need to be topped and tailed and any fibre pulled away. They can be eaten raw or boiled or steamed until just tender and served with a good knob of butter and a sprinkling of fresh, chopped mint, chervil or parsley. If you are feeling greedy, add a spoonful or two of crème fraîche.

If you are not in a hurry, shelling peas can seem therapeutic and if you have a garden it's a chore which is pleasant done out of doors. Hold each pod in one hand, seam side up, pointed end protruding and press the end with your thumb, it should pop and split so that it is then easy to pull the pod apart and scrape out the peas with your finger.

If you have a *mouli-légumes*, the pods can be made into a soup by boiling them in salted water with a chopped onion, two or three rashers of chopped bacon, two or three quartered potatoes, a bay leaf and sprigs of thyme or mint until the pods and potatoes are tender. Put the soup, a little at a time, through a *mouli-légumes*, discarding the fibrous remnants of the pods as you go. Return the soup to the pan, season well and add a sprinkling of chopped chives.

The weights given in the recipes which follow are for fresh peas in their pods. Frozen peas could be used, but you will only need half the amount, and they only need to be cooked for a very short time. Better still, when fresh peas are not available use the French or Belgian canned *petits pois* (again, halving the quantities and reducing the cooking time).

Market gardeners' soup
Hortillonnages

This soup from Picardy, which is sometimes known as *soupe des maraîchers*, makes a warming supper on a cool summer evening. It uses a mixture of vegetables, including peas, grown in the fertile land lacing the canals which is packed with market gardens, *les hortillonnages*.

1 firm round cabbage heart, cut into 8 pieces
50 g (2 oz) butter
4 leeks, sliced
2 litre ($3\frac{1}{2}$ pints) water
450 g (1 lb) potatoes, quartered
sprig of thyme
salt
freshly milled black pepper
1 small round lettuce, cut into 8 pieces
225 g (8 oz) peas, shelled
handful sorrel, chopped
6–7 sprigs of chervil, chopped

Blanch the cabbage for 5–10 minutes in boiling, salted water. Drain well and wipe out the pan. Melt half the butter in it, add the cabbage and the leeks, mix well, cover and leave to sweat for 10 minutes over a low heat. Add the water, potatoes and thyme and season with salt and pepper. Cover and simmer for 40 minutes. Add the lettuce, peas and sorrel and simmer for a further 15 minutes. Serve sprinkled with the chervil.

Pea soup
Potage aux pois

This tasty soup from Picardy can be made with fresh or even frozen peas but in this recipe it is made with split or whole dried peas. (If using fresh peas allow twice the quantity and halve the cooking time. Frozen peas will only need 20 minutes or so.) Whichever you use, it takes minimum preparation. In France you would use a whole piece of belly of pork, *lard de poitrine*, which would be blanched for 5 minutes in boiling water, drained and cut in cubes. In Britain, streaky bacon does very well and goes straight into the pot.

350 g (12 oz) dried or split peas
100 g (4 oz) streaky bacon, cut in cubes
1 teaspoon dried thyme
$1\frac{1}{2}$ litre ($2\frac{1}{2}$ pints) water
salt
freshly milled black pepper
50 g (2 oz) butter
bread croûtons

Soak the dried or split peas for an hour by covering them with boiling water. Drain. Put them with the bacon, thyme and fresh water into a saucepan. Bring to the boil and boil hard for 10 minutes. Remove any scum with a slotted spoon, lower heat and simmer, covered, for $1\frac{1}{4}$ hours or until tender. Purée the soup. Season to taste with salt and pepper. Melt the butter in a frying pan and fry the croûtons until golden; serve separately.

Peas with white onions
Pois à la falaisienne

This dish of peas comes from Falaise, the birthplace of William the Conqueror. It calls for fresh peas which the Normans call *pois de mai* but frozen peas – or dried peas, which they call *pois anglais* – can be used instead, though frozen peas will of course only take a few minutes and dried peas will need to be soaked and cooked for twice as long.

450 g (1 lb) peas, shelled
salt
50 g (2 oz) butter
4 spring onions, finely chopped
salt
freshly milled black pepper
2 tablespoons crème fraîche

Put the peas into a saucepan, cover them with boiling water and add salt. Simmer, uncovered, for about 20 minutes, until tender. Meanwhile, melt the butter in a frying pan and gently fry the onions until soft and beginning to brown. Season with salt and pepper, stir in the crème fraîche. Drain the peas and mix with the onions and crème fraîche.

Peas with cream
Petits pois à la crème

A classic Normandy recipe, which if it is made without the cream is known as *petits pois à la française.*

50 g (2 oz) butter
700 g (1½ lb) peas, shelled
2–3 tablespoons boiling water
1 sugar lump
sprig of parsley
3–4 lettuce leaves, torn into strips
6 spring onions
salt
3 tablespoons crème fraîche (optional)

Melt the butter in a saucepan and add the peas. Shake the pan to coat them all over. As soon as they turn to a brilliant green, add water, sugar, parsley, lettuce leaves, spring onions and salt. Cover and simmer for 15–20 minutes, until the peas are tender and most of the water is absorbed. Stir in the crème fraîche, if using, and serve.

Peas with tomatoes
Petits pois à la nantaise

This is a simple version of a well-known Breton vegetable dish. If you want something a little more elaborate, first fry 4 or 5 spring onions and the heart of a lettuce in the butter, then add the tomatoes, peas and other ingredients, dusting with parsley just before serving.

4 tomatoes
25 g (1 oz) butter
700 g (1½ lb) peas, shelled
sprigs of thyme and savory
salt
freshly milled black pepper
handful parsley, chopped

Put the tomatoes into a bowl and cover with boiling water. Leave a few minutes and skin. Melt the butter in a saucepan and add the tomatoes and let them soften without breaking for 5 minutes or so. Add the shelled peas, the thyme and savory, salt and pepper. Cover and simmer gently for about 20 minutes, until peas are tender. Serve dusted with the parsley.

Pigeon with peas
Pigeons aux petits pois

Sweet-tasting peas and gamey pigeons are a happy combination for which I have come across similar recipes in both Normandy and Brittany, the only difference being that in Brittany they add a sliced carrot and a turnip or two to the pot. French pigeons are specially reared for the table; our wood pigeons are tougher creatures and so if you use French recipes you must add at least an hour and probably more to the cooking time, as I have done in my adaptation below. Instead of fresh peas, you could use frozen or canned *petits pois*, allowing about 450 g (1 lb), but only add them five minutes or so before the end of the cooking time.

12 small onions
25 g (1 oz) butter
100 g (4 oz) streaky bacon, chopped
2 pigeons
1–2 tablespoons apple brandy or calvados
100 ml (4 fl oz) white wine
100 ml (4 fl oz) water
sprigs of thyme and parsley, tied in a bunch
1 bay leaf
salt
freshly milled black pepper
900 g (2 lb) peas

Peel the onions by first steeping them for a minute or two in boiling water. Melt the butter in a heavy-based casserole and fry the onions and bacon for a few minutes. Add the whole pigeons and brown them on all sides. Heat the apple brandy or calvados in a ladle or small pan, set it alight and pour it flaming over the contents of the pan. When the flames die down pour in the wine and water. Bring to the boil and add the thyme, parsley and bay leaf. Season with salt and pepper. Simmer, covered, for 2 hours. Half an hour before the end of the cooking time, add the shelled peas to the pan. Serve on a warm dish, the pigeons split in half surrounded by the peas and onions and pour the sauce over.

Duckling with peas
Caneton aux petits pois

This recipe comes from Nantes which through the centuries has vied with Rennes to be the capital of Brittany. It is famous for its ducks which at one time were raised on buckwheat which gave them a flavour all their own. Nearly a quarter of France's peas come from the same region, so it is natural the two should be teamed together to produce a dish that is sweet and succulent. When fresh peas are not in season, use frozen or canned *petits pois* but you'll need only half the weight of peas in the pod. Like Barbary ducks, Nantaise duck tend to be smallish and as the former are available here this is the kind I would use when cooking this dish in Britain.

1 duck, weighing about 1½ kg (3¼ lb)
50 g (2 oz) butter
100 g (4 oz) streaky bacon, chopped
100 g (4 oz) small onions
150 ml (¼ pint) dry white wine
150 ml (¼ pint) water
1 teaspoon sugar
1 lettuce heart
sprigs of thyme, savory and parsley, tied in a bunch
salt
freshly milled black pepper
900 g (2 lb) fresh peas

Prick the duck all over with a fork to allow the fat to run. Melt the butter in a heavy-based flameproof casserole, in which the duck will fit comfortably, and brown it well all over: this will take 10–15 minutes. Remove and discard all but about 1 tablespoon of the fat in the pan. Add the bacon and onions and fry them until they begin to brown. Return the duck and pour in the wine and water. Add the sugar, lettuce heart and herbs. Season with salt and pepper. Bring to the boil, cover and simmer for 45 minutes. Shell and add the peas 30 minutes before the end of the cooking time. (If using frozen or canned peas add them 5 minutes before duck is done.) Test the duck is cooked by inserting a skewer into a fleshy part: when done the juices should run clear. Transfer it to a serving dish and keep warm. Put the casserole over a high heat and reduce the liquid until it is almost completely gone (5–10 minutes), stirring as it reduces to prevent sticking. Discard the herbs and arrange vegetables and bacon around the bird.

FRENCH BEANS

French beans, which the French call *haricots verts* or *haricots princesse*, came along with other kinds of beans from the New World. They are superior in both flavour and tenderness to our common runner beans which originally were grown for their beautiful, scarlet flowers.

Prepare French beans by topping and tailing and removing any stringy fibres and cook them in fast boiling water, uncovered, to preserve their colour. The younger the beans, the shorter the cooking time, they are ready when they are soft but with a bit of bite. The new season's very young beans are delicious steamed and served tossed in melted butter and parsley as a first course. In Normandy they would stir in a tablespoon or two of cream.

French bean soup
Potage de Cormeilles

In this Normandy recipe French beans are cooked with potatoes and shallots in a stock with herbs to make a light and delicious summer soup. If you have no stock, you could sweat the vegetables in *graisse normande* (see Cabbages to Chicory section).

- 50 g (2 oz) butter
- 2 shallots
- 450 g (1 lb) French beans, topped and tailed
- 350 g (12 oz) potatoes, peeled and chopped
- 1 litre (1¾ pints) stock or water
- sprigs of thyme and parsley, tied together
- 1 bay leaf
- salt
- freshly milled black pepper
- 300 ml (½ pint) milk

Melt half the butter in a large saucepan and add the shallots, beans and potatoes. Let them sweat over a medium heat for 5 minutes, stirring from time to time to prevent them sticking. Pour over the stock or water, add the herbs and bay leaf and season with salt and pepper. Simmer, uncovered, for 45 minutes. Put through a food processor or liquidizer. Pour in the milk and heat until the first bubble appears. Remove from heat, adjust seasoning and add remaining butter.

French beans with potatoes
Haricots verts à la normande

This is a delicious way of serving fresh green beans. Beans and potatoes are cooked separately, then mixed together with a flavouring of butter and herbs.

225 g (8 oz) potatoes
450 g (1 lb) French beans
25–50 (1–2 oz) butter
handful chives, parsley and chervil, chopped
salt
freshly milled black pepper

Boil or steam the unpeeled potatoes for 20–30 minutes, until tender. Drain well. Boil the beans fiercely in salted water for 10–15 minutes. Peel the potatoes, holding them in a cloth if they are very hot. Slice them. Melt the butter in the pan, add the beans and potatoes and toss to coat them well. Sprinkle with the herbs and season with salt and pepper.

French beans with onions
Haricots verts à la mode de Bröons

This way of serving French beans from Bröons in Brittany's Côtes-du-Nord is delicious either as a simple first course or as an accompanying vegetable. Instead of small onions you could use shallots or spring onions.

50 g (2 oz) butter
4 small onions, finely sliced
450 g (1 lb) French beans, topped and tailed
salt
freshly milled black pepper
parsley, chopped

Heat the butter in a frying pan and fry the onions gently for 10–15 minutes, until soft and golden. Cook the beans by adding them to a pan of boiling, salted water and boiling them fiercely, uncovered, for 10–15 minutes until soft but still with a bite. Drain. Return beans to the pan, stir in the onions, heat through, season to taste with salt and pepper, turn into a warm serving dish. Sprinkle with chopped parsley and serve.

BROAD BEANS

The broad bean with its pretty white and purple flowers which scent the fields early in the year came to Europe via the Middle East. It appears right across the north of France from Flemish market gardens to the golden belt of Brittany.

Very young beans, in pods measuring around 5 cm (2 in) long –

probably those you have grown and picked yourself – can be topped and tailed like runner beans and eaten pods and all. You can cook them or, more imaginatively, eat them raw, dipping them into coarse sea salt. The beans which appear in the shops are older and must be shelled. To do this, wear rubber gloves to avoid staining your hands black. Very old beans are best avoided.

Broad beans can be cooked quite simply and served with melted butter or eaten in salads flavoured with vinaigrette, but because the pods are heavy, you need to allow at least 225 g (8 oz) unshelled beans per head. If time is pressing, buy frozen beans instead, allowing half as much as for beans in their pods. They can be used in any of the following recipes.

Broad bean soup
Soupe de fèves

This Breton soup is full of delicious surprises – mussels and bacon to name but two. Serve it in bowls with bread croûtons as a lunch or supper dish. It does create a lot of washing up but is so delicious it is worth the effort.

900 g (2 lb) fresh or 450 g (1 lb) frozen broad beans
1 litre (1¾ pints) water
sprigs of thyme
450 g (1 lb) mussels, washed and scrubbed
100 ml (4 fl oz) Muscadet or other dry white wine
2 shallots, chopped
150 g (6 oz) streaky bacon, chopped
1 onion, chopped
25 g (1 oz) butter
freshly milled black pepper
salt

Shell the beans and boil them uncovered in the water with the thyme until tender (how long depends on the age of the beans – frozen beans will take 5–10 minutes). Discard the thyme. To purée the beans and discard the skins, put the beans and the cooking liquid through a *mouli-légumes* and return to the saucepan in which they were cooked. Open the mussels by putting them into a large pan with the wine and shallots and bringing them to the boil. Remove the mussels as they open and, when they are cool enough to handle, shell them and add to the bean purée together with their strained cooking liquid. Heat the soup until it boils. Fry the chopped bacon and onion in the butter until golden and crisp. Season the soup with salt and pepper to taste and top with the onion.

Broad beans with artichokes
Ragoût de fèves léonard

Serve this Breton dish of broad beans and artichokes flavoured with bacon and savory or thyme either as a first course or as a vegetable accompaniment. It can be made from fresh or frozen broad beans.

- 450 g (1 lb) fresh or 225 g (8 oz) frozen broad beans
- 25 g (1 oz) butter
- 225 g (8 oz) streaky bacon, chopped
- 2 onions, finely chopped
- 150 ml ($\frac{1}{4}$ pint) Muscadet or other dry white wine
- 1 can artichoke bottoms, drained
- sprig of savory or thyme
- salt
- freshly milled black pepper
- 1 tablespoon chopped parsley

Shell the fresh beans. Melt the butter in a saucepan and gently fry the bacon and onions until soft and golden. Pour in the wine. Add the artichokes and savory or thyme. If using fresh beans, add them now. Season with salt and pepper and simmer for 30 minutes. If using frozen beans add them 5 minutes before the end of the cooking time. Sprinkle with chopped parsley and serve.

Broad bean purée with *andouilles*
Andouilles grillées à la purée de fèves

Andouilles and *andouillettes* are found all over France, although some regions are especially famous for them, notably Vire in Normandy. They are a kind of coarse sausage filled with chitterlings, and are very much an acquired taste. *Andouilles* are made with the large intestine of the pig, while *andouillettes* are made with the small intestine and these last are usually grilled or fried and served with apples.

Andouilles are sold ready cooked and are often sliced and served as a first course, but the slices can also be grilled and are served with baked or mashed potatoes, or with a delicate, green purée of broad beans. This same purée is also eaten as a garnish with lamb or pork.

900 g (2 lb) fresh or 450 g (1 lb) frozen broad beans
sprigs of thyme and parsley, tied together
1 bay leaf
salt
freshly milled black pepper
1–2 tablespoons crème fraîche
25 g (1 oz) butter
12 thick slices *andouille de Vire*
2–3 tablespoons oil
chives, snipped

Shell the beans and boil them with the thyme, parsley and bay leaf, uncovered to preserve their colour, until tender, the time will depend on their age. (Frozen will take 5–10 minutes.) Drain, discard the herbs and purée the beans. Season to taste with salt and pepper and mix in the crème fraîche and butter. Meanwhile brush the slices of *andouille* with oil and grill them on each side until brown. Serve them surrounded by the bean purée and sprinkle with the chives.

Fruits of Summer and Autumn

As late summer turned into autumn we stayed for a week at La Bégaudière, a Breton stone farmhouse just outside Dol-de-Bretagne. The sun was going down as we drove from St-Malo through lanes planted on either side with orchards laden with tiny, wrinkled cider apples, and fields of blue-green cabbages which were turning purple in the fading light. Arriving at the house we were soon sitting down and tucking into a delicious meal of mussels, lamb with haricot beans, a green salad in a vinaigrette dressing laced with shallots and a huge helping of *far forn aux pruneaux*, or battered prunes.

On the Saturday we went to the market in Dol, which ran right up the main street of medieval houses to a covered arcade at the top. By 10.30 a.m. it was packed, the traffic was snarled up on the incoming roads and there was nowhere to park. A whippy wind reminded us that summer was almost over and meant that the vendors cooking *crêpes* and hot sausages had a steady queue of customers.

There were stalls selling snowy white lace, clothes, hats and jewellery, clogs and shoes, onions, lettuces and shallots, dried flowers, pickled gherkins, parsley and chives, beetroot, farm chickens, guinea fowl and quails, vegetables of every kind, glistening apple cake and country bread. There was duck and goose *foie gras*, *rillettes*, *pâtés* and *charcuterie* of every kind and, of course, fish. Large and small crabs, mussels, boxes of oysters, sprats, winkles and sardines, conger eel, bream, plaice and turbot.

And fruit. We were too late for the cherries but there were still big fat strawberries next to baskets of raspberries and crates of plums, greengages, damsons and pears. And of course apples, those staple fruits of the north which form part of the mythology of Brittany. Country lore dictated that as each orchard was picked, the highest fruit would be left at the top of one of the trees; if it withstood the autumn gales longer than the dying leaves, it augured well for the following harvest. And legend tells how in the Arrée mountains, known as Roc Tréverzel, a treasure is hidden and protected by the *santig koz*, an ancient wooden saint. Anyone who comes close to finding this treasure is subjected to an irresistible temptation in the shape of an offering of Roc Tréverzel apples, which have the effect of making the bounty-hunter lose all sense of time and hold him in thrall for 100 years.

Legends or not, the French of the north waste no time in dealing with their fruits as they come into season, eating them raw, turning them into tarts or liqueurs, sorbets and jellies, or using them to flavour meats and fish. And there's many a family who has on the go a jar of *liqueur de vieux garçon*, which they call *confiture de vieux garçon* in the south of France and *Rumtopf* in Germany and for which the recipe is given in both *Simple French Cuisine* and *Kitchen Suppers*. Basically it is made by covering the soft fruits of summer in sugar and *eau-de-vie* and leaving until Christmas.

Cherries to sloes

Spiced cherries

Quail with cherries

Duck with cherries

Cherry soup

Brioche with cherries

Cherry tart

Cherry liqueur

Strawberry tart or tartlets

Strawberries in sparkling cider

Wells of love

Strawberry omelette

Strawberry mousse

Grandma's strawberries

Strawberries and melon

Strawberry liqueur

Stewed plums or prunes

Greengage tart

Damson spirit

Shuttered plums

Guinea fowl with prunes

Rabbit with prunes

Battered prunes

Quail with bilberries

Sloe liqueur

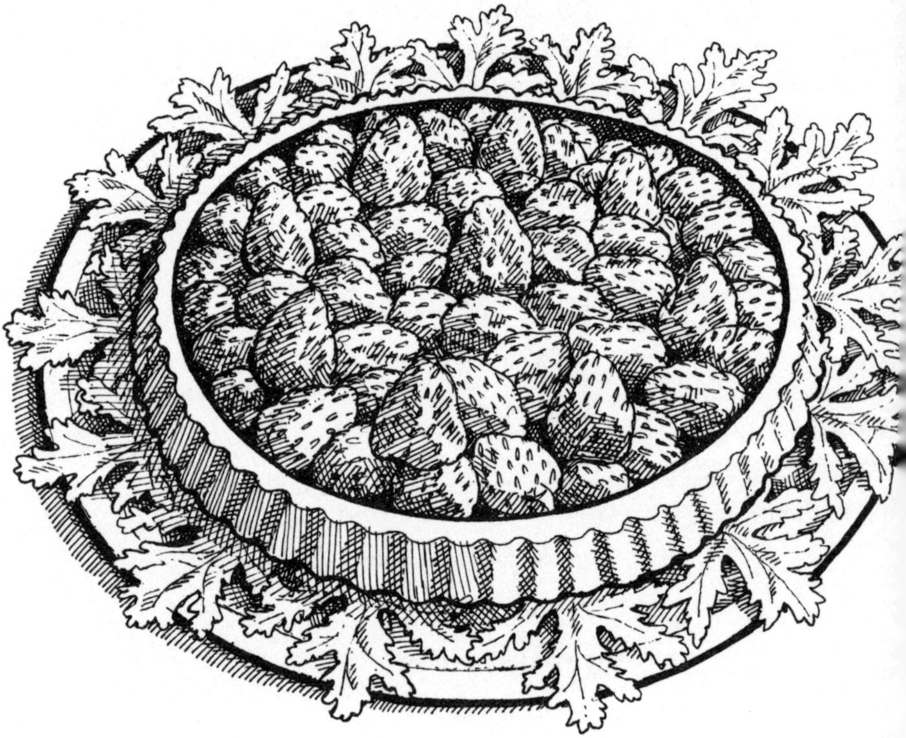

CHERRIES

The early-flowering cherries are one of the first signs of spring, their white blossom defying the cold winds of March and April, and when the first fruits begin to appear in the markets a couple of months later, we know it is summer. Picking cherries on a commercial basis is hard work but if you just want a basket or two, nothing is more agreeable than pulling down clusters of the fruit, their juice staining your fingers a deep red, tasting as you go. Poured into a pretty ceramic bowl they are at their most inviting left on the table for everyone to help themselves as they pass by.

In Flanders and the Nord, they make cherries into soup and, spiced, they are one of the specialities of Picardy. The Bretons spice them too, cook them with quail or turn them into a splendid liqueur. The Normans marry them with duck, turn them into tarts or serve them simply stewed with crème fraîche or fromage frais, especially around Jumièges which is as renowned for its cherries as it is for the magnificent ruined abbey set in a coil of the Seine as it snakes its way towards Honfleur and Le Havre.

For cooking purposes choose cherries which are slightly tart. These are usually dark red like Morellos or Dukes, but ask if you can taste one before you buy. White cherries which come later are much sweeter. On informal occasions it isn't really necessary to stone cherries which are to go into tarts or desserts, but for times when you can't avoid this chore, it's worth investing in a special implement sold in kitchen shops which can be used for stoning either cherries or olives.

Spiced cherries
Cerises au vinaigre

Although it is Picardy which is renowned for its spiced cherries, this recipe in fact comes from Brittany. It is not so dissimilar from the Provençal recipe I gave in *Simple French Cuisine* but uses white wine or cider vinegar instead of red wine and different spices. Eat these cherries as you would gherkins, with cold meats or as part of a mixed platter of crudités. They are ready after a fortnight but will keep for well over a year. When the jar is empty use the vinegar to flavour salads or meat and game sauces.

600 ml (1 pint) white wine vinegar or cider vinegar
rind of 1 orange or lemon, finely peeled
225 g (8 oz) light brown sugar
3 cloves
1–2 cinnamon sticks, broken in pieces
450 g (1 lb) ripe cherries, unstoned

Put the vinegar into a saucepan with the orange or lemon peel, the sugar, cloves and cinnamon. Bring to the boil and simmer until the sugar has dissolved. Remove from the heat and allow to cool. Wash and dry the cherries, and trim the stalks to about 1 cm (½ in). Put them into a glass preserving jar and pour over the cooled vinegar and spices. Seal and set aside for at least a fortnight before using.

Quail with cherries
Caille à la bretonne

Quail, which were once part of the hunter's bag, are nowadays farm-reared and available throughout the year. In this recipe from Brittany, they are stuffed with cherries, cooked with apples and served with a cherry sauce. Serve one or two quail per head depending on appetites.

450 g (1 lb) cherries, stoned
4–8 quail
4–8 rashers streaky bacon
3 tablespoons oil
450 g (1 lb) crisp eating apples, peeled, cored and sliced
2 tablespoons calvados
4 tablespoons dry cider or white wine
salt
freshly milled black pepper
sprig of fresh rosemary
25 g (1 oz) butter
1–2 tablespoons caster sugar

Put one or two cherries into the cavity of each bird, wrap each in a rasher of bacon and secure with string. Heat half the oil in a flameproof casserole and fry the apple slices gently for 5–10 minutes. Remove. Add the remaining oil and brown the quail all over. Heat the calvados in a ladle or small pan, light it and pour it over the birds. When the flames die down, add the cider or wine, salt and pepper. Put the apple slices and the sprig of rosemary on top. Cover and simmer for 30–40 minutes. Towards the end of this cooking time, melt the butter in a pan and stew the remaining cherries gently, for 5–10 minutes; they should be soft but hold their shape. Sprinkle with the sugar. Serve the quail on a long plate, surrounded by the cherries and apples. Reduce the sauce by rapid boiling and pour it over the quail.

Duck with cherries
Canard aux cerises de Pont-Audemer

Pont-Audemer stands by the river Risle just south of the Vernier marsh where wild ducks flourish. It is a town worth a detour, to see its seventeenth-century timbered, corbelled houses and its eleventh-century church, St-Ouen, which contains some wonderful stained glass, including a modern crucifixion by Max Ingrand. From such a delightful place comes this delightfully simple recipe in which cherries are gently stewed in wine, and the duck, either wild or farmed, is cooked in their juices and served surrounded by the whole fruit. Accompany the duck with a dish of potatoes in milk, *pommes de terre à la normande* (see Potatoes and Leeks section).

450 g (1 lb) cherries, stoned
100 ml (scant ¼ pint) light red wine
1 Barbary, mallard or plump duckling
50 g (2 oz) butter
2 level teaspoons flour
1 bay leaf
salt
freshly milled black pepper

Stone the cherries over the pan in which they are to be cooked, to catch the juice. Add the wine, bring to the boil and simmer, uncovered, for 4–5 minutes. Cover and set aside for 15 minutes to allow the cherries time to release their juice. Meanwhile, prick the duck all over with a fork (this will help the fat to run when it is browned). Melt half the butter in a flameproof casserole that will hold the duck comfortably and brown the bird well on all sides, over a medium heat. This will take 10–15 minutes. Remove the duck, discard all the fatty juices in the pan and wipe it out with kitchen paper. Add the remaining butter, let it melt, and stir in the flour and cook for 2 minutes, stirring constantly. Strain the cherries over a jug and gradually stir the juice into the flour. Return the duck breast side down, add the bay leaf, salt and pepper. Cover and simmer for 45 minutes–1 hour, depending upon whether you want it to be pink or well done. Turn it breastside up and add the cherries. Cover and simmer for a further 15 minutes. Put the duck on a warm serving dish surrounded by the cherries. Boil the sauce hard to reduce by about half and pour some over the bird, the rest into a sauceboat.

Cherry soup
Soupe aux cerises à la flamande

This cherry soup makes a simple but effective beginning or end to a summer lunch or dinner; it can be eaten either hot or cold but is really nicest when it is just warm, and it is especially appealing both visually and to the taste if a mixture of black and white cherries are used. The name is somewhat misleading, particularly as it is sometimes called *soupe aux cerises à l'anglaise*, because the English word 'soup' immediately conjures up something liquid and savoury, eaten as a starter or as a simple meal. But the French word *soupe* has a different meaning: it actually refers to the bread used to mop up whatever the peasant might be having for supper.

450 g (1 lb) cherries, stoned or unstoned
100 g (4 oz) caster or vanilla sugar
1 cinnamon stick

Put the cherries, sugar and cinnamon into a pan and barely cover them with cold water. Bring to the boil and simmer for 5–10 minutes until the sugar has dissolved and the fruit is soft but still holds its shape. Remove cherries to a bowl using a slotted spoon. Boil the liquid hard until reduced by half and pour over the fruit.

Brioche with cherries
Croûtons de badies

Cherries have all sorts of curious names in Brittany. They are known as *badies* around Rennes, whereas in Cancale they call them *roupettes à queues*, and elsewhere they are known as *kerez* or *badiou*. The original recipe calls for them to be stoned, which seems a pity for such a childish pudding treat as this. It's really only necessary if you are afraid someone may break a tooth or you feel too old to play Tinker Tailor. In Normandy, they serve apple purée on slices of fried bread or brioche.

225 g (8 oz) cherries
25–50 g (1–2 oz) caster or vanilla sugar
50 g (2 oz) butter
4 thick slices stale brioche or French bread
ground cinnamon

Put cherries and sugar into a saucepan and bring gently to the boil (add no water), stirring from time to time. Simmer for 5–10 minutes, until they are soft but still hold their shape. Melt the butter in a frying pan and fry the bread on both sides until golden. Put on to a serving dish or individual plates, pile the cherries on top of each piece of fried bread, sprinkle with cinnamon and serve immediately.

Cherry tart
Tarte aux cerises

In this cherry tart from Normandy, the stewed cherries, cream and fromage frais are piled into a cooked sweet pastry shell, which can be one you buy or make yourself (see Etceteras). The cherry mixture can be made well ahead of time, but only pile it into the pastry shell right at the last minute.

450 g (1 lb) cherries, stoned or unstoned
50–75 g (2–3 oz) caster or vanilla sugar
150 ml ($\frac{1}{4}$ pint) double cream
150 ml ($\frac{1}{4}$ pint) fromage frais
sweet or puff pastry shell, baked blind

Put the cherries and sugar into a saucepan and bring gently to the boil (add no water), stirring from time to time. Simmer for 5–10 minutes, until they are soft but still hold their shape. Remove from the heat and allow to cool. Whip the cream, stir in a spoonful or two of the cooking juices and fold in the fromage frais, taste and if necessary add more sugar. When ready to serve, spread the cream and cheese mixture over the pastry base and pile the cherries on top using a slotted spoon. The juice can be handed separately in a jug.

Cherry liqueur
Cerises à l'eau-de-vie

Mur de Bretagne, in the heart of Brittany where Corot loved to paint, produces a cherry liqueur on a grand scale with the sour cooking cherries grown in the area, and there was a time when every household in Haute-Bretagne would offer their own home-made version to friends and family. The cherries are steeped for up to a year in sugar syrup and apple brandy. In this country use one of the less expensive varieties of calvados, or make it with vodka or white rum. Serve it right at the end of the meal in the drained and still warm coffee cups, or in small glasses. Whichever you use, put two or three cherries in each and top up with liqueur; everyone eats the cherries by picking them up by their tails.

350 g (12 oz) caster sugar
150 ml ($\frac{1}{4}$ pint) water
450 g (1 lb) white cooking cherries
600 ml (1 pint) apple brandy, vodka or white rum

Dissolve the sugar in the water over a low heat, then let it cool. Cut the cherry stalks to about 1 cm ($\frac{1}{2}$ in). Put the fruit into a 1 litre preserving jar, add the sugar water and fill to the top with the spirit. Seal and leave for 3–12 months before indulging.

STRAWBERRIES

It is Plougastel in Brittany's Finistère which is most famously associated with the strawberry. Local folklore tells how the good people of the region aroused the devil's anger by spurning his attempts to buy them with gold. (It probably wasn't too much of a temptation because they lived by bartering and hardly knew what gold was.) Their stubbornness threw him into such a rage that he bombarded their fields with millions of stones so that nothing would grow. But God took pity on the Bretons, and his saints lent a hand: St James filled the estuary with scallops, St Peter explained how to navigate, St John created a miraculous spring, and all those stones were turned into strawberries by St Thomas.

Like all folklore, it is rooted in reality because the juicy strawberries we eat nowadays did have their beginnings in Plougastel, but not until the eighteenth century. A French naval officer called Freziers introduced the inhabitants to a plant from Chile which had huge, yellow berries tasting faintly of pineapples. These were crossed with wild strawberries from Virginia and the ancestor of the modern strawberry was born.

It wasn't too long before the new fruit became an English obsession and the early crop, grown in the sheltered climate of the Plougastel peninsula, were exported directly to Plymouth from where they were sent to fruit markets all over England. The trade continues to this day and during the season, which lasts from May to July, strawberries from Plougastel are eaten all over Europe.

The first summer strawberries are delicious on their own, dipped perhaps into a bowl of sugar and then into crème fraîche or whipped cream which can be lightened by folding in a beaten egg white or two. If the fruit is not quite ripe, it is greatly improved by macerating for an hour or two in either 2–3 tablespoons of lemon juice or wine, or perhaps a mild fruit or wine vinegar.

Strawberry tart or tartlets
Tarte aux fraises

In Normandy it feels as if summer has really arrived when every restaurant's sweet trolley and every *pâtissier*'s window gleams with strawberry tarts and tartlets. Everyone has their own idea as to the kind of pastry to use and exactly how it should be mixed. The only point of agreement is that the strawberries must not be cooked but are placed on a baked pastry shell and then covered with a hot redcurrant glaze, which is often jazzed up with a dash of kirsch or other spirit. You will only need to use about half the glaze as given in the recipe, but it's worth making this quantity and storing what you don't use for another time, adding more water as necessary. This is an easy and pretty dessert to make especially if you buy a pre-cooked shell. (If you prefer make your own, see Etceteras.) Small tartlet shells can be filled in the same way, as indeed can an open sponge flan.

350 g (12 oz) strawberries, hulled
1 pre-baked 20 cm (8 in) sweet pastry shell
100 g (4 oz) redcurrant jelly
2 teaspoons water
dash kirsch, noyau or other fruit spirit

Arrange the strawberries in the pastry shell, packing them tightly together. Melt the redcurrant jelly in a small saucepan with the water, whisking until smooth. Stir in the liqueur. Brush the glaze generously over the surface of the strawberries, making sure it covers any exposed pastry and the rim of the tart. Set aside to cool and set.

Strawberries in sparkling cider
Fraises au cidre bouché

In this recipe the strawberries are macerated for an hour or two in sugar and just before they are served they are sprinkled with *cidre bouché*, sparkling cider. Drink the rest of the bottle as you eat them. In Brittany they are served with crisp sweet biscuits, *galettes bretonnes*, or perhaps *crêpes-dentelles*, thin, lacy pancakes which can be bought in packets or tins. Here you could serve them with sponge fingers or almond twirls.

450 g (1 lb) ripe strawberries
2–3 tablespoons caster or vanilla sugar
150 ml (¼ pint) sparkling cider

Put strawberries into a bowl or individual glasses and sprinkle with the sugar. Cover and refrigerate. Just before serving add the sparkling cider.

Wells of love
Puns ar garantez

To make these little wells of love, the Bretons macerate strawberries in sugar and a special kirsch made from wild cherries. You could use noyau or cherry liqueur instead. Just before serving, the strawberries are covered with beaten egg yolks and capped at the last minute with the stiffly whipped whites.

225 g (8 oz) strawberries
3 tablespoons caster or vanilla sugar
2 tablespoons kirsch
3 eggs, separated

Divide strawberries between four individual glasses or bowls and sprinkle with 1 tablespoon of sugar and 1 of kirsch. Leave for an hour or so. Beat the egg yolks with 1 tablespoon of sugar and 1 of kirsch until thick and creamy; pile on top of the strawberries. Just before serving, beat the egg whites until stiff, fold in the last tablespoon of sugar and put a dollop on top of each glass or bowl.

Strawberry omelette
Omelette sivi

This is a delicious way of eating strawberries on a chilly evening. In Brittany they mark the cooked omelette in squares with a red hot branding iron, setting a strawberry in each square. In the absence of such a tool, we have to make do with putting the omelette under a hot grill. In Normandy they make a similar omelette, filled with sliced apples or pears stewed in butter until soft, and flamed in calvados.

225 g (8 oz) strawberries
2 teaspoons kirsch or noyau
4 eggs
salt
2 tablespoons caster or vanilla sugar
2 tablespoons crème fraîche
50 g (2 oz) butter
1–2 teaspoons icing sugar

Hull the strawberries, cut them in half and put them into a bowl with the spirit. Beat the eggs with a little salt, the sugar and the crème fraîche. Heat the grill. Melt the butter in a frying pan and when it is sizzling, pour in the eggs. Stir them briskly and cook the omelette over a high flame, lifting the edges as they cook to allow the runny centre to spread underneath. Pile strawberries into the centre and fold the omelette in half. Sprinkle with icing sugar and put under the hot grill for the sugar to melt and brown.

Strawberry mousse
Coupe de fraises

This delicate dessert calls for strawberries which have ripened in the sun and are full of flavour. They are puréed and mixed with whipped cream and beaten egg whites. Allow time for the finished mousse to chill in the fridge for an hour or two. Serve in individual glasses with almond biscuits or twirls.

350 g (12 oz) ripe strawberries
juice of 1 lemon
150 ml (¼ pint) whipped cream
2 egg whites
3–4 tablespoons caster or vanilla sugar

Put the strawberries into a bowl with the lemon juice and leave to macerate for 1–2 hours, then put them into a blender and blend until smooth. Fold in the whipped cream. Beat the egg whites until stiff and fold into the mixture; add sugar to taste. Spoon into individual glasses, cover and refrigerate.

Grandma's strawberries
Fraises mam goz

The Breton *mam goz*, grandma, knew what she was doing with these strawberries. Red wine and water are simmered with cinnamon, sugar and orange flower water to form a sweet scented syrup in which to macerate the fruit. It's wonderful at the height of summer but also a perfect way of dealing with the forced strawberries available out of season. Serve with or without whipped cream.

150 ml ($\frac{1}{4}$ pint) red wine
150 ml ($\frac{1}{4}$ pint) water
100 g (4 oz) sugar
1 cinnamon stick
1 tablespoon orange flower water
450 g (1 lb) strawberries

Put the wine, water, sugar, cinnamon and orange flower water into a saucepan, bring to boiling point and boil hard, uncovered, for 5 minutes. Allow to cool. Put strawberries into a bowl, pour over the wine syrup, discarding the cinnamon stick. Cover and refrigerate for at least 2 hours.

Strawberries and melon
Petits gris aux fraises

Brittany melons grown around Rennes and Nantes are nicknamed *petits gris*, their dull outer skin giving no hint of the red flesh within. Galia or charentais melons will do very well instead. In this recipe they are filled with strawberries and flavoured with a mixture of strawberry liqueur (see below), hydromel and lemon juice. Hydromel, a distilled drink flavoured with honey, has roots going back to Celtic times. Known as *boisson des dieux* it went out of favour in the early part of this century but is nowadays experiencing a revival. It is drunk as an aperitif or a digestif. If you haven't any use a tablespoon of honey instead.

4 small ripe melons
4 tablespoons strawberry liqueur
2 tablespoons hydromel
squeeze of lemon juice
225 g (8 oz) strawberries, cut in half
toasted almonds

Cut the tops off the melons and scoop out the seeds using a spoon. Cut a sliver off the base of each so they will stand upright. Mix the liqueur with the hydromel and lemon juice and stir into the strawberries. Fill each melon cavity with some of the fruit and pour over any remaining juices. Chill for an hour and serve sprinkled with toasted almonds.

Strawberry liqueur
Liqueur de fraises

Make this strawberry liqueur at the peak of the summer with firm, ripe strawberries. The fruit is steeped in alcohol for a month, then strained. The strawberries lose all their colour, staining the liqueur a brilliant scarlet, but rather than throw them away, purée them and mix with cream to make a delicious, boozy fool. The liqueur will be ready to drink at Christmas, but if you can be persuaded to set it aside for a year, it will be even better. The alcohol you use can be almost any kind, choosing from the fruit *eaux-de-vie* widely available in France, vodka or white rum, apple brandy, or armagnac, even gin. The same recipe can be used for other soft fruits like raspberries, red, white and black currants, loganberries and tayberries etc.

450 g (1 lb) firm, ripe strawberries
150 g (6 oz) caster or vanilla sugar
1 bottle *eau-de-vie* or other spirit

Choose a 1 litre preserving jar and fill it right to the top with strawberries. Pour in the caster or vanilla sugar. Fill to the top with spirit. Seal and leave for at least one month in a cool, dark place. Turn the jar over occasionally to distribute the sugar. Strain and bottle.

PLUMS AND PRUNES

Several varieties of plums are grown in northern France, to be eaten mostly just as they are or used to make jams, tarts and compotes. The best, most French agree, have yellow or green skins and the best of all are greengages and the small mirabelles, yellow streaked with red. Damsons, *prunes de Damas*, the plum from Damascus, with their deep purple skins and strong, bitter flavour are best from old orchards and make wonderful compotes, the stones make an especially flavoursome noyau, which can be used to give fillip to fruit salads, ice creams etc.

Prunes, *pruneaux*, are dried varieties with red or purple skins and the best come from Agen or Touraine. Californian prunes which are widely available here come from the same variety as Agen prunes. Apart from being made into compotes and used to flavour cakes, puddings and tarts, prunes play their part in savoury dishes throughout the region.

Stewed plums or prunes
Compote de prunes ou pruneaux

The best plums to use for compotes are greengages, mirabelles or damsons. If you are using prunes, soak them for several hours in cold water or steep them for half an hour or so in boiling water. Whichever fruit you use there's no need to stone them, but if you prefer to do this, the stones are easy to remove if the fruit is cut in half.

450 g (1 lb) plums or prunes
300 ml (½ pint) water or a mixture of red wine and water
100 g (4 oz) caster or vanilla sugar
1 cinnamon stick

Put the fruit into a saucepan with all the other ingredients. Bring to the boil and simmer very gently until tender. Plums will take 10–15 minutes, prunes up to twice as long.

Greengage tart
Tarte aux vertes bonnes

The French name for a greengage is *reine-claude* after the wife of François I who, while her husband was busy making war, busied herself encouraging her friends to cultivate the trees and gave the fruit her name. But in Normandy this tart is made with *vertes bonnes*, a special variety of greengage which grows in the Seine valley along the borders of the river. It calls for a sweetened shortcrust pastry which is sprinkled with biscuit crumbs to absorb the juices of the fruit. Make the pastry at least half an hour before you want to cook the tart, as it must rest before being rolled out, otherwise it will shrink in the oven. If greengages are not available, the tart can be made with other varieties of plums.

225 g (8 oz) sweet shortcrust pastry (see Etceteras)
50 g (2 oz) plain biscuits
450 g (1 lb) greengages
300 ml (½ pint) double cream
50 g (2 oz) caster or vanilla sugar

Heat the oven to Gas 6/400°F/200°C. Line a 22 cm (9 in) flan tin with a removable base with the pastry. Prick it all over with the prongs of a fork. Crush the biscuits into fine crumbs in a bag using a rolling pin, and sprinkle them over the pastry, covering the base completely. Cut the greengages in half and cut out the stones. Pack them tightly, skinside down, on top of the crumbs. Bake for 30–35 minutes. When cool enough to handle, remove the tart from the tin. Whip the cream with the sugar and pile on top of the tart just before serving. Eat warm or cold.

Damson spirit
Noyau

If you want to give an almond flavour to sweets, ice creams, fruit salads or cakes, make this easy noyau. In this recipe damson stones are used but you could use any plum or peach, apricot or cherry stones.

Use a small preserving jar with a close-fitting lid. Fill it with damson stones which you have cracked with a hammer. Top up completely with apple brandy, *eau-de-vie* or vodka. Put on the lid and set aside for at least three months, the longer the better.

Shuttered plums
Jalousies

Jalousies grace the window of many a *pâtisserie*. They are quick and easy to make if you use ready-made puff pastry. They can be filled with any sort of plum or other fruits, or more simply still with almost any kind of jam.

Heat the oven to Gas 7/425°F/220°C. Roll the puff pastry into two strips each about 10 cm (4 in) wide and twice as long. Lay one strip on a damp baking sheet. Cut three or four plums in half, remove the stones, and place down the middle, leaving a clear border which should be brushed all round with water. Fold the second strip in half lengthwise and cut horizontal slits at regular intervals, leaving a rim all round. Open it out – it will look like a slatted shutter – and lay it on top of the fruit. Press the edges of the pastry together all round. Brush with beaten egg and sprinkle lightly with sugar. Bake for 10–15 minutes, until golden brown.

Guinea fowl with prunes
Pintadeau aux pruneaux

Guinea fowl are lean birds which when roasted can be dry, but there is no danger of that in this adaptation of a Breton recipe. The meat is soft and tender and sweetly flavoured by the prunes soaked in *lambig*, Brittany's apple brandy. It could be served with a purée of apples or *purée bretonne*, which is a mixture of mashed potatoes and carrots.

24 pitted prunes
2–3 tablespoons apple brandy or calvados
25 g (1 oz) butter
2 tablespoons oil
1 guinea fowl
3 onions, sliced
300 ml (½ pint) strong dry cider
sprigs of thyme and parsley, tied in a bunch
1 bay leaf
salt
freshly milled black pepper

Soak the prunes in the apple brandy or calvados for 30 minutes. Melt the butter with the oil in a heavy-based casserole and brown the guinea fowl well all over. Remove to a plate. Add the sliced onions and fry them gently until turning golden. Return the bird to the casserole and pour in the cider. Let it bubble hard for a few minutes. Add the prunes and their liquid, followed by the thyme, parsley and bay leaf. Season with salt and pepper. Cover and simmer for 45–50 minutes. Remove the guinea fowl to a warm dish, surround it with the onions and prunes; discard the herbs. Keep the dish warm while you boil the liquid in the pan over a high heat until it has reduced by half. Put into a sauceboat and serve separately.

Rabbit with prunes
Lapin aux pruneaux

Rabbit and prunes seem to have a natural affinity and northern France has many different recipes. This one from Haute-Bretagne is quick and easy to prepare. Eat it with baked jacket potatoes or a mixture of mashed potatoes and celeriac.

10 g (½ oz) butter
12 small onions
1 teaspoon caster sugar
1 rabbit, cut into 8 pieces
1 tablespoon flour
2 tablespoons oil
150 ml (¼ pint) Muscadet or other dry white wine
12 prunes
sprigs of thyme and parsley, tied in a bunch
1 bay leaf
salt
freshly milled black pepper

Melt the butter in a heavy-based casserole, add the onions and sprinkle with the sugar. Shake over a high heat until the onions are golden brown. Remove and set aside. Roll the rabbit pieces in the flour until well coated. Heat the oil in the casserole and brown the rabbit pieces all over, in two batches is necessary. Add the wine, prunes and herbs and season with salt and pepper. Put the little onions on top, bring to the boil, cover and simmer for 45–60 minutes.

Battered prunes
Far forn aux pruneaux

Breton *farz* or *fars* come in many forms, sweet or savoury. This one, flavoured with prunes, is baked, *far forn*, and eaten like cake. Once it was part of every wedding feast – guests would wrap a piece in their handkerchief to take home to those left behind.

Both sweet and savoury *farz* are made with varying quantities of buckwheat or wheat flour, eggs, milk and water. The savoury version, served either sliced or broken into pieces, is sometimes called *farz pod* because it is boiled in a muslin bag in the same pot as the meat or vegetables. The best-known dish in which it appears is the *kig ha farz*.

Sometimes these boiled *farz* are called after the shape of the bag which might be like a sleeve, *farz manch*, a bag, *farz sac'h*, or a pocket, *farz poch*. Then there are small dumpling-like *farz* known as *kunpoud* or *pouloud* which are often sweetened with raisins. Savoury *farz* were invented by people to whom bread was almost unknown, but nowadays not very many can spare the time to make them.

However, baked sweet *farz* appear on many restaurant menus and in every bakery. Apart from those made with prunes they are often filled with raisins, dried apricots, poached apples or pears.

225 g (8 oz) prunes
2–3 tablespoons calvados or brandy
3 eggs
100 g (4 oz) caster or vanilla sugar
125 g (5 oz) flour
550 ml (scant 1 pint) milk
pinch salt
butter

Soak the prunes in the calvados or brandy for 1–2 hours. Heat oven to Gas 7/425°F/220°C. Beat the eggs well and beat in the sugar, followed by the flour. Gradually beat in the milk and salt. Stir in the prunes and spirit. Butter a shallow earthenware 2 litre (3½ pint) dish. Pour in the mixture. Bake for 10 minutes, then lower the heat to Gas 5/375°F/190°C for 30 minutes until the *far* is puffed and golden. Eat warm or cold, cut into slices.

BILBERRIES AND SLOES

Bilberries grow wild in the damp woodlands, heaths and moors of Brittany and Britain. In late summer, some may even creep into the shops. If you can't get hold of them use blueberries instead, their cultivated cousins, which are now quite widely available and are sweet and rich in vitamins and as good to eat raw as cooked.

Sloes are also only usually found wild. The fruit of the blackthorn which grows in thickets and hedgerows, they look like small plums with their dust of blue bloom and their French name is *prunelles sauvages*, little wild plums. In Brittany they call them *blosses*. They are hard and bitter, and at their best after the first frost, which softens their skins and improves their flavour. They are sometimes made into a jelly, but more often used to flavour liqueur.

Quail with bilberries
Cailles aux myrtilles

The bilberries give an unusual and special flavour to this dish which is enhanced by the addition of calvados, cider and herbs. Spring chicken are good cooked in the same way, but increase the cooking time to an hour. Serve with steamed new potatoes and watercress.

225 g (8 oz) bilberries or blueberries
4 quail
4 rashers streaky bacon
2 tablespoons olive oil
2 tablespoons calvados or brandy
150 ml (¼ pint) dry cider
sprigs parsley, thyme and chervil
salt
freshly milled black pepper
1 tablespoon caster sugar
25 g (1 oz) butter
2 tablespoons redcurrant jelly
2 tablespoons crème fraîche
few sprigs watercress, to garnish

Put two or three bilberries or blueberries inside each quail. Wrap each in a rasher of bacon and secure with string. Heat the oil in a heavy-based casserole just large enough for the four birds to sit in comfortably. Brown them all over. Heat the calvados or brandy in a ladle or small saucepan, light it and pour it flaming over the birds. When the flames die down, pour in the cider, add the parsley, thyme and chervil and season with salt and pepper. Cover and simmer for 35–40 minutes. Put the remaining bilberries or blueberries into a small pan with the sugar and butter and heat gently, let them simmer until they are soft but still hold their shape. Set them aside until the birds are done. To serve, put them on a warm serving dish and cover them with foil. Reheat the bilberries or blueberries. Boil the sauce in which the quail were cooked until it reduces by half, stir in the jelly and the crème fraîche, and pour over the birds. Serve with the berries at one end of the dish and the watercress at the other.

Sloe liqueur
Liqueur de blosses

This is similar to our sloe gin but uses apple brandy as the spirit base. Whichever you use, the method is the same.

Pick sufficient sloes to fill a 1 litre jar. Prick each one with a darning needle, cut off its stalk and put into the jar. Layer with sugar as you go, allowing 100–150 g (4–6 oz) sugar for each kilo (2 lb). Top up completely with spirit, using either apple brandy, calvados or gin. (Or you could use *eau-de-vie* or vodka.) Leave for at least three months. Strain, discard the sloes and bottle.

Apples and pears

The climate of the north of France, particularly in Normandy and Brittany, is perfect for apples and pears and the orchards, which in spring were covered in rose-pink and white blossom, in autumn are weighed down with fruit. From kitchens and *pâtisseries* mouthwatering smells emerge as everyone gets down to the serious business of making flans and sweet dishes from the sheer abundance. And if you thought it was only the English who combined pork and apples, you're in for a pleasant surprise, because the French do, too, as well as using them to sweeten and give flavour to almost every other kind of meat.

At last in this country, supermarkets are leading the way in selling more interesting and traditional apples and pears and it is certainly worth experimenting with different kinds. Remember when cooking with apples that you don't need simply to buy Bramleys; they are fine when baked but are too mushy for many of the dishes. Go instead for hard, firm eating varieties, buy then slightly underripe and keep them for a few days before using. The same advice is even more appropriate for pears because once ripe they deteriorate rapidly, so it's best to buy them when still hard and use them once the neck yields when gently pressed.

Both apples and pears tend to go brown when peeled, but this can be prevented if you sprinkle them with lemon juice or put them into a bowl of water to which you have added a little salt, lemon juice or vinegar, as you prepare them.

Pork chops with apple sauce
Côtes de porc aux pommes

There are recipes from all over northern France for pork chops with apples. In this one, the chops are first marinated in calvados or pommeau, before being simmered in cider. The apples are gently stewed to a pulp in a separate pan while the chops are cooking.

4 lean pork chops or escalopes
1 tablespoon calvados or pommeau
25 g (1 oz) butter
700 g ($1\frac{1}{2}$ lb) tart eating apples, peeled, cored and sliced
2 tablespoons oil
2 shallots, chopped
salt
freshly milled black pepper
sprigs of fresh thyme or $\frac{1}{2}$ teaspoon dried
150 ml ($\frac{1}{4}$ pint) dry cider
handful parsley, chopped

Put the meat into a glass or china dish, sprinkle with the calvados or pommeau and set aside for 30 minutes. At the end of this time, melt the butter in a frying pan, add the apple slices and set over a very low heat to stew gently. Heat the oil in a flameproof casserole and brown the chops for 3 or 4 minutes on either side. Remove to a plate. Add the shallots to the casserole and cook until golden, but not brown. Remove to the plate. Return the chops to the pan, top with the shallots, season with salt and pepper and sprinkle with thyme. Pour in the cider, let it bubble, cover and simmer for 15 minutes until the juice runs clear when pricked with a pointed knife. Put the cooked chops and shallots on to a warm serving dish, cover loosely with foil and keep them warm. Boil the sauce hard until reduced by half, pour it over the chops, sprinkle them with the parsley and serve them surrounded by the apples.

Rabbit with apples
Lapin aux pommes

Make this Normandy dish, in which the rabbit absorbs the sweet flavours of cider, apples and herbs, either using a whole, jointed rabbit or, for a delicious and informal family supper, use the cubed rabbit sold frozen in some supermarkets. Serve with steamed or boiled potatoes dusted with parsley.

50 g (2 oz) butter
1 rabbit, cut into 8 pieces
300 ml ($\frac{1}{2}$ pint) strong dry cider
450 g (1 lb) hard sweet apples, peeled, quartered, cored and sliced
salt
freshly milled black pepper
sprigs of parsley and savory, tied in a bunch

Melt butter in a heavy-based casserole and fry the rabbit pieces all over until golden, in two batches if necessary. Lower the heat, cover and cook gently for 15 minutes. Meanwhile, heat the oven to Gas 4/350°F/180°C. Remove the rabbit to a bowl and pour the cider into the casserole. Boil it hard until reduced by half. Add the apple slices, put the rabbit on top and season with salt and pepper. Add the herbs, cover and put into the oven for 35–40 minutes.

Guinea fowl with apples
Pintadeau à la normande

In this recipe, which is also suitable for chicken or pheasant, the bird is braised between layers of apples laced with either cider or apple juice and becomes moist, tender and sweetly flavoured.

50 g (2 oz) butter
900 g (2 lb) sweet firm dessert apples, peeled, quartered and cored
½ teaspoon ground cinnamon
300 ml (½ pint) strong dry cider or apple juice
1 tablespoon oil
1 guinea fowl
salt
freshly milled black pepper
4 tablespoons crème fraîche

Heat the oven to Gas 5/375°F/190°C. Melt half the butter in a flameproof casserole and fry the apple slices, sprinkled with cinnamon, over a medium heat for 5–10 minutes, until soft but not brown. Remove to a bowl. Pour the cider or apple juice into the casserole, boil hard until reduced to 2–3 tablespoons, and pour over the apples. Add the remaining butter and the oil to the casserole and brown the guinea fowl all over. Remove and wipe out the casserole with kitchen paper. Lay half the apples over the base, put the guinea fowl, breast side down, on top and cover with the remaining apples and juices; season with salt and pepper. Put on the lid and transfer to the oven for 30 minutes. Remove, turn the bird breast side up, add the crème fraîche, cover and put back into the oven for a further 20 minutes. Put the bird on a serving dish and keep warm. Stir the apple and crème sauce over a medium heat until it reduces and thickens. Serve the sauce either surrounding the guinea fowl or in a sauceboat.

Roast pork on a bed of apples
Rôti de porc

In Haute-Bretagne they roast their pork surrounded by a bed of apples which half way through the cooking time are mashed to a pulp. I came across a similar recipe when writing *Simple French Cuisine from Provence and Languedoc*. It would be interesting to know whether it was the Bretons who taught it to the Provençals, or the other way round.

1½ kg (3 lb) roasting pork
1½ kg (3 lb) hard sweet eating apples, peeled, cored and sliced
50 g (2 oz) butter
salt
freshly milled black pepper

Heat the oven to Gas 6/400°F/200°C. Lay the pork in the middle of a shallow earthenware dish and surround by the apples, dotting them with the butter. Roast for 25 minutes per 450 g (1 lb). Half way through the cooking time, crush the apples to a pulp and season the meat with salt and pepper. Allow to rest in the turned-off oven for 15 minutes before serving in the dish in which the pork and apples were cooked.

Andouillettes baked with mustard and apples
Andouillettes à la mode de Carentan

Andouillettes are sold all over France and you either adore them or loathe them! In Normandy they are a speciality of Vire, Caen, Avranche and Rouen. They are made from the small intestine of the pig, stuffed with strips of pork or beef chitterling and stomach and flavoured with spices. They are usually grilled and served with plenty of mustard. This recipe comes from Carentan in Normandy's Manche, which was a Roman town and nowadays is a dairy centre, renowned for its cattle market. This recipe also works extremely well with spicy or herby sausages instead of *andouillettes*, which are not easily found outside France.

100 g (4 oz) softened butter
2 tablespoons mustard
700 g (1½ lb) *andouillettes*
6 apples, peeled, cored and thickly sliced
salt
freshly milled black pepper

Heat the oven to Gas 6/400°F/200°C. Mix half the butter with the mustard. Split the *andouillettes* in half lengthwise and spread the cut side with the mixture. Melt the remaining butter in a shallow oven dish that can go on top of the stove. Fry the apples until they begin to soften, then season with salt and pepper. Lay the *andouillettes* on top and bake for 20–30 minutes.

Sausages braised with apples
Saucisses aux pommes

On lean days, this is a cheap and cheerful Breton recipe for almost any sort of sausage, although the better the sausage the better the dish. It is quick to make and delicious served with mashed potatoes and a green vegetable.

25 g (1 oz) butter or
  1 tablespoon oil
450 g (1 lb) sausages
450 g (1 lb) sweet dessert
  apples, peeled, cored and
  sliced
salt
freshly milled black pepper
½ teaspoon cinnamon

Heat the butter or oil in a heavy-based pan and when it sizzles, brown the sausages all over. Add the apple slices. Lower the heat, and season with salt, pepper and cinnamon. Cover and simmer for 25 minutes. Remove the sausages to a warm serving dish, raise the heat and reduce the liquid surrounding the apples by half. Pour over the sausages and serve.

Black pudding with apples
Boudin noir aux pommes

Mortagne-au-Perche in Normandy's Orne region lays claim to being the capital of *boudin noir* and a brotherhood of pudding tasters, *Confrérie des chevaliers du goûte-boudin* who run an annual contest which attracts entries from all over Europe including Scotland. *Boudin noir* is much lighter than the English black pudding, being made from a mixture of pig's blood, cream, pork fat and onions. Traditionally eaten all over France as part of the feast after Christmas Eve Mass, *boudin noir* is good grilled or fried and served with a sauce of fried apples and onions. Needless to say, the same sauce goes well with ordinary sausages.

450–700 g (1–1½ lb) *boudin noir*
100 g (4 oz) butter
2–3 onions, finely chopped
4 eating apples, peeled, cored and sliced
1 teaspoon runny honey
salt
freshly milled black pepper

Grill or fry the *boudin noir*. Melt half the butter in a frying pan and gently fry the onions. Put the remaining butter in a saucepan, add the apples and honey and season with salt and pepper. Simmer, covered, until soft. Mix with the onions. Serve the sausages surrounded by the mixture of onions and apples.

Steak with apples
Steak au vinaigre de cidre

Yes, in Normandy, they even eat steak with apples! In this recipe they are mixed with onions and the gravy itself is flavoured with cider vinegar. Try it, it's extremely tasty.

4 steaks
juice of 1 lemon
freshly milled black pepper
25 g (1 oz) butter
1 tablespoon oil
2 onions, finely chopped
225 g (8 oz) apples, peeled, cored and sliced
100 ml (4 fl oz) cider vinegar

Put the steaks into a non-metallic dish, squeeze over the lemon juice and season with pepper. Leave to marinate for 1 hour. Melt the butter with the oil and fry the onions for a few minutes until they begin to soften, add the apple slices and cook together until they too are soft. Heat the grill pan for 5 minutes until very hot. Brush lightly with oil and grill the steaks, 2–3 minutes on each side for rare, 4–6 minutes for well done. Place them on a serving dish and keep them warm. Pour the cider vinegar into the grill pan, put it over the heat and let it bubble and reduce by half. Pour over the steaks and serve topped by the mixture of onions and apples.

Quails in their nests
Cailles en douillons

You need very large apples for this old Normandy method of cooking quails because when they are scooped out, they must be big enough to hold a bird. Some versions suggest wrapping the apples and quails in shortcrust pastry and if you want to try this, make sure you roll the pastry very thin.

25 g (1 oz) butter
2 tablespoons oil
4 quail
salt
freshly milled black pepper
2 tablespoons calvados
4 large apples
300 ml ($\frac{1}{2}$ pint) dry cider

Heat the oven to Gas 6/400°F/200°C. Heat the butter and oil in a flameproof, shallow oven dish and quickly brown the birds all over; season with salt and pepper. Put the calvados into a ladle or small pan, heat it, set it alight and pour it over the birds; when the flames die down set the birds aside. It's easier to core apples unpeeled, so prepare them by slicing off the top third of each and scooping out the cores and sufficient flesh to make hollows large enough to hold the birds. Now peel the apples and slice a sliver off the base of each so that they can stand upright. Place them in the dish and settle a bird in each whichever way up it fits most easily. Chop the remaining pieces of apple and put them round the whole apples with half the cider. Bake for 30 minutes, basting after 15 minutes. Transfer to a warm serving platter. Add the remaining cider to the dish and boil on top of the stove until it has reduced by half. Pour over the apples and quail.

Flamed sugared apples
Pommes flambées à la bretonne

Variations of this simple dessert appear all over the place. In this one, the apples are flavoured with cinnamon and flamed in calvados, but they are equally good flavoured with finely grated orange peel or nutmeg and flamed in some other spirit such as rum or brandy. Pears can be prepared in the same way and flamed perhaps in Poire William or your own pear liqueur.

3–4 tablespoons caster or vanilla sugar
4 sweet firm dessert apples, peeled, quartered and cored
75 g (3 oz) butter
½ teaspoon cinnamon
2 tablespoons calvados

Put the sugar on a plate and roll the apple quarters in it. Heat the butter in a frying pan and fry the apples over a medium heat, turning them frequently, until they soften and begin to caramelize. Sprinkle with the cinnamon. Heat the calvados in a small pan or ladle, light it and pour it flaming over the apples. Serve straight from the pan on to individual plates.

Apple mousse
Mousse de pommes

This is our English apple snow, Normandy version, but the cinnamon and cider in which the apples are cooked turn it a pale amber rather than white. It is served with a mixture of warm crème fraîche and cider.

700 g (1½ lb) apples, peeled, cored and sliced
150 g (6 oz) caster or vanilla sugar
pinch of ground cinnamon
4 tablespoons strong dry cider
2 egg whites
150 ml (¼ pint) crème fraîche

Put the apples, 50 g (2 oz) of the sugar, the cinnamon and 2 tablespoons of the cider into a saucepan and simmer gently, uncovered, until the apples are soft and most of the moisture has evaporated, stirring occasionally to prevent apples sticking and burning. Purée, cool and refrigerate. Half an hour or so before serving, beat the egg whites and fold in 50 g (2 oz) sugar, followed by the apple purée. Spoon the mixture into four bowls or glasses and return to the fridge. Just before serving, make a sauce by heating the crème fraîche with the remaining sugar and cider. Serve in a jug.

Apple tart
Tarte aux pomme normande

The secret of a successful apple tart is to make it in stages during the day. Left to the last minute it appears far too daunting but taken step by step it is really quite easy. It is nicest eaten warm either decorated with apricot glaze or whipped cream.

225 g (8 oz) sweet shortcrust pastry (see Etceteras)
900 g (2 lb) firm eating apples, such as Discovery or Cox's, peeled, quartered and cored
50 g (2 oz) caster or vanilla sugar
apricot glaze (see below) or whipped cream

Make the pastry and refrigerate for 30 minutes. Prepare the apples and put them into a bowl of water with either a little salt, lemon juice or vinegar to prevent them from going brown. Drain and chop half of them and put them in a saucepan with a couple of teaspoons of water and the sugar. Cook gently until they are soft and all the liquid has evaporated. Mash them and set aside to cool. Line a 22 cm (9 in) flan tin with a removable base with the pastry and prick the base all over with a fork. Refrigerate the tin in a plastic bag until ready to cook. Heat the oven to Gas 6/400°F/200°C. Spread the cooled apple purée over the pastry base. Drain and slice the remaining apples and arrange them on top in concentric, overlapping circles. Bake for 25–35 minutes until pastry is golden and the apples are turning deep brown at the edges. Brush the apples and pastry edge with apricot glaze or, if you prefer, allow the tart to cool and decorate with whipped cream.
To make apricot glaze: Empty a jar of apricot jam into a saucepan and add 4 tablespoons of water. Melt the jam gently until it bubbles, beating with a whisk to remove lumps. (If the lumps persist, rub the mixture through a sieve with the back of a spoon.) Brush this hot glaze over the tart. The rest can be stored in a screw-topped jar to be used another time, but you'll probably need to add a further tablespoon or two of water.

Creamy apple tart
Tarte aux pommes du pays de Bray

This version of apple tart comes from the rich dairy region of the pays de Bray. The apples are first gently stewed, then baked in a pastry shell with crème fraîche beaten with eggs. It is nicest eaten warm.

150 g (6 oz) sweet shortcrust pastry (see Etceteras)
50 g (2 oz) butter
450 g (1 lb) eating apples, peeled, cored and chopped
225 ml (8 fl oz) crème fraîche
2 eggs
50 g (2 oz) caster or vanilla sugar

Line a 20 cm (8 in) loose-bottomed flan tin with the pastry. Prick the base all over and refrigerate in a plastic bag while you prepare the filling. Heat the oven to Gas 6/400°F/200°C. Melt the butter in a frying pan and add the chopped apples. Fry for 10–15 minutes, until soft. Beat the crème fraîche with the eggs and the sugar. Spread the apples over the pastry base, pour over the cream mixture and bake for 30–35 minutes until puffed and golden.

Apple turnovers
Choquarts

These apple turnovers from Brittany are similar to Normandy's *chaussons*. They appear in the shops when the apple harvest begins and are sold in the region of St-Malo as *pommés*. They are very easy to make: the fruit melts to a purée and the pastry, with its egg glaze mixed with the juice from the fruit, is crisp and golden brown. For best results, eat warm.

225 g (8 oz) crisp eating apples, peeled, cored and thinly sliced
½ teaspoon cinnamon
juice of 1 lemon
50 g (2 oz) caster or vanilla sugar
225 g (8 oz) bought puff pastry
1 egg yolk

Put the sliced apples into a bowl and sprinkle with the cinnamon, lemon juice and sugar. Leave to macerate for 1 hour. Divide the pastry into four. Roll each piece into a ball between floured hands, then roll out into a circle, using a saucer as a cutting guide. Set aside in a cool place. When ready to cook, heat the oven to Gas 7/425°F/220°C and put a baking sheet inside to heat. Using a slotted spoon, fish out the apple slices from their juices, and divide between the four circles of pastry, laying them on one half only and leaving a border of pastry free. Dampen the edges all round with water. Fold the pastry over, forming a half moon, and press the edges together to seal well. Mark all round the sealed edges with the prongs of a fork. Cut a small slit in the top of each turnover for the steam to escape. Break the egg yolk into the bowl containing the remaining juices and beat well. Brush all over each turnover. Put on to the hot baking sheet and bake for about 20 minutes, until puffed and golden. Eat warm.

Apple jelly
Gelée de pommes

If you grow apples or have friends who do, the problem of what to do with the windfalls is solved by making apple jelly. Simply chop them up, cutting out any bruised or wormy pieces, and put them – skin, cores, pips and all – into a large saucepan. (The same recipe can be made with crab apples but cook them whole.) Cover with water, flavouring it as you will with either a few mint or scented geranium leaves or spices like cloves, cinnamon or root ginger. Bring to the boil and simmer until the fruit is soft and pulpy. Transfer fruit and juice to a jelly bag suspended over a bowl and leave overnight. Don't be tempted to squeeze it if you want clear rather than cloudy jelly.

The next day measure the juice and add 1 kg (2 lb) of sugar to every litre (2 pints) and a squeeze of lemon or orange juice. Heat gently until the sugar has dissolved, then raise the heat and boil steadily until setting point is reached. Test after 10 minutes or so: remove the pan from the heat, put a little of the jelly on to a cold saucer, let it cool for a minute or two, then push with the tip of your finger. If it wrinkles, it is done. If not, boil again and test every 5 minutes, taking the pan from the heat each time. Allow the jelly to cool a little before transferring to hot jars (they can be heated in a low oven). Seal, label and date, and store in a cool, dark, dry place.

Spiced pears
Poires au vinaigre

In Brittany they eat raw pears with butter, or stew or bake them with sugar, but a speciality of the region is to spice them and this is a perfect way of dealing with those small, hard pears that come into the shops in early autumn. They are delicious with duck or other game and go well with Boxing Day turkey.

1 kg ($2\frac{1}{4}$ lb) pears
100 g (4 oz) soft brown or granulated sugar
300 ml ($\frac{1}{2}$ pint) red wine vinegar
300 ml ($\frac{1}{2}$ pint) red wine

Peel the pears. If they are small, leave them whole, otherwise cut in quarters. Put them in a wide-mouthed flameproof casserole. Add the sugar, vinegar and wine. Simmer, covered, for one hour. Uncover and turn the pears over carefully, then simmer, uncovered, for another hour, until tender. Put into a sterilized jar and pour over the liquid. Top up if necessary with more vinegar. Keep at least two weeks before eating.

Pears or apples in dressing gowns
Douillons ou bourdelots

Normandy's pears or apples cooked in pastry are called *douillons* or *bourdelots*; the names are interchangeable, but the first usually refers to pears and the second to apples. The name *douillon* is said to be derived from *douillette*, a child's dressing gown. You may come across them in the Nord called *rombosses* or *moines*. Like our own baked fruit dumplings, Normandy's versions are often made with shortcrust or yeast pastry. I find puff pastry is lighter, but whichever you use, make sure it is rolled out very thinly.

225 g (8 oz) puff pastry
4 ripe pears or apples
caster or vanilla sugar
butter
ground cinnamon
1 egg yolk
2 tablespoons redcurrant jelly or smooth apricot jam
1 tablespoon calvados or rum (optional)

Divide the pastry into four and roll out each piece into a square big enough to enclose a pear or an apple. Very carefully, using an apple corer, hollow out the core, but leave the base of the fruit intact. Remove the peel. Roll the fruit in sugar and stand each in the centre of a pastry square. Fill each hollow with a sliver of butter and a little cinnamon. Dampen the edges of the pastry with water and shape the pastry around the fruit so that it is completely enclosed. Put on to a baking sheet and brush with beaten egg; refrigerate until ready to cook. Heat the oven to Gas 7/425°F/220°C. Bake the dumplings for 30–35 minutes until golden brown. Melt the jelly or jam in a small pan, with the calvados or rum if using (otherwise thin it with a tablespoon of water). Pour it over the fruit when serving.

White wolf
Le loup blanc

A refreshing Breton dessert for a warm autumn evening is made by first gently poaching pears, then puréeing them and topping with a mixture of stiffly beaten egg white and whipped cream. Sweetened, puréed strawberries or raspberries (in their raw state) are delicious with the same topping.

4 pears, peeled, quartered and cored
3–4 tablespoons caster or vanilla sugar
2 egg whites
150 ml ($\frac{1}{4}$ pint) whipped cream

Put the pears into a saucepan with a little water and 2 tablespoons sugar. Cover and simmer gently for about 10 minutes until soft (time will vary according to the ripeness of the pears). Drain well and purée them, taste and, if necessary, stir in a further tablespoon of sugar. Half fill four glasses or dishes. When cold, cover and put in the fridge. Beat the egg whites until stiff and fold into the whipped cream, together with the remaining sugar. Cover the pear purée with the creamy mixture and return to the fridge for at least 15 minutes.

Pear tart
Tarte aux poires

Make this spectacularly pretty tart from Normandy on the day it is to be eaten because puff pastry goes limp by the next day. To prevent the pears making the pastry soggy, the pastry shell is lined with a thin layer of powdered macaroons which soak up the juice. The fruit is arranged in the pastry shell in the shape of a flower, each sliced pear half forming one of the petals.

225 g (8 oz) puff pastry
25–50 g (1–2 oz) macaroons, finely crushed
3 firm ripe pears, peeled, halved and cored
1–2 tablespoons caster or vanilla sugar
2–3 tablespoons smooth apricot jam

Roll out the pastry and use it to line a 20 cm (8 in) flan tin with a removable base. Refrigerate, covered, for 30 minutes. At the end of this time, heat oven to Gas 7/425°F/220°C. Sprinkle the crushed macaroons evenly over the pastry base. Thinly slice the pear halves crosswise and slide each into place on the pastry base. (This is easy to do if you slip a flexible spatula or palette knife under each cut half, fan the slices out slightly by pressing them down with the palm of your hand and slide the pear half into place in the shell with the pointed end towards the middle.) Bake for 20 minutes, remove from oven and sprinkle the pears with the sugar. Return to the oven for 10–15 minutes. Heat the apricot jam in a small saucepan with 1 tablespoon of water, stir until smooth and bubbling. Remove the cooked tart from the tin and brush the surface, including the pastry rim, with the apricot glaze. Serve warm or cold.

Baked caramel pears
Rochas granvillaise

Rochas are a variety of pears grown in Normandy and no sooner had I come across this recipe for cooking them, than I discovered them on sale in my local English supermarket! You can of course use other kinds of pears, and you'll find that apples are delicious baked in the same way, in fact they used to be a favourite breakfast snack and were cooked in the baker's oven once the bread was done. People would buy them on the way to work from street vendors crying: *'la roulée, à la roulée.'*

butter
8 pears
juice of 2 lemons
100 g (4 oz) caster sugar

Heat oven to Gas 5/375°F/190°C. Generously butter an ovenproof dish in which the pears can stand upright in a single layer. Peel the pears but leave the stalks on. Stand them in the dish as you go, sprinkling each with lemon juice. Dust them with the sugar. Put a little water in the base of the dish and bake them for 45–60 minutes, until tender and the sugar has turned a deep golden brown. Serve warm.

Crusty pears
Poires en croûte

This delicious Normandy way of eating pears is included in *Kitchen Suppers*, but I felt I couldn't omit it from this book. If you can't track down brioche buns or loaves, use a tea bread instead, though it isn't quite as good. Other fruit, such as apples, peaches, greengages and apricots can be cooked in the same way.

3 brioche buns or ½ brioche loaf
50 g (2 oz) softened butter
50–75 g (2–3 oz) caster or vanilla sugar
4–6 dessert pears, peeled, cored and sliced
juice of 1–2 lemons
½ teaspoon cinnamon
½ teaspoon nutmeg

Heat the oven to Gas 6/400°F/200°C. Cut the buns in half horizontally, or cut six 2 cm (¾ in) thick slices of brioche loaf. Butter one side and lay them, butter side down, in a shallow ovenproof dish. Butter the top sides. Sprinkle with half the sugar. Pile the pear slices on top of the brioche but leave a border of brioche exposed. Sprinkle them with lemon juice to prevent them turning brown, then sprinkle over the cinnamon, nutmeg and remaining sugar. Bake for 20–30 minutes until golden and the edges of the bread are nicely browned.

Pear liqueur

In the *Auberge de Rose* in Châteaudun we came across a bottle of Poire William liqueur with a whole pear in it and couldn't resist having some. Never mind that two glasses cost almost as much as a complete menu, it was the end of the holiday so we didn't care. How do they put a whole pear into a bottle? The answer is when it is tiny. The process begins in the spring by inserting a branch with its immature fruit into the bottle. The fruit then grows and ripens through the summer; it is then cut down and the bottle filled with *eau-de-vie*, corked and left in the sun for a month. After this sugar is added, the bottle is re-corked and left to mature for at least three months but after a year it will be even better. As well as being a delicious liqueur to offer at the end of a supper, added in small quantities it gives fire to pear or apple dishes, sorbets and ice creams.

To make your own you don't need a whole tree but just one pear, and it will have to be made in a jar not a bottle.

1 ripe William pear
1 cinnamon stick
piece of orange peel
½ whole nutmeg
600 ml (1 pint) *eau-de-vie* or vodka
150 g (6 oz) sugar

Put the pear and spices in a 1 litre preserving jar, top up completely with *eau-de-vie* or vodka and leave in a warm, sunny place for a month. Add the sugar and reseal. Leave at least three months before using.

Cider, wine and beer

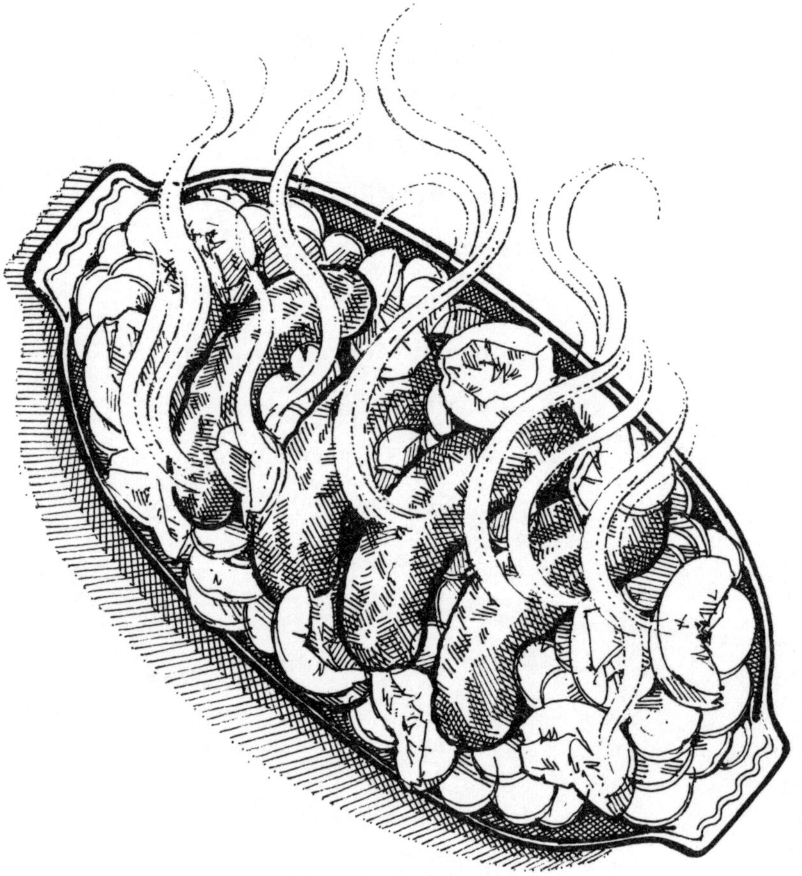

CIDER

Cider dates back at least to the Romans who probably brought it to northern France and England. Although Normandy and Brittany are principally associated with this drink, it is produced in Picardy too. Once it was very much a farming industry, but nowadays most of the production of this golden juice, *liqueur d'or*, is no longer carried out by the small grower but is done on a commercial scale.

Normandy cider is the finest, the best coming from the Pays d'Auge, and centres to note are Bonnebosc, Livarot, Cambremer, Vimoutiers and Pont l'Evêque. Brittany's cider is rougher but the best comes from La Guerche, Pleudihan, Merdignac and Fouesnant.

Special apples are grown to produce *cidre*, cider. The fruit is first crushed and pressed to release the juice, which is then fermented in barrels or huge vats. There are many different types, ranging from pale amber to deep mahogany and from the still *bon bère*, made from unadulterated apple juice, to *cidre bouché*, a sparkling cider with a champagne-type cork, fashionable as an aperitif. Like wine, cider has good and bad years, but it should always be drunk young, last year's harvest producing this year's drink.

The best cider is carefully blended to provide a fine dry drink that is comparable to wine – look out for cider marked 'Cru de Cambremer' which has been chosen at an annual tasting – and the locals like to drink it with simple dishes of shellfish, chicken, lamb or pork. In Brittany it is a refreshing accompaniment to pancakes and *crêpes* and is still served in pottery bowls in many cafés and bars. The old faïence bowls made in Quimper have become collectors' pieces. It is delicious, though heady, as a cool, summer drink, and in Normandy it is often drunk diluted with water. Rough farm cider is best drunk with caution, it is at least as potent as our West Country scrumpy and guaranteed to give you a *gueule de bois*, or hangover. In *The Cook's Encyclopaedia*, Tom Stobart recounts how his father would use old scrumpy to scrub out the boiler and dissolve the rats. So be wary!

Pear cider, or *poiré* was once only available home-brewed but is now being commercially produced and can be found all over France. It makes a refreshing drink but does not lend itself to cooking as it is too acidic and loses its flavour when heated.

When cooking savoury dishes with cider choose a strong, dry kind. You can buy French *brut* or *sec* in some outlets in the UK, it has a higher alcoholic content than our own and is more expensive. Sweet or even medium sweet ciders (*cidre doux*) contain added sugar and their flavour is only suitable for some sweet dishes. Most recipes in which cider is used call for it to be reduced in volume to intensify the flavour, either by hard boiling at the beginning or end of cooking. Once opened, store what you don't use in a stoppered bottle and keep it in the fridge to use in other dishes. It loses its fizz but this does not matter although like wine, if kept too long, it will turn to vinegar.

Normandy cider sauce
Sauce normande

This cider, butter and cream sauce can be served with meat or vegetables.

75 g (3 oz) butter
1 onion, finely chopped
25 g (1 oz) flour
225 ml (8 fl oz) cider
salt
freshly milled black pepper
pinch of nutmeg
4 tablespoons crème fraîche
juice of ½ lemon

Melt 25 g (1 oz) of the butter in a saucepan and fry the onion until golden. Add remaining butter and, when it has melted, stir in the flour. Cook for 2 minutes, stirring constantly. Gradually stir in the cider and when the sauce thickens, season with salt, pepper and nutmeg. Using a whisk, beat in the crème fraîche and add the lemon juice.

Scallops with cider
Coquilles St-Jacques au cidre

In Britain scallops are expensive and hard to find as most are exported to Europe or the States. In fact the scallops you eat in France might easily have come from our own shores. When buying ask the fishmonger for both shells, as the deeper one is a perfect serving dish. If they have not been cleaned wash them under running cold water and pull away the grey-brown frill and black thread of intestines. Like most molluscs they need only a very short cooking time.

4 scallops
25 g (1 oz) butter
2 shallots, chopped
100 ml (4 fl oz) strong dry cider
salt
freshly milled black pepper
2 tablespoons crème fraîche
juice of ½ lemon

Remove the white nut and orange coral from the half shell and cut into bite-sized pieces. Wash and dry. Melt the butter in a frying pan, add the shallots and let them sweat for a few minutes. Moisten with the cider. Add the scallop pieces and season with salt and pepper. Bring just to boiling point and poach gently for 4–5 minutes. Remove the scallop pieces to a warm plate. Raise the heat and boil the juices hard to reduce by half. Stir in the crème fraîche, followed by the lemon juice and continue stirring until the sauce bubbles. Return the scallop pieces to the sauce, then pile the mixture into the deep shells or small dishes and serve.

Plaice with cider
Carrelet au cidre

In this Normandy recipe, fillets of plaice are baked on a bed of chopped shallots, onions, mushrooms and herbs, moistened with cider. Instead of fillets you could use a whole fish and it doesn't have to be plaice but could be any other sort of flat fish such as lemon sole or dabs. These last, one of the sweetest flavoured and least expensive of all flat fish, are often passed off as small plaice but are easily recognized because they lack the plaice's bony nodules on the head and their dark skin is rough.

50 g (2 oz) butter
3 shallots, chopped
1 onion, chopped
225 g (8 oz) mushrooms, chopped
parsley, thyme and tarragon, chopped
450–700 g (1–1½ lb) fillets of plaice or a whole fish
300 ml (½ pint) dry cider
salt
freshly milled black pepper
handful breadcrumbs

Heat the oven to Gas 5/375°F/190°C. Generously butter a gratin dish and scatter over the chopped shallots, onion, mushrooms and herbs. Lay the fish on top. Pour over the cider and season with salt and pepper. Sprinkle with the breadcrumbs and dot with the remaining butter. Bake for 20–30 minutes.

Tripe in cider
Tripes à la mode de Caen

Few people nowadays attempt to make Caen's most famous dish. It needs to be made in large quantities in a special earthenware dish with a narrow opening. The tripe, around 2 kg (4½ lb), is scraped and washed several times before being blanched for an hour in salted water. (This process can of course be shortened by buying from a butcher who sells it ready prepared, when the blanching process can be reduced to a few minutes.) It is then cut up and mixed with the chopped flesh of a calf's and an ox foot. The dish itself is lined with pork rinds, the bones of the feet, sliced carrots and onions, herbs and garlic, cloves, salt, black and cayenne pepper. The tripe and meat are laid on top, it is covered with cider, the lid is sealed and it is cooked very slowly for 8–10 hours. It is served hot with all the bones and herbs removed and the fat skimmed away.

It is simpler to order it in a restaurant or to follow the French housewife, who rarely suffers from our Puritan guilt, and buy a wedge, a jar or can of the real thing (when cold it is set in stiff jelly) from a *charcuterie* in France and heat it up at home.

Mackerel with cider
Maquereaux au cidre

In Brittany, we watched the fishing boats come in laden with spanking fresh mackerel, their silvery sides gleaming with blues and greens. It was like being back in Devon when I was a child, when my grandmother would stand there eulogizing about mackerel just out of the sea. Always buy them from the boats when the opportunity is there and never buy them tired when their eyes sag in their heads and all the spunk has gone out of them. Try them cooked in this Breton way flavoured with parsley and cider. Wash the mackerel, cut off the fins and make sure the cavity is clear of blood or any blackness but leave the heads on.

2 shallots, chopped
handful parsley, chopped
4 mackerel
150 ml (¼ pint) strong dry cider
salt
freshly milled black pepper
25 g (1 oz) butter

Heat the oven to Gas 6/400°F/200°C. Put the chopped shallots and half the parsley in the base of a shallow oven dish and put the fish on top. Pour over the cider and season with salt and pepper. Dot with the butter. Bake for 15–20 minutes. Serve sprinkled with the remaining parsley.

Dover sole with cider
Sole au cidre

The sole, which we designate the Dover sole, is the king of all flat fish. It is found all round the coasts of northern France but principally at Dieppe in Normandy and further north in Boulogne and Dunkerque. In Normandy they accord it royal treatment and in their most classic recipe, *sole à la normande*, garnish it with oysters, mussels, prawns, *langoustines*, smelt, mushrooms and truffles. A dish to order when you eat out, if you can afford it! In this recipe the fillets are treated very simply. They are poached in the oven in cider and served with a thickened sauce made with the cooking juices. This recipe is suitable for other kinds of fish fillet too.

4 fillets of sole
3 shallots, chopped
300 ml (½ pint) strong dry cider
salt
freshly milled black pepper
1 tablespoon butter
1 tablespoon flour
1 tablespoon chopped parsley

Heat the oven to Gas 5/375°F/190°C. Lay the fillets in a buttered dish. Sprinkle over the chopped shallots and cover with the cider. Add salt and pepper. Put into the oven and poach for 10–15 minutes. Transfer the fish to a hot dish and keep warm in the turned-off oven with the door ajar. To make the sauce, melt the butter in a saucepan, stir in the flour, cook for 2 minutes and gradually stir in the cooking liquid. Pour the sauce over the fish and scatter with the chopped parsley.

Sailor's pot
Matelote normande

Only in Normandy is a *matelote* made with sea fish, everywhere else it is a freshwater stew. There are lots of different recipes depending upon the area of Normandy in which it is prepared. Basically you need three or four sorts of any firm white fish, such as haddock, cod, hake, conger eel, coley, dogfish – otherwise known as huss or rock salmon – ling, monkfish etc. Serve the *matelote* with bread croûtons.

1 kg ($2\frac{1}{4}$ lb) mixed firm white fish, cut in slices
sprigs of thyme and parsley
1 bay leaf
salt
freshly milled black pepper
300 ml ($\frac{1}{2}$ pint) strong dry cider
50 g (2 oz) butter
225 g (8 oz) mushrooms, quartered
450 g (1 lb) mussels
100 ml (4 fl oz) crème fraîche

Heat the oven to Gas 6/400°F/200°C. Put the fish into a flameproof casserole, add the thyme, parsley and bay leaf, season with salt and pepper and pour over the cider. Dot with half the butter. Put into the oven for 25 minutes. Towards the end of this cooking time, heat the remaining butter in a frying pan and fry the mushrooms until golden. Scrub and wash the mussels well and steam them open in a saucepan with a little water.

To serve, put the fish into a wide shallow dish and surround with the mushrooms and mussels. Put the dish into the turned-off oven with the door ajar to keep warm. Reduce the cooking juices by half and stir in the crème fraîche before pouring over the fish.

Chicken with cider
Coq au cidre

This is Normandy's version of the Burgundian's *coq au vin*. Naturally it contains, cider, apples and a little crème fraîche.

50 g (2 oz) butter
1 tablespoon oil
1 chicken, cut in 8 pieces
1 onion, chopped
1 tablespoon flour
300 ml ($\frac{1}{2}$ pint) strong dry cider
sprigs of parsley and thyme, tied in a bunch
1 bay leaf
1 stick celery, sliced
salt
freshly milled black pepper
150 g (6 oz) small onions
1 teaspoon caster sugar
150 g (6 oz) button mushrooms
2 crisp eating apples, peeled, quartered and cored
2 tablespoons crème fraîche

Heat half the butter and the tablespoon of oil in a heavy-based flameproof casserole and brown the chicken all over, in two batches if necessary. Remove the pieces to a warm plate as you go. Add the chopped onion to the casserole and fry until golden. Stir in the flour, and gradually mix in the cider. Bring to the boil, return the chicken pieces to the casserole and add the parsley, thyme, bay leaf and celery. Season with salt and pepper. Cover and simmer for 45 minutes. Meanwhile, peel the small onions (this is easy if you steep them for a few minutes in boiling water). Melt the remaining butter in a small pan and cook the onions gently with the sugar until golden brown; add the mushrooms and cook a further 15 minutes. About 15 minutes before the end of the cooking time, add the onions, mushrooms and apple quarters to the casserole.

To serve, put the chicken, onions, mushrooms and apples on to a serving dish. Boil the sauce hard until reduced by half, stir in the crème fraîche, check the seasoning and pour over the chicken.

Mint sauce
Sauce à la menthe

It seems that lamb and mint sauce is not just an English fancy. In Granville, situated in Normandy's 'sleeve', the Manche, they have their own version but the sauce is made with cider and crème fraîche and the lamb is heavily studded with garlic. It is good eaten with haricot beans or flageolets and roast potatoes. Of course Granville does have a tenuous connection with England, having been fortified by the English in the fifteenth century when they tried, unsuccessfully, to capture Mont-St-Michel. Later its port was a haven for pirates but it settled down in the nineteenth century to become a fashionable seaside resort with a famous carnival held every year at Mardi Gras.

You will find a recipe for roast lamb in the Parsley, Chervil, Tarragon and Chives section.

150 ml ($\frac{1}{4}$ pint) cider	salt
2 sprigs of mint	freshly milled black pepper
3–4 tablespoons crème fraîche	

While your lamb is roasting, put the cider and mint into a saucepan and bring to the boil. Remove from the heat and set aside to infuse for 30 minutes. Once the lamb is cooked and left to rest before carving, pour away the fat from the roasting tin and pour in the cider (discarding the sprigs of mint). Put the tin on the stove over a medium heat and let the cider bubble and reduce by half. Stir in the crème fraîche and season with salt and pepper. Pour any of the juices that have collected round the lamb into the sauce, give it a stir and pour into a warm sauceboat or small bowl.

Cider with honey and cinnamon
Cidromel

When buckwheat was grown extensively in Brittany, the bees produced a delicious dark honey. Nowadays the honey of northern France is more likely to be made from lime-flowers, clover, rape or heather. Here, as in other regions of France, honey is fermented with water to make mead, *la boisson des Celtes*, hydromel, and is sold most often under the Breton names of *chouchenn* or *chammilard*. It's for those who have a sweet tooth and is drunk either as an aperitif or digestif. A simpler drink is this Normandy *cidromel*, which is an infusion of cider, honey and cinnamon.

4 tablespoons honey
2 teaspoons ground cinnamon
1 litre ($1\frac{3}{4}$ pints) strong cider

Put the honey and cinnamon into the cider and set aside in a cool place for 2 hours. Strain and return to the bottle. Seal and leave for a month before drinking.

Cider cup
Le cup cidre

This Normandy cider cup makes an economical and refreshing drink for a summer party. Make it well ahead of time to allow for the tea to cool before being mixed with the other ingredients.

50 g (2 oz) caster sugar
700 ml ($1\frac{1}{4}$ pints) fresh tea
700 ml ($1\frac{1}{4}$ pints) strong dry cider
4 oranges
ice

Dissolve the sugar in the freshly made hot tea and set aside until completely cold. Mix the cider and tea together in a bowl and squeeze in the juice of three of the oranges. Garnish with the remaining orange cut in thin slices. Add ice and serve.

Cider ice
Sorbet au cidre

This cider ice from Normandy is sweetly refreshing after a rich main course. Serve it straight from the freezer in tall glasses, topped perhaps with a few extra drops of calvados. Don't throw away the vanilla pod but wash and dry it and put it in a jar of sugar (see Etceteras).

300 ml (½ pint) water
100 g (4 oz) sugar
zest and juice of 1 lemon
vanilla pod
300 ml (½ pint) dry cider
2 egg whites
1 tablespoon calvados

Put the water, sugar, grated zest of the lemon and the vanilla pod into a saucepan and boil for 3 minutes. Allow to cool and strain into a shallow container. Add the lemon juice and the cider. Freeze until almost set, break up with a fork, until you have a mass of amber crystals. Beat the egg whites until stiff, fold them into the ice with the calvados and freeze again.

WINE

Very little wine is produced in northern France and it is not until you reach southern Brittany that you see the first straight lines of vineyards, but this does not prevent the inhabitants from drinking it or using it in cooking.

There are two main wines produced in Brittany. The first, Gros Plant, is light and sharp and is generally reserved for drinking with seafood, especially oysters. The second is Muscadet, which is dry and fruity and also excellent with seafood as well as being pleasant drunk on its own.

Wine which is simply labelled Muscadet AC is light and just a little dull; a better wine is labelled Muscadet des Coteaux de la Loire and comes from the region east of Nantes. Neither can compare in flavour with the wines produced further south of the Loire, Muscadet de Sevre-et-Maine or Muscadet sur lie. This last is produced by leaving the wine to mature on the lees – the yeast sediment that remains after fermentation – and results in a wine with a fresh, prickly flavour. To retain this quality, the wine must be bottled on the premises, so look out for labels stating '*mise en bouteille à la propriété*' etc. Muscadet should be drunk young.

You might come across some not bad red wine labelled *Vin de Pays des Marches de Bretagne* which comes from the mouth of the Loire, some of which is extremely palatable.

Some wines are produced in the Rhuys Peninsula where the wild plants are similar to those of the Midi but it has a pretty poor local reputation. It is said to drink it you need four men and a wall: one pours it, one drinks it, the other two hold him and the wall prevents him falling backwards.

White wine sauce
Sauce honfleuraise

Perhaps this delightful sauce, served with grilled or fried fish, was the inspiration of Mère Toutain, owner of a small inn in Honfleur which was the meeting place of Eugène Boudin and the first Impressionists. The port itself is still brimming with fish and is as captivating as ever, although filled to bursting in the summer with tourists.

25 g (1 oz) butter
100 ml (4 fl oz) Muscadet or other dry white wine
½ lemon, sliced
sprigs of parsley, thyme and tarragon
1 bay leaf
1 clove garlic, crushed
1 clove
1 tablespoon breadcrumbs
salt
freshly milled black pepper

Put all the ingredients into a saucepan, bring to the boil and simmer for 15 minutes. Strain over the fish.

Red mullet with saffron
Rougets au safran

In this tasty Breton recipe, red mullet are baked in wine and left overnight until cold when the cooking juices turn to a delicate jelly. Eat them on a warm summer's evening. In Normandy they use paprika instead of saffron and add cream to the sauce. Red mullet have very big scales, so when you ask the fishmonger to clean the fish for you, ask for them to be trimmed and scaled too. (The livers are a delicacy, so should not be removed.)

4 red mullet
1 shallot, chopped
sprigs of thyme and parsley
1 bay leaf
2–3 threads saffron or generous pinch saffron powder
1 teaspoon coriander seeds
5 tomatoes
100 ml (4 fl oz) Muscadet or other dry white wine
salt
freshly milled black pepper
several thin slices carrot
1 lemon, sliced

Heat the oven to Gas 5/375°F/190°C. Lay the red mullet in a shallow ovenproof dish with the chopped shallot, thyme, parsley, bay leaf, saffron and coriander seeds. Add 4 of the tomatoes, cut in quarters, pour over the wine and season with salt and pepper. Bake for 10–15 minutes. Remove and leave to get cold. Garnish with the carrot, the remaining tomato, thinly sliced, and the lemon.

Trout in wine sauce
Truites cauchoises

In this Normandy recipe the trout are baked in a hot oven on a bed of shallots and served with a cream sauce flavoured with wine and herbs. It is very quick to prepare and lovely to eat. The same recipe is delicious with trout or salmon fillets.

50 g (2 oz) butter
2–3 shallots, chopped
4 trout
salt
freshly milled black pepper
100 ml (4 fl oz) Muscadet or other dry white wine
4 tablespoons crème fraîche
sprigs of thyme
1 bay leaf
juice of 1 lemon

Heat the oven to Gas 6/400°F/200°C. Generously butter a flameproof gratin dish and sprinkle the chopped shallots over the base. Season the cavities of the trout with salt and pepper and lay the fish on top of the shallots, dot with the remaining butter and pour over the wine. Bake for 15–20 minutes. Put the trout on to a warm serving platter. Put the gratin dish on to the top of the stove and let the juices bubble. Stir in the crème fraîche. Add the thyme and bay leaf and stir for a few minutes over a medium heat until the sauce reduces by about half. Squeeze in the lemon juice, pour over the fish and serve.

Pork parcels
Bouligots de la Rance

I like the origins of this recipe in which boned pork is rolled in vine leaves. It comes from the region bordering the river Rance which rises in the Landes de Menez and meanders westwards before turning north and widening into the estuary between Dinard and St-Malo. Once vineyards lined the river and they produced a pleasant if somewhat tart wine. Now the vines run wild in abandoned vineyards or by the side of the lanes. As well as using the leaves, sometimes the tendrils and the small, crabby grapes go into the dish.

You could make it using leaves from a home-grown vine and the little grapes which so rarely ripen in our English climate; or use preserved vine leaves packed in brine which come from Greece and are sold in ethnic shops and some supermarkets. They must be soaked to rid them of their saltiness by putting as many as you need into a large bowl, cover with boiling water and leave for 5 minutes; drain them and rinse under cold water.

- 10–14 vine leaves
- 25 g (1 oz) butter
- 2 shallots, chopped
- 4 boned pork chops or escalopes
- 2 tablespoons oil
- 150 ml ($\frac{1}{4}$ pint) dry white wine, such as Muscadet or Gros Plant
- salt
- freshly milled black pepper
- handful small seedless tart grapes

Chop two of the vine leaves. Melt the butter in a heavy-based pan and gently fry the chopped leaves and shallots, but don't let them brown. Flatten the pork by beating with a rolling pin. Put a little of the cooked mixture in the centre of each piece and roll into a cylinder. Wrap each of these pork rolls in two or three vine leaves and tie securely with string. Heat the oil in the pan and sear the wrapped pork rolls all over. Add the wine, salt and pepper and the grapes. Simmer, covered, for 20–25 minutes. Cut away the string from the pork rolls and transfer them with the grapes to a warm serving dish. Raise the heat and boil the sauce in the pan until it is reduced by half. Pour over the meat and grapes and serve.

Chicken in white wine
Poulet au vin blanc

In this Breton recipe, chicken, carrots and shallots are flamed in apple brandy before being flavoured with herbs and simmered gently in wine. Right at the end the sauce is thickened with an egg yolk and a little crème fraîche, turning quite a simple dish into a feast.

50 g (2 oz) butter
1 chicken, divided into 8 portions
2 carrots, sliced
3 shallots, chopped
2 cloves garlic, crushed
2 tablespoons apple brandy or calvados
150 ml ($\frac{1}{4}$ pint) Muscadet or other dry white wine
pinch of nutmeg
parsley, chervil and tarragon, tied in a bunch
salt
freshly milled black pepper
1 egg yolk
2 tablespoons crème fraîche

Melt the butter in a heavy-based casserole and fry the chicken all over until golden, in two batches if necessary. Remove to a plate. Add the carrots and shallots and fry for a few minutes, stirring often. Add the garlic. Return the chicken pieces to the casserole. Heat the apple brandy or calvados in a ladle or small saucepan, set it alight and pour it flaming over the chicken. When the flames die down, add the wine, nutmeg and bunch of herbs. Season with salt and pepper, cover and simmer for 50–60 minutes.

To serve, remove the chicken to a hot serving dish. Boil the sauce rapidly for a few minutes until reduced by at least half. Mix the egg yolk with the crème fraîche in a small bowl. Stir in a tablespoon or two of the reduced liquid and tip the mixture into the remaining sauce. Stir for a few moments until it thickens but do not let it boil or it will curdle. Pour the sauce over the chicken.

Salsify in wine sauce
Salsifis à la normande

The long, thin roots of salsify (which has white skin – the black-skinned is scorzonera but is sometimes called black salsify) are very popular in Normandy. They are sometimes available here in supermarkets or upmarket greengrocers. Both varieties should be well washed and scraped before eating and put into a bowl of acidulated water to prevent them turning brown. They are delicious grated raw in salads or eaten, as in this recipe, in a winey sauce. If you have no wine to spare use cider instead.

700 g (1½ lb) salsify
1 lemon
salt
50 g (2 oz) butter
1 onion, chopped
25 g (1 oz) flour
100 ml (4 fl oz) dry white wine
100 ml (4 fl oz) milk
freshly milled black pepper
nutmeg
2 tablespoons crème fraîche

Wash and scrape the salsify using a swivel-bladed peeler, cut into three or four pieces and put into a bowl of water with the juice of half the lemon. Bring a saucepan half-filled with water to the boil, add salt, put in the lengths of salsify, cover and simmer until tender. This will take about 30 minutes but may take longer if the roots are very thick. Meanwhile, make a sauce by melting the butter and frying the onion until golden. Stir in the flour and cook for 2 minutes stirring constantly. Gradually mix in the wine and milk and when the sauce thickens and boils, season with salt, pepper and nutmeg. Drain the cooked salsify well and put it into a warm dish. Stir the crème fraîche into the sauce, squeeze over the juice from the remaining half lemon and pour over the vegetable.

BEER

The practice of brewing grains to make an alcoholic drink goes back almost to the beginning of time. The Babylonians did it, as did the Egyptians, Greeks and Romans. But beer was being made in northern Europe long before the Romans appeared on the scene. However, it wasn't until much later that the practice of malting barley and adding hop shoots was invented. This last development came from Germany and a liking for hop-flavoured beer was brought via Flanders to Britain by soldiers returning from the Hundred Years' War.

If beer is our national drink it is the soul of the north-western regions of France, too, figuring largely in its cooking and being drunk with almost everything. Even with beer soup! A by-product of the brewing is the wonderful pâtés and *charcuterie* for which the whole region is famous which stem from the days when the pigs were reared on the dregs from the breweries.

The beer of the north comes under various guises: *légères*, *claires*, *mousseuses*, *fines* – light, clear, sweet and dry. Most of it is bottled and similar to lager but fizzier. Motte-Cordonier, a pale ale from Lille, and Porter 39, a brown ale from Maubeuge, are famous, and in July there is a beer festival at Maubeuge.

It is the female flowering hop shoots which are used to make beer and in the beer-producing regions of France it is possible to buy the male hop shoots, *jets de houblons*, in the markets in spring. They are eaten as a vegetable, gently scraped and washed then boiled in salted water with a squeeze of lemon juice until tender before being drained and eaten with butter or cream.

Beer soup
Soupe à la bière

In Flanders, beer is *de rigueur* in much of the cooking and this soup, at least until recently, was much in favour. As with most traditional recipes, there are lots of variations. Some contain no eggs and are thickened with flour. Sometimes beef stock is added. Some suggest adding a small glass of gin right at the end. It's even recommended that the soup is washed down with yet more beer. All recipes agree that it should be served with plenty of country bread toasted or baked at the top of a hot oven.

1 litre (1¾ pints) brown beer
150 g (6 oz) caster sugar
4 egg yolks
150 ml (¼ pint) crème fraîche
salt
freshly milled black pepper

Bring the beer to the boil in a large saucepan, add the sugar and simmer for 5 minutes. Put the yolks into a soup tureen, and mix in the crème fraîche. Gradually beat in the beer. Season to taste with salt and pepper.

Leek tart
Quiche flamande

In this Flemish quiche – which can be eaten hot, warm or cold – the leeks are complemented with spices and the bitter-sweet flavour of beer. Crème fraîche is mixed with milk to make a light and creamy filling. It includes no cheese. Discard the tough green part of the leeks and wash them well, they can be gritty, by splitting them lengthwise almost to the base and spreading them open under running cold water.

225 g (8 oz) shortcrust pastry
25 g (1 oz) butter
1 tablespoon oil
450 g (1 lb) leeks, sliced
sprig of fresh thyme or ½ teaspoon dried
nutmeg
cinnamon
salt
freshly milled black pepper
300 ml (½ pint) pale ale or lager
100 g (4 oz) smoked ham, cut in strips
4 tablespoons crème fraîche
4 tablespoons milk
3 eggs

Roll out the pastry and line a 20 cm (8 in) flan tin; prick the base all over with a fork, cover and refrigerate. Heat the butter and oil in a saucepan, add the leeks and fry gently for 5 minutes. Add thyme, a pinch each of nutmeg and cinnamon, salt and pepper, and pour in the beer. Bring to the boil, lower heat and simmer, uncovered, for 1–1½ hours, until the leeks are very tender and nearly all the liquid has evaporated. Heat the oven to Gas 5/375°F/190°C. Spread the leeks over the pastry base, dot with the ham. Mash the crème fraîche in a bowl, gradually mix in the milk and beat in the eggs. Season with salt, pepper and a further pinch of nutmeg and cinnamon. Pour the mixture over the leeks and ham. Bake for 30–35 minutes until the quiche is puffed and golden.

Chicken with beer
Coq à la bière

This recipe comes from the Nord where cocks were specially bred for fighting, and those that didn't come up to scratch ended up in the pot. Fed on the best, their flesh was meaty and very tasty. This dish is similar to *coq au vin* but the bird is cooked in beer rather than wine and it is flamed with gin not brandy. Traditionally it is eaten with plainly boiled or steamed potatoes, or sometimes *pommes pont-neuf*, a grand name for French fries which are thinner, crisper and, according to us Francophiles, superior to our chips.

- 50 g (2 oz) butter
- 2 tablespoons oil
- 1 chicken, divided into 8 portions
- 2 tablespoons gin
- 300 ml (½ pint) pale ale or lager
- 1 clove garlic, chopped
- sprigs of parsley
- 1 bay leaf
- sprig of fresh thyme or ½ teaspoon dried
- salt
- freshly milled black pepper
- 2 sugar lumps
- 150 g (6 oz) small onions
- 100 g (4 oz) smoked streaky bacon, chopped
- 150 g (6 oz) mushrooms, quartered
- 1 teaspoon sugar
- 2 tablespoons crème fraîche

Heat half the butter with 1 tablespoon of the oil in a heavy-based casserole and fry the chicken pieces on all sides until golden, in two or three batches as necessary. Pour off all but about 1 tablespoon of the fat, and return the chicken to the pan. Heat the gin in a ladle or small saucepan, light it and pour over the chicken, shaking the pan until the flames die down. Pour in the beer, and add the garlic and herbs. Season with salt and pepper and add the lumps of sugar. Cover the pot and simmer gently for 45 minutes. Meanwhile make the garnish. Put the unpeeled onions into a small saucepan, cover with cold water, bring to the boil and simmer for 10 minutes. Drain and cool, before removing skins which will come away easily. Put the remaining butter and oil into a saucepan, add the bacon and fry until beginning to brown. Add the onions and mushrooms and the teaspoon of sugar and cook gently. When the chicken is done (test by piercing flesh with a skewer – the juices should run clear), put it on a serving platter, surround with the onions, mushrooms and bacon, and keep warm either in the oven or covered loosely with a piece of foil. Boil the cooking liquid until it is reduced by half, stir in the crème fraîche and pour over the chicken.

Pork braised with beer
Carbonnades de porc

The word *carbonnades* derives from *charbons ardents*, live coals, stemming from the days when the pot was buried in the hot embers to allow the contents to braise gently while the household went about their other business. Often these dishes call for long cooking times but this Flemish version using pork is quite quick. You could use beef but might have to increase the cooking time. It is sweet and tasty and especially delicious with a mixed purée of Brussels sprouts and potatoes to soak up the sauce surrounding the meat.

4 tablespoons oil
2 onions, chopped
700 g (1½ lb) boneless pork shoulder, cut in cubes
1 clove garlic, chopped
1 tablespoon flour
1 tablespoon tomato purée
1 teaspoon wine vinegar
300 ml (½ pint) pale ale
2 sugar lumps
3 tablespoons sliced gherkins
salt
freshly milled black pepper

Heat half the oil in a heavy-based pan and add the onions, fry for a few moments until beginning to brown. Transfer to a plate and set aside. Add the remaining oil and the pieces of pork, in two or three batches, and let them brown over a medium heat, turning them over from time to time, transferring them to the plate as you go. Return the onion and pork to the pan, add the garlic, stir in the flour and let it cook a couple of minutes, stirring all the time. Add the tomato purée and the vinegar, mix well and pour in the pale ale. Bring to the boil, then add the sugar, gherkins, salt and pepper. Lower the heat, cover and allow to simmer gently for 1–1½ hours until the meat is tender.

Sausages in beer
Saucisses à la bière

In this bitter-sweet dish from Flanders, spicy sausages are cooked in beer on a bed of potatoes and apples. The potatoes almost completely absorb the beer and the apples melt to a sweet purée, while the sausages remain moist and full of flavour. Use a light French bottled beer like Bière de Garde, sold in bottles in some supermarkets, or an English pale ale. The same recipe works wonderfully with cider when it should then perhaps be called *saucisses à la normande*.

50 g (2 oz) concentrated butter
2 tablespoons oil
450 g (1 lb) spicy or herb sausages
900 g (2 lb) potatoes, peeled and sliced
450 g (1 lb) apples, peeled, quartered and cored
salt
freshly milled black pepper
200 ml (7 fl oz) light beer
handful parsley, chopped

Heat the oven to Gas 5/375°F/190°C. Heat the butter and oil in a flameproof shallow dish and brown the sausages all over. Add potatoes and fry them for a few minutes, turning them over once or twice. Top with the apples, and season with salt and pepper. Pour over the beer and bring to the boil. Cover either with a lid or foil and bake for 40 minutes. Sprinkle with the parsley and serve.

Autumn and Winter Matters

As the leaves in the orchards turn from shades of red and chestnut through to yellow and orange and the first of the autumn gales begin to blow, so the English holidaymaker's thoughts turn towards home. The dash to the ferries is a race to get to the port while it's still light enough to catch a glimpse of farms and villages shrouded in a rainswept landscape. The corn has been harvested in the vast fields of the Nord and waits in huge carpet-bales to be taken away, guarded by the mechanical harvesters which look like prehistoric monsters made out of giant Meccano. The ploughed earth waits for the winter sowing.

On the coast the warm, golden days of early autumn become fewer and the sunlit coves and beaches no longer look warm and inviting. The sea is whipped to a frenzy and the wind moans over the dunes, sending scurries of sand flying into the faces of the cockle hunters and the people walking their dogs. Everyone thinks of being indoors and looks forward to a hearty meal, though nowadays not perhaps in front of a roaring fire but with central heating and the inevitable television.

French clocks go back at the end of September and for a month, until we change ours, we share the same time as they do. As the evenings draw in chestnuts, wild mushrooms and pumpkins appear in the shops. Pheasant is on the menu along with wild boar, roast woodcock, rabbit and hare. Now is the time to buy *foie gras*, *rillettes*, *confits* and *magrets de canard* from local producers in Brittany and Normandy and to indulge if you're lucky in a dish of *canard à la rouennaise* in the Hôtel de la Poste at Duclair in the Seine valley, helped down with a shot of *trou normand* or even a *trou canard*.

As the last of the dying leaves are snatched from the trees, autumn gives way to winter and as the fog rolls down over the hills and into the valleys, the market stalls are filled with cabbages and greens, cauliflowers, Brussels sprouts and heads of chicory wrapped in purple paper to keep out the light. There are great bundles of leeks and piles of potatoes and the fish stalls are laden with gleaming shellfish and spanking fresh fish.

As Christmas and New Year approach, the shop counters and markets of even the smallest town are filled with the sort of abundance you'd only expect to find at Harrods. There are dozens and dozens of oysters packed in boxes, smoked salmon, truffles and caviar, dried fruits and fresh fruits, pâtés and every kind of *charcuterie*, farm-reared ducks, geese and turkeys and the *pâtisseries* are overflowing with tempting offerings.

In the dog days of January and February when the sky is heavy with snow and the land lies in the grip of the frosts, what could be more heartwarming than sharing the northern French custom of drinking a cup of strong coffee laced with one of their local spirits, apple brandy, calvados or gin?

From calva to gin

Fine CALVADOS
Fine

CALVADOS AND *LAMBIG*

It was a Normand living in Provence who first introduced me to calvados by bringing out a bottle, heavily laden with dust and cobwebs, which had, he said, been produced by his grandfather. We solemnly sipped it while he eulogized about the *trou normand*, and the Provençals among the guests rolled their eyes in disbelief and afterwards told us he brings out the same bottle every time, topping it up with a more recent brew as the level drops! Whatever the truth of the matter, it tasted good to me, warm and smooth with more than a hint of fire and spiced with apples.

Apples, and to a much lesser extent pears, are distilled in Normandy and Brittany to make fruit brandies, each litre taking 30 litres of cider. The apple brandy, calvados, is named after the Normandy region in which it is produced and is subject to strict controls as to quality and quantity, but because production is limited, many farmers produce it illegally and the quality cannot be guaranteed, though sometimes you might come across a really good *calvados fermier*. The best true calvados, matured in casks like the finest malt whisky, comes from the valley known as the Pays d'Auge and this is a name worth looking out for on labels. If you see the word *fine* on a label it means the calvados is 2–3 years old and is still quite young; *vieux (VSOP)* signifies it is at least 5 years old and *hors âge*, *âge inconnu* or *Napoléon* means it is at least 6 and up to 12–15 years old.

Apple brandies produced outside the *département* of Calvados are sold as *eau-de-vie de cidre* in both Normandy and Brittany, though in the latter region they are often sold under the Breton name of *lambig*, the best of which is reputed to come from Rhuys. None has the fineness of calvados and the worst are ferocious firewaters similar to a really bad American apple-jack. The art of distilling apples was taken to the States by early French settlers, where it earned the nickname 'essence of lockjaw'. The French have more euphemistic nicknames for their apple brandies, from *dour vulnerer*, sweet temptation, to *renard boiteux*, slippery fox.

The Normands have such an affection for their calvados that they find any excuse to drink it. At cafés, even at breakfast time, you'll hear them asking for a *calva* or, if they want just a dash of it in their coffee, a *café calva*. This dash is sometimes called a *mic*, or a *micamo*, which is short for *mic à mort*, a drop of death. In Brittany, you are likely to hear the same drink called a *mécano* but an *eau-de-vie* or *gnôle* with a dash of coffee is a *jambinet*. If all this seems too much, fortify yourself with a *canard normand* – a lump of sugar dipped in calvados and sucked like a sweet.

Calvados is expensive to buy in this country but now that customs restrictions are lifted, it is worth bringing some back from your holiday in France and using it not only to drink but to give flavour to your cooking. It appears in many dishes throughout this book and below are just a few to whet your appetite.

The Norman hole and apple sorbet
Trou normand et sorbet de pommes

During the drawn-out affair of a gargantuan Normandy meal, a glass of calvados is traditionally offered between courses; this is the *trou normand*, the Norman hole. No one seems exactly sure whether these ambiguous words describe the pause for breath before the feasting begins again, or the ability of the calvados to carve a hole in the stomach to make room for more food. Nowadays restaurants often offer an apple sorbet doused with calvados in its place.

1 kg (2¼ lb) apples
100 g (4 oz) caster sugar
½ teaspoon cinnamon
500 ml (scant 1 pint) water
calvados

Put the apples into a pan with the sugar, cinnamon and water and simmer gently until soft. Purée and freeze. Remove from freezer 15 minutes before serving. Add a dash of calvados to each portion.

Apple juice with calva
Pommeau

Drunk chilled as an aperitif in Normandy and parts of Brittany too, *pommeau* also has a place in cooking; use it in any of the recipes in place of cider. It is a mixture of unfermented apple juice and calvados. Buy a bottle or two when on holiday as it's not expensive, or make your own version at home – simply mix two to three parts of apple juice to one of calvados.

Rouen duck and *le trou canard*
Canard à la rouennaise et le trou canard

There are very few places, except perhaps one or two exclusive restaurants, where you will be offered *canard à la rouennaise*. For a start it is essential that the duck comes from a special breed – a cross between tame and wild – reared in the Seine valley at Yvetot and Duclair; then it must be strangled so that none of the blood, which gives the dish its special flavour, is shed. It must be partially roasted, then divided and the breast sliced and put into a sauce of wine and shallots; the carcase is crushed in a special press and the juices strained into the sauce. The legs and wings are coated in breadcrumbs and grilled until golden; finally the breast slices are served coated in the sauce, surrounded by the legs and wings.

After this gargantuan dish a glass of *trou canard* is drunk but it is surely the cook, as much as the sated diners, who needs it most. Quantities are for one.

2 shots orange bitters
pinch of sugar
¼ apple, peeled
2 shots Angostura bitters
2 teaspoons calvados

Put all the ingredients into a glass in the order given and mix well.

Toddy
Toddy à la normande

In Jersey they make a classic whisky toddy by combining whisky, sugar, lemon juice and hot water. In Normandy they have the same habit but use calvados instead and stir the brew with a cinnamon stick.

For each glass:
1 clove
2 tablespoons calvados
1 slice lemon
1 teaspoon caster sugar
1 cinnamon stick

Warm the glass before putting in the clove, calvados, lemon and sugar and topping up with boiling water. Stir with the cinnamon stick.

Crab gratin
Dormeurs gratinés

In French markets, crabs range from small dark brown swimming crabs, *étrilles* destined for the soup pot, to the larger, prickly spider crab, *araignée*, and the *tourteau* sometimes called *dormeur*, sleeper, which is our common or edible crab. In this recipe the crab meat is cooked with onion and garlic before being flamed in calvados or apple brandy and moistened with wine. The mixture is then piled back into the shells and put into a hot oven to brown.

4 medium-sized cooked crabs
75 g (3 oz) butter
2 onions, chopped
2 cloves garlic, chopped
2 tablespoons calvados or apple brandy
150 ml ($\frac{1}{4}$ pint) dry white wine
2 tablespoons tomato purée
salt
cayenne pepper

Heat the oven to Gas 7/425°F/220°C. Break off the claws, crack them (use a small mallet or nut crackers) and scoop out the meat. Remove the flesh from the body, chopping the white meat and setting it and the brown meat aside. Discard the bag-like stomach sac, the gills and grey-green lungs (known as dead man's fingers). Break away the underside edge of each shell before washing it out. Melt 50 g (2 oz) of the butter in a shallow pan and fry the onions and garlic until golden. Add the white meat from the body and claws, stir until hot. Put the calvados or apple brandy into a ladle or small pan, heat it and set it alight. Pour it flaming over the contents of the pan. When the flames die down, stir in the wine, the brown meat and the tomato purée. Season with salt and cayenne pepper and stir gently until hot through. Spoon the mixture into the shells, dot with the remaining butter and put into the oven for 5 minutes.

Arthur's wild boar
Fricassée de marcassin de Paimpont

Paimpont is the modern name for the forest of Brocéliande which is where, according to Breton legends, King Arthur held his court. However, there's nothing legendary about the wild boar which used to flourish there in huge numbers, and I include this recipe because they still roam freely in France's forests and are also reared in this country. If unobtainable, you could use venison instead. A *marcassin* is a young boar up to six months old; older boars need longer marinating, up to a week, to make them tender. Serve with croûtons of bread.

700–900 g (1½–2 lb) wild boar, cut in cubes
300 ml (½ pint) dry white wine
2 tablespoons calvados or apple brandy
3 cloves garlic, chopped
sprigs of thyme
2 bay leaves
freshly milled black pepper
4 tablespoons oil
2 onions, chopped
2 carrots, sliced
sprigs of parsley
salt

Put the meat with the wine, calvados or apple brandy, 1 clove of garlic, some sprigs of thyme, 1 bay leaf and a seasoning of black pepper into a non-metallic dish. Cover and leave to marinate for three days, turning the meat over once each day.

To cook: drain the meat in a colander over a bowl to catch and reserve the marinade liquid. Dry the meat between pieces of kitchen paper. Heat the oil in a heavy-based casserole and brown the meat all over in several batches, transferring it to a plate as you go. Add the chopped onions and sliced carrots to the casserole and stir over a medium heat for a few minutes. Pour in the liquid from the marinade and add the 2 remaining cloves of garlic, some fresh sprigs of thyme and parsley and the second bay leaf. Return the meat to the pan and season with salt and pepper. Bring to the boil and simmer, covered, for 1½–2 hours, until the meat is tender.

Chicken with calvados and cream
Poulet vallée d'Auge

This chicken dish is one of Normandy's most elegant and is quick and easy to prepare. Chicken pieces are sautéed, then flamed in calvados and flavoured with crème fraîche. It is delicious with a dish of baked mushrooms, a simple green salad and plenty of French bread.

50 g (2 oz) butter
1 tablespoon oil
1 corn fed or free-range chicken, divided into 8 portions
salt
freshly milled black pepper
1 tablespoon calvados
4 tablespoons crème fraîche

Heat the butter and the oil in a heavy-based, flameproof casserole and fry the chicken pieces until they just turn golden but not brown. Season with salt and pepper. Cover and simmer gently for about 25 minutes until cooked. Test by piercing with a skewer – the juices should run clear. Remove chicken, pour away the fatty juices and return chicken to the casserole. Heat the calvados in a small pan or ladle, light it and pour over the chicken. Add the crème fraîche, let it bubble for a few minutes and serve.

Lamb chops with calvados
Côtes d'agneau à la rouennaise

This is a classic dish from Normandy. Lamb chops are gently cooked with onions and shallots in a little cider. They are then served with a sauce made with their own pan juices, thickened with puréed chicken livers and flavoured with calvados. Purée the livers in a food processor or use a mortar and pestle. Traditionally the chops are served with pieces of bread cut into heart-shaped croûtons and fried in butter.

50 g (2 oz) butter
1 onion, chopped
1 shallot, chopped
4 chump chops
150 ml (¼ pint) dry cider
salt
freshly milled black pepper
2 chicken livers, puréed
2 tablespoons calvados

Put 40 g (1½ oz) of butter into a heavy-based pan and fry the onion and shallot for 5–10 minutes over a low heat until golden. Remove. Add the chops and brown all over. Return the onion and shallot, raise the heat and pour in the cider. Season with salt and pepper. Cover and simmer for 15–20 minutes. Put the chops on to a warm serving dish, cover and keep warm. Boil the sauce hard until reduced by half, lower heat, add the puréed livers, pour in the calvados and add the remaining butter. Stir until amalgamated, without letting the sauce boil. Pour the sauce over the chops and serve.

Trout with calvados
Truite normande

In this Normandy recipe, trout are coated in milk – give any left over to the cat – and flour before being fried, flamed in calvados and served with a simple creamy sauce.

150 ml (¼ pint) milk
2 tablespoons flour
4 trout
50 g (2 oz) butter
2 tablespoons calvados
2 tablespoons crème fraîche
pinch of nutmeg
juice of 1 lemon

Put the milk in a shallow dish and the flour in another. Dip each trout first in milk, then coat it in flour. Heat the butter in a frying pan and fry the trout, allowing 3–4 minutes on each side. Heat the calvados in a ladle or small saucepan, set it alight and pour it flaming over the trout. Transfer the fish to a hot dish. Mix the crème fraîche with the remaining cooking juices, stir in the nutmeg and lemon juice, pour over the fish and serve.

BÉNÉDICTINE

Normandy produces northern France's most famous sweet liqueur, Bénédictine, which is made from a secret formula mixing alcohol, brandy and honey with 27 aromatic plants. Like so many of the good things in life, it was invented by a monk. He was a Venetian, Bernardo Vincelli, who early in the sixteenth century found himself in the monastery at Fécamp. He needed something to bring some cheer to the gloomy northern winters and Bénédictine was the result. Somehow the recipe got mislaid only to be unearthed some three and a half centuries later by a local historian, Alexander Legrand, who recreated the elixir and in doing so made his and his family's fortune.

Bénédictine is one of those sweet drinks which not everybody likes and the Americans preferred it laced strongly with brandy; this is the origins of 'B and B' a much drier version of the liqueur.

Although normally simply drunk as a digestif, it is also occasionally used in cooking.

Bitter-sweet apples
Pommes à l'aigre-douce

Apples, Golden Delicious in this Normandy recipe, are gently stewed in butter with raisins, Bénédictine and lemon juice with just a hint of cinnamon. Eat them as they are or with a dollop of cream. If you have no Bénédictine use calvados, brandy or some other liqueur.

50 g (2 oz) butter
6 Golden Delicious apples, peeled, quartered and cored
50 g (2 oz) raisins
pinch of cinnamon
2 tablespoons Bénédictine
juice of ½ lemon

Put the butter, apples, raisins, cinnamon, Bénédictine and lemon juice into a saucepan. Cover and put over a high heat for 3 minutes. Lower heat and simmer until apples are soft but still slightly firm. Put apples and raisins into a warm dish. Reduce sauce over a high heat and pour over the fruit.

Poachers' rabbit
Garenne aux bracos normands

A *garenne* is a wild rabbit which is tastier than a domestic rabbit but more likely to be tough, so in this recipe it is marinated overnight in cider and Bénédictine as well as herbs and juniper. Sweet, seedless grapes are added towards the end and the dish is usually served with apple slices which have been gently stewed in butter until soft and then seasoned with salt and pepper. Plain, steamed potatoes dusted with parsley are a pleasant addition. If you have no Bénédictine use calvados, brandy or some other liqueur.

1 rabbit, cut into 8 portions
300 ml (½ pint) strong dry cider
2 tablespoons Bénédictine
sprigs of parsley and thyme
2–3 sage leaves
1 bay leaf
6 juniper berries, crushed
1–2 tablespoons flour
50 g (2 oz) butter
salt
freshly milled black pepper
225 g (8 oz) seedless white grapes

Put the rabbit, cider, Bénédictine, herbs and juniper berries into a non-metallic dish and leave to marinate overnight. Next day, take the rabbit pieces out of the marinade and wipe them dry with kitchen paper. Roll them in the flour until well coated. Melt the butter in a heavy-based casserole and brown the pieces of rabbit all over, in two batches if necessary. Pour in the liquid from the marinade, bring to the boil. Season with salt and pepper and simmer, covered, for 45–50 minutes. Turn the rabbit pieces over, add the grapes and simmer for a further 5–10 minutes, taking care they don't begin to break up. Put rabbit and grapes on to a serving dish and keep warm. Boil the liquid hard until reduced by half, pour over the rabbit and serve.

GIN

Gin, *genièvre*, is the *gnôle du pays* or *eau-de-vie* of Flanders, but it is more akin to Dutch gin than to our own as the scent of juniper is very pronounced. It was invented as a medicine in Holland at the end of the eighteenth century and soon took Europe and especially England by storm where it gathered all sorts of unflattering names, from mother's ruin to poor man's rot-gut.

Coffee laced with spirit is a favourite in Flanders just as it is throughout France. There, gin is used, of course, and the concoction is known as a *bistouille.*

If you use French or Dutch gin in following the recipes given below, halve the amount of juniper berries – I have doubled the amount to counteract the milder flavour of our English gin.

Quail with juniper
Cailles au genièvre

In this recipe gin gives the quail a sweet, intense flavour which is enhanced by adding crushed juniper berries right at the end of the cooking time. Serve one or two quail per person depending on appetites.

4–8 quail
4–8 rashers streaky bacon
75 g (3 oz) butter
2 tablespoons oil
salt
freshly milled black pepper
2–3 tablespoons gin
12 juniper berries, crushed
4–8 slices French bread
few sprigs of watercress

Wrap each bird in a rasher of bacon and tie securely with string. Heat half the butter and 1 tablespoon of the oil in a heavy-based flameproof casserole and brown the quail all over, in two batches if necessary, over a medium heat. Season with salt and pepper. Heat the gin in a ladle or small saucepan, set it alight and pour it flaming over the birds. When the flames die down, cover, lower the heat and cook gently for 25–30 minutes. Add the crushed juniper berries. Heat the remaining butter and oil in a frying pan and fry the bread until golden on both sides. Serve the quail on these bread croûtons, pouring over the cooking juices and garnishing with sprigs of watercress.

Pheasant with gin
Faisan à la brabançonne

The pheasant in this dish is stuffed with Petit Suisse cream cheese and crushed juniper berries, then wrapped in vine leaves and bacon before being braised with gin on a bed of chicory.

Vine leaves preserved in brine can be bought from delicatessens – before using soak them in boiling water for a few minutes to rid them of their saltiness. Store unused ones in the fridge. One cock pheasant will feed four people but if you have big appetites, you will need two. Guinea fowl or free-range chicken can be used instead.

1 pheasant
12 juniper berries, crushed
50 g (2 oz) butter
1 Petit Suisse cheese
salt
freshly milled black pepper
3–4 vine leaves
2–3 rashers streaky bacon
1 tablespoon oil
4 heads chicory
1 sugar lump
2 tablespoons gin
watercress or lamb's lettuce

Wipe the pheasant all over with kitchen paper. Mix the juniper berries with 12 g ($\frac{1}{2}$ oz) of the butter and mash well together, before mixing in the Petit Suisse and seasoning with salt and pepper. Spoon the mixture into the cavity of the bird. Lay the vine leaves, then the bacon rashers over the breast of the pheasant and secure with string. Heat remaining butter with the oil in a heavy-based casserole in which the pheasant will fit snugly. Brown the bird all over on a medium heat. Remove and add the heads of chicory. Add salt, pepper and the lump of sugar. Put the pheasant on top. Heat the gin in a ladle or small pan, set it alight and pour over the bird. When the flames die down, cover and simmer gently for about 1 hour. Divide the pheasant into four pieces, put them on a platter, surrounded by the chicory and keep warm. Reduce the sauce by about half by boiling fiercely. Pour over the bird and serve garnished with the watercress or lamb's lettuce.

Roast woodcock
Bécasse rôtie

Woodcock are considered so fine that they are eaten ungutted. But nowadays they are rare birds and when they are sold are very expensive. In this recipe, in which they are roasted and doused in gin, you could always use quail instead. Serve the birds on croûtons of bread fried until golden in oil.

4 woodcock
4 rashers fat streaky bacon
100 g (4 oz) butter
4 tablespoons gin
salt
freshly milled black pepper

Heat the oven to Gas 7/425°F/220°C. Wrap each bird in a rasher of bacon and secure them with string. Put them into a well-buttered gratin dish and dot with the remaining butter cut in small pieces. Roast for 30 minutes, basting and turning the birds several times. After about 15 minutes, sprinkle each bird with gin and season with salt and pepper. A few minutes before the end of the cooking time, remove the bacon and return the birds to brown the breasts.

Kidneys with juniper and gin
Rognons à la liégeoise

The original recipe was for calves' kidneys which are not so easy to find, so I have used lambs' kidneys. They are braised with onion and bacon before being flavoured with crushed juniper berries and the sauce enriched with gin and white wine. Serve these kidneys with steamed potatoes sprinkled with parsley.

450–700 g (1–1½ lb) lambs' kidneys
50 g (2 oz) butter
2 onions, chopped
4 rashers streaky bacon, chopped
1 teaspoon juniper berries, crushed
2 tablespoons gin
2 tablespoons dry white wine
salt
freshly milled black pepper

Cut the kidneys in half and remove the fatty core. Melt the butter in a heavy-based flameproof casserole and fry the onions and bacon until golden. Add the kidneys and seal them quickly on both sides. Cover and simmer gently for 5 minutes. Add the crushed juniper berries and cook for 5–8 minutes more. Remove to a warm serving dish. Pour the gin and wine into the pan juices, bring to the boil and let the sauce reduce by at least half. Season with salt and pepper and pour over the kidneys.

Juniper liqueur
Liqueur de genièvre

If you live where junipers flourish, you might like to make your own juniper liqueur. Sweeter than gin it makes an interesting digestif at the end of a meal. Remember the longer it is kept, the better it is likely to be.

- 1 tablespoon green juniper berries
- 1 tablespoon blue juniper berries
- ½ lemon, finely sliced
- ¼ cinnamon stick
- 1 litre *eau-de-vie*
- 225 g (8 oz) caster sugar

Put the berries and lemon slices into a 1 litre jar with the cinnamon and fill to the top with the *eau-de-vie*. Cork and leave for two months. At the end of this time, put the sugar into a saucepan with a little water, bring to the boil and simmer until the bubbles become small and there is practically no steam. Leave to cool. Strain the *eau-de-vie* into a bottle, add the syrup, bottle and cork. Keep at least two weeks before drinking.

Hare pâté without hare
Pâté de lièvre sans lièvre

This unlikely sounding pâté from Dol in Brittany is surprisingly successful. Despite the fact that it really does contain no hare, it looks and tastes rich and gamey and is very cheap and simple to prepare. It's just the sort of frugal recipe you can imagine pleasing Breton grandmothers! It doesn't contain any gin either, but it does use juniper berries, so this seems an appropriate place to include it.

225 g (8 oz) red kidney beans, soaked (see Etceteras)
1 carrot, sliced
1 onion, stuck with 2–3 cloves
1 clove garlic
parsley, thyme
3 bay leaves
150 g (6 oz) streaky pork rashers, minced
1 egg, beaten
150 ml ($\frac{1}{4}$ pint) red wine
1 teaspoon juniper berries, crushed
grating of nutmeg
salt
freshly milled black pepper
3–4 rashers streaky bacon, cut in half lengthwise

Put the soaked beans into a large pan, cover with cold water and add the carrot, onion stuck with cloves, garlic, parsley, thyme and 1 bay leaf. Bring to the boil and simmer for 45–60 minutes, until tender. Drain well and put through a *mouli-légumes* to make a smooth purée and extract the skins. Heat the oven to Gas 3/325°F/160°C. Mix the bean purée with the minced pork and stir in the egg and wine, followed by the juniper berries and nutmeg. Season well with salt and pepper. Put into a buttered ovenproof dish and arrange the bacon rashers in a criss-cross pattern over the top. Cover with foil. Bake for 1 hour, remove foil and bake a further 30 minutes. Test it is done by inserting a skewer – it should come out clean. If not, continue the cooking for a little longer. Set aside to cool and after 1 hour, weight the foil down with a plate and something heavy on top. Leave in a cool place for at least 12 hours before eating.

Flesh pot
Potjevleisch

There are many versions of this traditional pâté which comes from Dunkerque. It can be made with one or several varieties of meat and poultry and is the sort of thing to buy from a local *charcuterie* rather than attempt to make yourself, but it is interesting to know how it is done.

First a rabbit and chicken are boned and cut in pieces. An earthenware terrine is then lined with pieces of fat pork, and the rabbit, chicken, chopped onion, slices of bacon, small pieces of veal and sliced carrots are put in layers in the dish. Finally they are topped by pieces of duck, sprigs of thyme and bay leaves and seasoned with salt and pepper. The whole thing is then laced liberally with gin, covered with a layer of pork rinds and sufficient jellied stock is poured in to come right to the top. The dish is then covered with a lid sealed with a flour and water paste and it goes into a slow oven in a bain-marie for 3–4 hours.

Mushrooms and chestnuts

Fried parasol mushrooms

Penny buns with cream

Grilled penny buns

Lemon sole with mushrooms

Trout with mushrooms

Chicken with morels

Lamb with mushrooms and cream

Normandy pancakes

Canned and dried chestnuts

To peel chestnuts

Boiled chestnuts

Roasted or grilled chestnuts

Chestnut soup

Rabbit with chestnuts

Baked chestnut cake

Chocolate chestnut cake

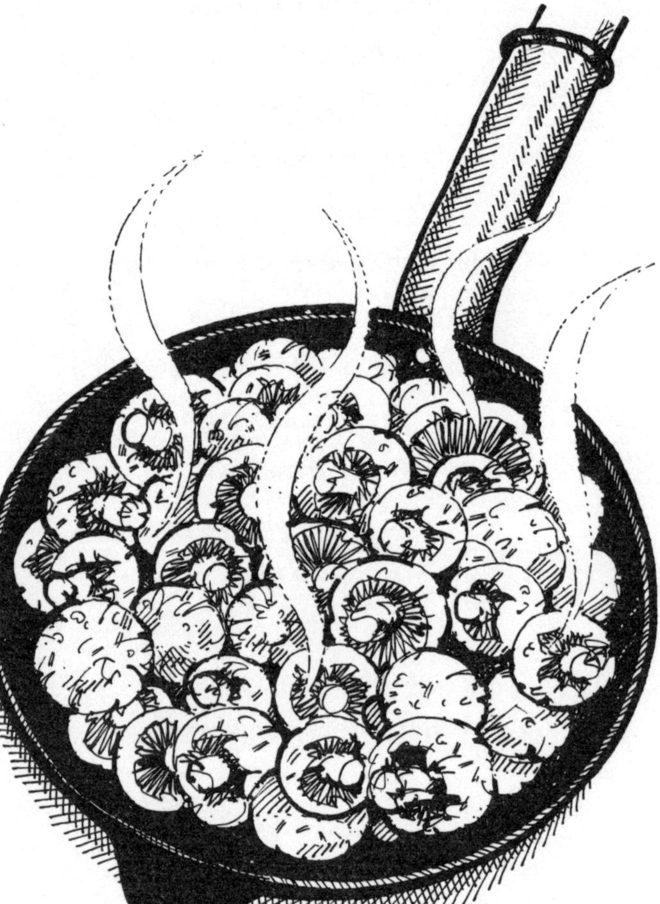

MUSHROOMS

For most of us, the word mushroom conjures up the cultivated kind readily on sale in greengrocers and supermarkets. The French prefer to buy their mushrooms wild from a market stall, and those who can tell the edible sort from a poisonous toadstool (the Bretons call them *kabell-touseg* and the French *capuchons de crapaud*), like to search them out in woods and fields. The ones they find are not so very different from our own indigenous varieties but somehow their French names, *bolets*, *cèpes*, *chanterelles*, *girolles*, *pieds de mouton*, *coulemelle* etc. make them seem much more seductive.

Wild mushrooms must have been in abundance in the forest of Paimpont, the legendary Brocéliande where Merlin was imprisoned in an enchanted circle by the fairy Viviane. The story tells that he could easily have broken her spell if he had wished but that he had no desire to do so. I like to think she was a good cook and enchanted him with the dishes of wild mushrooms she prepared. The following three recipes come from that area.

When preparing the recipes, if you haven't wild mushrooms to hand use cultivated instead, experimenting with some of the more interesting ones now on sale.

Fried parasol mushrooms
Coulemelles au beurre

The *coulemelle* is the parasol mushroom (*Lepiota procera*). The stalks are inedible so must be discarded but the heads are considered a great delicacy. To prepare avoid washing but brush away any lingering dirt.

50 g (2 oz) butter
350 g (12 oz) parasol mushrooms or field mushrooms
juice of ½ lemon or 1–2 tablespoons Muscadet or other dry white wine
salt
freshly milled black pepper
handful parsley, chopped

Melt the butter in a frying pan. When it is sizzling, add the mushrooms and fry them over a medium heat, turning them over and over until soft and tender. Add the lemon juice or wine, season with salt and pepper and serve dusted with parsley.

Penny buns with cream
Cèpes à la paimpontaise

There are several different kinds of *cèpes* or *bolets* (*Boletus* family) but the one that interests the gourmet is *Boletus edulis*. The Victorians called it penny bun because it looked like a bun both in shape and colour. It is full of flavour but can be maggoty so must be well cleaned, and if the tubes on the underside look damp or discoloured they should be peeled away.

350 g (12 oz) penny bun mushrooms or field mushrooms
2 tablespoons oil
50 g (2 oz) butter
6 tablespoons crème fraîche or clotted cream
1 clove garlic, chopped
1 shallot, chopped
generous handful parsley, chopped

Slice the mushrooms. Heat the oil in a frying pan and toss them over a high heat until they are almost cooked. Drain them. Lower the heat, add the butter to the pan and, when it has melted, return the mushrooms. Turn them over and over for a minute or two more, then stir in the crème fraîche. Serve on a hot plate, sprinkled with the garlic, shallot and parsley.

Grilled penny buns
Cèpes grillées

1–2 cloves garlic, cut in slivers
350 g (12 oz) *cèpes* or flat mushrooms
6–8 tablespoons oil
25 g (1 oz) butter, cut in small pieces
generous handful parsley, chopped

Insert the slivers of garlic into the *cèpes* or mushrooms and lay them in a glass or china dish. Sprinkle over the oil and leave them to marinate for half an hour, turning them over from time to time. Heat the grill. Lay the mushrooms in a single layer in the pan and grill, turning them frequently. Serve on a hot plate, dot with the butter and sprinkle with the chopped parsley.

Lemon sole with mushrooms
Sole limande à la normande

This is a simple adaptation of a classic Normandy dish. Quick to prepare it is graceful enough for any dinner party. It can be made with other kinds of flat fish such as plaice, flounder or dab.

4 large fillets lemon sole
150 ml (¼ pint) dry cider
salt
freshly milled black pepper
75 g (3 oz) butter
225 g (8 oz) mushrooms, sliced
4 tablespoons crème fraîche
handful parsley, chopped

Heat the oven to Gas 5/375°F/190°C. Lay the fish in a single layer in a buttered oven dish. Pour over the cider, season with salt and pepper and dot with one third of the butter. Bake for 10–15 minutes. Meanwhile, heat the remaining butter in a frying pan. When it sizzles, add the mushrooms and cook over a medium heat, stirring occasionally until they are soft and hot through. Put the cooked fish on a warm dish (keep the liquid), garnish with the mushrooms, cover with a loose piece of foil and put back in the switched-off oven, the door ajar. Pour the liquid into the frying pan and boil hard until reduced by two-thirds. Stir in the crème fraîche and boil for a moment or two to let the sauce thicken. Pour over the fish, dust with the parsley and serve.

Trout with mushrooms
Truites gratinées

This recipe for trout cooked on a bed of onions, shallots and mushrooms, comes from Lisieux, a thriving, industrial town in Calvados. However, it is also the town where Ste-Thérèse lived, and thousands of pilgrims come every year to see the house where she was brought up and the convent in which she died in 1897 at the age of 24 after writing her *History of a Soul*. It's perhaps frivolous but it would be nice to think that, before she embraced the austere life of a Carmelite, she was allowed occasionally to enjoy a trout caught in the local river, cooked in this simple fashion.

50 g (2 oz) butter
1 onion, finely chopped
2 shallots, finely chopped
handful parsley, chopped
225 g (8 oz) mushrooms, finely sliced
4 trout
225 ml (8 fl oz) dry white wine or dry cider
2 lemons
salt
freshly milled black pepper
2–3 tablespoons breadcrumbs

Heat the oven to Gas 6/400°F/200°C. Generously butter a shallow flameproof gratin dish. Spread the base with the chopped onions and shallots, the parsley and half the mushrooms. Lay the trout on top. Sprinkle over the wine or cider and the juice of 1 lemon. Season with salt and pepper. Sprinkle over the rest of the mushrooms and the breadcrumbs. Dot with the remaining butter. Put on the stove and heat until the wine or cider bubbles. Transfer to the oven for 15 minutes. Serve garnished with remaining lemon cut in quarters.

Chicken with morels
Poulet aux morilles à la mode de Normandie

Fresh honey-combed morels, (*Morchella vulgaris*) with their hollow, fleshy, slightly brittle caps, are on sale – at a price – in French markets from spring through to autumn. To prepare them, remove stalks, cut the caps in half lengthwise and soak them for 5–10 minutes in salted water to encourage the insects inside to evacuate. Rinse well to remove all traces of sand or grit. Dry with kitchen paper. Dried morels need to be soaked for an hour, then trimmed, split and rinsed before using. This recipe also works well with rabbit.

2 tablespoons oil
50 g (2 oz) butter
1 onion, chopped
1 maize-fed or free range chicken divided into 8, or use chicken pieces
2 cloves garlic, crushed
sprigs of tarragon, parsley, thyme
150 ml (¼ pint) dry cider
salt
freshly milled black pepper
225 g (8 oz) morels or mushrooms
juice of ½ lemon
2 tablespoons crème fraîche
pinch of cayenne

Heat the oil with half the butter in a heavy-based casserole and brown the chicken pieces (in two batches if necessary). Remove to a plate. Fry the onion gently for a few minutes and return the chicken to the casserole. Add the garlic, herbs and cider, bring to the boil, season with salt and pepper, cover and simmer for 50–60 minutes. Heat the remaining butter in a frying pan and fry the mushrooms gently for 5–10 minutes. Remove the chicken pieces to a warm serving dish, garnish with the mushrooms, squeeze over the lemon juice, cover with foil and keep warm. Raise the heat under the casserole and boil the sauce fiercely until it has reduced by half. Discard the herbs, stir in the crème fraîche and a pinch of cayenne. Pour sauce over the chicken and serve.

Lamb with mushrooms and cream
Sauté d'agneau

This recipe from St-Michel Bay uses the tender, sweet lamb which graze on the spring and summer pastures provided by the salt marshes, which in autumn and winter are under the sea. Mont-St-Michel is just inside Normandy but the Bretons have a claim to it, because not only does much of the granite with which it is constructed come from Brittany, but also before the river Couesnon changed its course, the abbey was on the Breton side, and there is a Breton saying: *le Couesnon, par sa folie, a mis le Mont en Normandie* (in its lunacy, the Couesnon put the Mont in Normandy).

In this quick and simple recipe, finely sliced pieces of lamb are sautéed in butter and oil with mushrooms, then flamed in calvados or apple brandy and the sauce is thickened with cream. It goes well with plain rice.

450–700 g (1–1½ lb) boneless lamb leg steaks
1 lemon
freshly milled black pepper
50 g (2 oz) butter
1 teaspoon oil
225 g (8 oz) mushrooms, finely sliced
1 tablespoon calvados or apple brandy
2–3 tablespoons crème fraîche
salt

Cut the lamb into fine strips and put into a non-metallic dish. Squeeze over the lemon juice and season with pepper. Cover and leave to marinate for at least 1 hour. At the end of this time heat the butter and oil in a frying pan and fry the pieces of meat quickly until sealed all over. Cover and lower the heat, and cook very gently for 5 minutes. Remove and cover with foil to keep warm. Add the mushrooms to the frying pan and fry quickly over a high heat. Remove and put with the lamb. Wipe out the frying pan with kitchen paper, return the meat and mushrooms to the pan and put over a high heat. Put the calvados or apple brandy into a ladle or small pan to heat. Light it and pour it flaming over the meat and mushrooms. When the flames die down, stir in the crème fraîche and season with salt and pepper. Serve immediately.

Normandy pancakes
Ficelles normandes

Pancakes are not confined to Brittany. They make them all over northern France and this recipe is to be found in both Normandy and Picardy (there they are known as *ficelles picardes* and the milk and water are replaced by pale ale). They are filled with a mixture of ham and mushrooms in a béchamel sauce and glazed in a hot oven.

8 *crêpes* (see Etceteras)
75 g (3 oz) butter
150 g (6 oz) mushrooms, sliced
50 g (2 oz) flour
300 ml (½ pint) milk
salt
freshly milled black pepper
pinch of nutmeg
225 g (8 oz) cooked ham, cut in cubes
2 tablespoons crème fraîche
2 tablespoons chopped parsley

Prepare the *crêpes*. Heat the oven to Gas 5/375°F/190°C. Melt 50 g (2 oz) of the butter in a saucepan and fry the sliced mushrooms until soft. Stir in the flour and cook for 2 minutes, stirring all the time. Gradually mix in the milk and, when it is bubbling and thick, season with salt, pepper and nutmeg. Add the ham, crème fraîche and parsley. Generously butter a shallow oven dish. Fill each *crêpe* with some of the ham and mushroom mixture, roll them up and lay them in the dish. Pour over any remaining sauce. Dot with the remaining butter and put into the oven for 10 minutes.

CHESTNUTS

The French call them *marrons* and *châtaignes*, but in Brittany they call chestnuts *kistin*. *Marrons* are superior to *châtaignes*, containing only one nut instead of two or three to each prickly shell. Like the people of the Auvergne, Breton peasants relied on chestnuts as part of their staple diet and ate them every which way: roasted or boiled, stuffed into cabbages, made into cakes or to flavour soups and stews and for highdays and holidays used them to stuff poultry just as we do the Christmas turkey.

Skinned chestnuts were simply boiled and served in a bowl covered with milk or buttermilk. In Dol they stew them, *frigousse de marrons*, in salted water, sweetened with a lump of sugar and flavoured with butter and a tablespoon of the juices from a roast. The cooked chestnuts retain their shape but are soft and succulent and delicious with fried or grilled sausages.

At Dol-de-Bretagne, we came across chestnut pans known as *harrassoires*, shallow saucepans punched with holes in which the nuts are cooked over the fire and it is in this region, southwards through Rennes to Redon, that the trees flourish by canal and river banks and in woods alongside old oaks, beeches and birch.

Canned and dried chestnuts

When fresh chestnuts are not available, or too time-consuming to prepare, either canned or dried chestnuts can be used in the recipes. Make sure you use the unsweetened kind when buying cans. Dried chestnuts must be soaked for 24 hours before being boiled until soft.

To peel chestnuts

Chestnuts are a chore to peel although once you have accomplished the laborious task you will be able to decide whether the purists are right and they really are superior to canned or dried.

Score each chestnut on its rounded side. Boil them for 8–10 minutes in a large pan of salted water. Remove each chestnut with a slotted spoon, hold it in a cloth and use a knife to help you slip off the outer husk. Rub off the inner skin with the cloth. If the inner skins prove stubborn, put the chestnuts into cold water, add a spoonful of oil and bring to the boil. Simmer until the skin rubs away easily, holding and rubbing the chestnuts one at a time in a cloth.

Boiled chestnuts
Marrons bouillis

Boil chestnuts for about an hour in a large pan of salted water flavoured with a sprig of celery. Drain them and eat them with butter. Each person slits his or her own with a knife and eats the soft flesh with a teaspoon.

Roasted or grilled chestnuts
Marrons grillés

Lightly score each chestnut on its rounded side. Put into a pan punched with holes and cook over an open fire, in a hot oven or over a high heat, turning them over from time to time, until they are black and give slightly. Eat with butter and a glass of sweet cider.

Chestnut soup
Potage aux marrons

Wherever there are chestnuts in France, there are recipes for chestnut soups. This one comes from Redon in Brittany, which on the fourth Saturday in October holds an annual fair, the Foire Teillouse, to which people come from miles around to buy chestnuts. This sweetly flavoured soup makes a comforting starter for a supper on a chilly autumn evening and is even more delicious if you use a game stock made from, say, duck or pheasant.

- 50 g (2 oz) butter
- 100 g (4 oz) streaky bacon, chopped
- 2 onions, chopped
- 2 carrots, sliced
- 1 leek, sliced
- 1 × 450 g (1 lb) can unsweetened chestnut purée
- 2 cloves
- sprigs of thyme
- 1 bay leaf
- 1 clove garlic, left whole
- 1 litre (1¾ pints) stock or water
- salt
- freshly milled black pepper
- sprigs of parsley

Melt the butter in a large saucepan and sweat the bacon, onions, carrots and leek, covered, for 10 minutes over a low heat. Stir in the chestnut purée (break it up with a fork) and add the cloves, thyme, bay leaf and garlic. Pour in the stock or water, mix well, season with salt and pepper, cover and simmer for 45–60 minutes. Purée, check the seasoning and serve decorated with sprigs of parsley.

Rabbit with chestnuts
Frigousse rennaise aux châtaignes

In this recipe, the rabbit is cooked in dry cider and flavoured with tomato, garlic and herbs. Sometimes wild mushrooms are added as well and a Muscadet or dry white wine is used instead of the cider. If you buy a rabbit from a game dealer, ask for the liver which is added right at the last minute and is a treat to be fought over. This dish is delicious with mashed turnips or steamed or boiled potatoes.

1 pkt dried chestnuts
4 tablespoons oil
1 rabbit, cut into 8, or equivalent rabbit portions, plus the rabbit's liver, if available
150 g (6 oz) streaky bacon, chopped
150 g (6 oz) shallots, sliced
2 tablespoons tomato purée
sprig of thyme
1 bay leaf
2 cloves garlic, chopped
300 ml ($\frac{1}{2}$ pint) dry strong cider
salt
freshly milled black pepper

Soak the chestnuts overnight in cold water. Heat the oil in a heavy-based casserole and fry the rabbit pieces on all sides, removing them to a warm plate. Add the streaky bacon and the shallots and cook over a low heat until soft but not brown, stirring often. Stir in the tomato purée. Return the rabbit pieces to the casserole, add the drained chestnuts, thyme, bay leaf and garlic. Raise the heat, pour over the cider and bring to the boil. Season with salt and pepper and simmer, covered, for 1–1$\frac{1}{4}$ hours. Add the rabbit liver, stir it into the sauce and simmer for a further 5 minutes. Put rabbit, liver and chestnuts on a warm serving dish. Boil the sauce hard for 5 minutes until it has reduced by about half. Pour over the rabbit and serve.

Baked chestnut cake
Gâteau St-Conwoïon

The river port of Redon in Ille-et-Vilaine with its celebrated chestnut fair, the Foire Teillouse is also famous for its chestnut gâteaux. This one is baked, covered with caramelized sugar and is rather like a cold soufflé. It is a delicious indulgence masked with whipped cream.

1 × 450 g (1 lb) can unsweetened chestnut purée
3 eggs, separated
150 g (6 oz) caster sugar
25 g (1 oz) butter
150 ml ($\frac{1}{4}$ pint) double cream, whipped

Heat the oven to Gas 5/375°F/190°C. Mash the chestnut purée and gradually beat in the egg yolks and half the sugar. Put the remaining sugar into a cake tin with a tablespoon of water and the butter and heat gently over a low heat until the sugar melts. Raise the heat and let it bubble and turn golden. Tip the tin about so that the sides are lightly coated. Beat the egg whites until stiff and fold into the chestnut purée. Turn the mixture into the tin and transfer to the oven. Bake for 40–45 minutes, until the gâteau is puffed and risen and a skewer, when plunged into the centre, comes out clean. Allow to cool, when it will sink a little. Turn it out when completely cold on to a round plate and mask with whipped cream or sprinkle with icing sugar.

Chocolate chestnut cake
Gâteau aux marrons

Wherever there are chestnuts, there are recipes combining them with chocolate, as in this second gâteau from Redon. Like the one above, it is also very rich but makes a moreish dessert at the end of a meal, eaten perhaps with macaroons or, for those who are not worried about their figures, a dollop of whipped cream. Make up the same recipe for a Christmas log, *bûche de Noël*, by making in a loaf tin lined with greaseproof paper; when the log is set, roll it on to a dish, peel away the paper, mark it with the prongs of a fork to simulate bark and sprinkle sparingly with sieved icing sugar.

225 g (8 oz) plain, bitter chocolate
150 g (6 oz) butter
1 × 450 g (1 lb) can unsweetened chestnut purée
100 g (4 oz) vanilla sugar
2 tablespoons white rum

Grease a loose-bottomed cake tin with butter and line with a circle of greaseproof paper cut to fit the base. Melt the chocolate and butter together either in a low oven or in the microwave. Beat the chestnut purée with the sugar until light and creamy. Beat in the melted chocolate and butter and the rum. Turn the mixture into the prepared tin. Cover and put into the fridge to harden for 2–3 hours or overnight. To serve, turn cake out carefully on to a serving dish.

Potatoes and leeks

Cheese and leek soup

Leek gratin

Potato and leek gratin

Potato and leeks in milk

Potato and watercress soup

Potatoes in milk

Potatoes with bacon

Potato cake

Warm potato and celery salad

Grated potato cake

Potatoes with onions

Mashed potatoes with celeriac

Breton fish casserole

Skate with cream

Dogfish with wine

Pheasant with potatoes

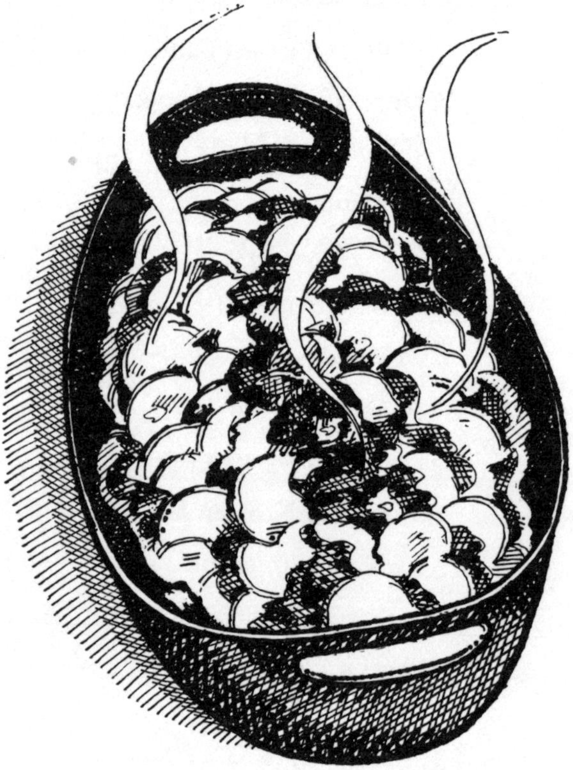

There's a romantic story that the potato became popular in France due to the single-minded efforts of an agriculturalist with the grand name of Antoine-Auguste Parmentier, and when you come across the description *parmentier* on a restaurant menu, you may be sure it has a lot to do with potatoes.

Although the potato had been around in Europe for quite some time – ever since the Spanish discovered it in South America – the French regarded it with deep suspicion (who says it is the English who are conservative about their food?) and they even thought it was a cause of leprosy. However, Parmentier was forced to live on potatoes while imprisoned by the Prussians and he realized they could be a source of food for the starving peasants. He approached the king, Louis XVI, and they devised a plan to convince people what a valuable vegetable it really was. Fields of potatoes were planted in the Bois de Boulogne and heavily guarded – but not so heavily that it was impossible for the crops to be stolen. It seems that from then on everybody loved potatoes and there is not a region of France which does not have its own potato dishes.

Leeks, their origins lost in the mist of time, have nothing to do with potatoes except they go beautifully together, and there are many recipes from northern France to prove it. Only in Brittany were they relegated to mere chickenfeed or their use restricted to flavouring the *pot-au-feu*. Now they feature in soups or are eaten cold with a vinaigrette when they are known as *asperge du pauvre*. They are delicious, too, steamed or cooked in butter and glazed with sugar or honey.

Cheese and leek soup
Potage de poireaux gratiné

This is not dissimilar to *vichyssoise*, which is the name given to the chilled leek soup first served by a French chef, Louis Diat, at the Ritz-Carlton in New York in 1917. The word *vichyssoise* actually means 'in the style of Vichy' but the soup Diat made really belongs to American cooking and is not to be found in French cookery books. The leek soup below stems from Flanders. It is pale and creamy with a topping of bubbling cheese and is quick and cheering on a cold winter's day. In France I would use Gruyère, but here I use mature cheddar which is full of flavour and has the advantage of melting without becoming stringy.

50 g (2 oz) butter
450 g (1 lb) leeks, finely sliced
350 g (12 oz) potatoes, peeled and sliced
1 litre ($1\frac{3}{4}$ pints) water or stock
2 bay leaves
nutmeg
salt
freshly milled black pepper
100 g (4 oz) cheese, grated

Gently melt the butter in a heavy-based casserole, add the leeks, cover and allow to sweat for 10–15 minutes. Add the potatoes, water, bay leaves, nutmeg, salt and pepper, bring to the boil and simmer for 45 minutes. Heat the grill or the oven to Gas 7/425°F/220°C. Put the soup through a food processor or *mouli-légumes* and return to the casserole. Sprinkle the cheese over the surface and put the soup under the grill or at the top of the oven for 5–10 minutes, until the cheese melts and bubbles and begins to brown.

Leek gratin
Poireaux de Rouen à la sauce crème

Eat this dish of leeks either as a first course or as an accompaniment to a simple roast of lamb or chicken. It is quick to prepare, the leeks being simply boiled then coated in a sauce of lemon juice, butter and cream, *sauce à la normande*, topped with cheese and browned either at the top of the oven or under the grill.

900 g (2 lb) leeks
100 g (4 oz) butter
juice of 1 lemon
150 ml ($\frac{1}{4}$ pint) crème fraîche
salt
freshly milled black pepper
75 g (3 oz) cheese, grated

Wash the leeks well (discard the green tops) and simmer them in salted water for 15–20 minutes until they are soft: use a wide-mouthed casserole that can go from stove to oven or grill. Drain very well, pressing them to extract all the moisture. Return them to the casserole. Melt the butter in a saucepan and let it turn a pale brown, add the lemon juice and gradually stir in the crème fraîche. Season with salt and pepper. Pour the sauce over the leeks, sprinkle with the cheese and put either at the top of the oven heated to Gas 6/400°F/200°C, or under a hot grill to brown, for 5–10 minutes.

Potato and leek gratin
Gratin à la normande

This is a light gratin of potatoes and leeks and because they are cooked in stock or water, it makes a sober contrast to some of Normandy's creamier dishes.

50 g (2 oz) butter
450 g (1 lb) leeks, sliced, green ends discarded
900 g (2 lb) old potatoes, finely sliced
450 ml (¾ pint) stock or water
1 teaspoon dried thyme
1 bay leaf
pinch of nutmeg
salt
freshly milled black pepper
1–2 tablespoons chopped parsley

Heat the oven to Gas 6/400°F/200°C. Melt half the butter in a flameproof gratin dish and add the leeks. Cover with foil and leave to sweat over a low heat for 10 minutes. Mix in the potatoes and add the stock or water, thyme, bay leaf and nutmeg. Season with salt and pepper, bring to the boil and dot with the remaining butter. Bake for 40 minutes until the potatoes are soft and the gratin is golden brown. Sprinkle with the parsley before serving.

Potato and leeks in milk
Pommes de terre aux poireaux en blanquette

This leek and potato dish from Normandy goes beautifully with lamb or pork. The vegetables are cooked in milk in the oven in a covered dish and so do not brown. Hence the name *en blanquette*, meaning in a white sauce.

50 g (2 oz) butter
1 lb leeks, sliced
25 g (1 oz) flour
300 ml (½ pint) milk
salt
freshly milled black pepper
900 g (2 lb) potatoes, peeled and finely sliced
2 tablespoons crème fraîche
freshly snipped chives

Heat the oven to Gas 5/375°F/190°C. Melt half the butter in a shallow flameproof dish and add the leeks. Cover and let them sweat while you make the sauce. Melt the remaining butter in a small pan, sprinkle in the flour and stir for 2 minutes. Gradually add the milk and stir until the sauce boils and thickens. Season with salt and pepper. Add the potatoes to the leeks, and pour the sauce over. Spread the *crème fraîche* over the top, cover and bake for 45 minutes. Serve sprinkled with the chives.

Potato and watercress soup
Soupe au cresson à la paysanne normande

Known as *cresson de fontaine*, the watercress of northern France has been famous for centuries. In this recipe from Normandy this simple potato and watercress soup is turned into something special by putting grated cheese and 1 or 2 thin slices of tomato into each bowl before pouring in the soup. The heat of the soup melts the cheese and is sufficient to lightly cook the tomato. Serve with croûtons fried in butter or oil.

25 g (1 oz) butter or 2 tablespoons oil
450 g (1 lb) potatoes, peeled and quartered
1 bunch watercress
1 litre ($1\frac{3}{4}$ pints) water
salt
freshly milled black pepper
50 g (2 oz) grated hard cheese
1 tomato, thinly sliced

Heat the butter or oil in a saucepan, add the potatoes and just the leaves of the watercress. Let them sweat, covered, over a low heat for 10 minutes. Pour in the water and season with salt. Simmer, covered, for 30–40 minutes. Purée and add pepper to taste. Put a little cheese and 1 or 2 slices of tomato into each bowl. Pour over the soup and serve.

Potatoes in milk
Pommes de terre à la normande

Quicker than a potato gratin, the potatoes in this dish are cooked with onions, milk and herbs on top of the stove and then put under a hot grill to brown. The potatoes absorb almost all the milk and are full of flavour.

50 g (2 oz) butter
2 onions, chopped
900 g (2 lb) potatoes, finely sliced
450 ml (¾ pint) milk
salt
freshly milled black pepper
sprigs of thyme and parsley, tied in a bunch
1 bay leaf

Melt half the butter in a wide-mouthed flameproof casserole and fry the onions over a medium heat until just beginning to take colour. Mix in the potatoes, pour over enough milk barely to cover (you may not use it all) and season with salt and pepper. Add the thyme, parsley and bay leaf. Cover and simmer gently for about 20–30 minutes, until the potatoes are tender. Remove lid, dot the top with the remaining butter and put under a hot grill for 5 minutes, until the top bubbles and turns golden brown.

Potatoes with bacon
Pommes de terre au lard

In both Normandy and Brittany I have come across variations on this potato dish; sometimes it is cooked on top of the stove but I prefer the other method of baking it in a warm oven. It results in a finished dish in which the potatoes will be coloured an appetizing tomato red, they will have absorbed nearly all the sauce and the kitchen will be filled with a tantalizing smell of garlic, bacon and herbs.

25 g (1 oz) butter or 2 tablespoons oil
1 onion, chopped
100 g (4 oz) streaky bacon, chopped
1 tablespoon tomato purée
150 ml (¼ pint) water
150 ml (¼ pint) strong dry cider or dry white wine
2 cloves garlic, chopped
sprigs of thyme and parsley, tied in a bunch
1 bay leaf
700 g (1½ lb) potatoes, peeled and sliced
salt
freshly milled black pepper

Heat the oven to Gas 5/375°F/190°C. Heat the butter or oil in a flameproof casserole or gratin dish and add the chopped onion and bacon and fry for a few minutes until golden. Stir in the tomato purée, followed by the water and the cider or white wine. Add the garlic, thyme, parsley and bay leaf and stir in the potatoes. Season with salt and pepper. Bring to the boil, transfer to the oven and bake for 1½ hours or until potatoes are soft and have absorbed almost all the sauce.

Potato cake
Galette de pommes de terre

This recipe comes from Vannes, the capital of Morbihan, which in the ninth century was the seat of the first Duke of Brittany, Nominoë, and is now a thriving agricultural market town and tourist centre.

The flat cake is baked until golden in a hot oven and can be served with a Beaumanoir sauce (see Index). Eat it hot or cold as an accompaniment to a roast or a salad. If preferred the mixture can be formed into small individual cakes.

450 g (1 lb) potatoes
100 g (4 oz) flour
50 g (2 oz) butter
pinch of nutmeg
salt
freshly milled black pepper
1 egg yolk, beaten

Boil or steam the unpeeled potatoes until soft, drain and set aside until cool enough to handle. Heat the oven to Gas 7/425°F/220°C. Remove the skins and mash the potatoes, mixing in the flour and butter. Season with nutmeg, salt and pepper. Butter a baking sheet and spread the mixture over the surface in the shape of a flat pancake about 1 cm (½ in) thick. Brush with beaten egg and bake until golden.

Warm potato and celery salad
Salade du pays de Caux

Serve this Normandy potato salad, also called *salade cauchoise* or *salade normande* as a warming starter in winter.

450 g (1 lb) potatoes
juice of ½ lemon
1 tablespoon vinegar
salt
freshly milled black pepper
1 celery heart, cut in fine strips
225 g (8 oz) ham, cut in cubes
150 ml (¼ pint) crème fraîche

Steam or boil the potatoes in their skins. Peel and slice the potatoes as soon as they are cool enough to handle. Put them into a salad bowl and stir in the lemon juice, vinegar, salt and pepper. Add the celery and ham and mix in the crème fraîche.

Grated potato cake
La rapée de pommes de terre

This recipe from Dol-de-Bretagne is quite basic but it is a delicious accompaniment to grilled fish or meat. Grate the potatoes if you prefer, although I find they are less watery if cut into matchstick strips. Only add the salt right at the end, otherwise the cake will stick.

25 g (1 oz) butter
1 tablespoon oil
4 medium potatoes, cut into fine matchstick strips
salt
freshly milled black pepper
handful parsley or chervil, chopped

Heat the butter and oil in a small heavy-based frying pan and when it sizzles add the potatoes. Press them down well, cover and cook over a low heat for 15–20 minutes. Turn them over. Don't worry if the cake breaks up at this point, simply press it back together. Cook, covered, for a further 15–20 minutes. Uncover, lift an edge with a spatula and if it is not golden brown, raise the heat and cook for a few minutes longer. Your nose will tell you when it is ready. Season with salt and pepper and sprinkle with the parsley or chervil. Serve from the pan.

Potatoes with onions
Pommes de terre aux oignons

The secret of cooking these potatoes with onions is to fry them over a low heat until they slowly brown. You can use sliced left-over potatoes but, better still, steam or boil them in their jackets ahead of time and peel them when they are just cool enough to handle, and the skin comes away paper thin.

2–3 tablespoons oil
225 g (8 oz) onions, sliced
450 g (1 lb) potatoes, cooked and thinly sliced
salt
freshly milled black pepper
chopped parsley

Heat the oil and cook the sliced onions until golden. Add the potatoes and fry slowly, turning once or twice, until golden brown. Season with salt and pepper and sprinkle over the parsley.

Mashed potatoes with celeriac
Pommes de terre au céleri-rave

Celeriac gives mashed potatoes a subtle, nutty flavour which goes well with pork, rabbit or sausages. Once peeled and cut celeriac, like potatoes, goes black if exposed to the air, so put immediately into cold water.

700 g (1½ lb) celeriac
700 g (1½ lb) potatoes
50 g (2 oz) butter
salt
freshly milled black pepper
1 tablespoon chopped parsley

Peel the celeriac, cut into even pieces and put into a saucepan of cold water. Peel and add the potatoes, cut into similar-sized pieces and add to the pan. Bring to the boil, add salt and simmer covered for 20–30 minutes until soft. Drain well and mash. Beat in the butter, add salt and pepper to taste. Put into a dish, fork the surface and sprinkle with parsley.

Breton fish casserole
Cotriade

A *cotriade* is a warming winter stew, sometimes flavoured with tomatoes, in which a variety of fish are cooked with potatoes and onions. All around the coast of Brittany you will come across different versions. There is the *cotriade de Brigneau* which contains conger eel, rock salmon, wrasse, hake, mackerel and sardines, while that of Belle-Ile contains a whole host of firm white fish as well as mussels, lobster and other shellfish. Another is made simply with sardines and leeks and in the gulf of Morbihan they might add a smattering of crabs.

Make it when you have hungry guests to feed, it's an ideal dish for an informal supper party. Quantities in the recipe are for six people. Serve the *cotriade* with bread which has been rubbed with garlic, sprinkled with oil and toasted in the top of a hot oven.

50 g (2 oz) butter
3 onions, chopped
2 leeks, sliced
3 cloves garlic, chopped
1½ kg (3 lb) potatoes, peeled and quartered
½ teaspoon dried thyme
sprigs of parsley, plus 2–3 tablespoons chopped
1 bay leaf
salt
freshly milled black pepper
few threads of saffron
2–3 tablespoons tomato purée
2 fish heads
1½ kg (3 lb) fish, cut into chunks: choose 3 or 4 kinds from cod, hake, haddock, coley, dogfish, conger eel, red mullet, mackerel, etc.
juice of ½ lemon
handful parsley, chopped

Choose a very large saucepan and melt the butter in it. When it sizzles add the onions and leeks and fry until golden. Stir in the garlic and add the potatoes, thyme, sprigs of parsley and bay leaf. Mix well over the heat before adding salt, pepper and saffron and covering with water. Bring to the boil, cover and simmer for 10–15 minutes until the potatoes are beginning to soften. Stir in the tomato purée, add the fish heads and the fish, bring to the boil and simmer, uncovered, for 5–10 minutes. Put the fish and vegetables on to a warm serving plate (discarding the heads), squeeze over the lemon juice and sprinkle with the chopped parsley. Strain the liquid into a warm soup tureen. Eat the *cotriade* in warm shallow soup bowls, putting a little soup and some fish into each.

Skate with cream
Raie à la crème

This Normandy recipe is one of the simplest and pleasantest ways of preparing and eating skate. You will find one wing (actually a fin) is enough for two. Ask the fishmonger to cut each in half for you. Look out for thick, firm pieces tinged slightly pink and don't worry about the slight smell of ammonia which disappears on cooking. Be careful not to overcook, because the cartilaginous mesh with which the wings are laced will turn to gelatine and give a gluey taste. Eat the wings by pulling out the flesh between the rays with the prongs of your fork.

450 g (1 lb) potatoes, peeled and cut in even-sized pieces
salt
700–900 g (1½–2 lb) skate wings, cut in 4 portions
1 tablespoon wine vinegar
freshly milled black pepper
225 ml (8 fl oz) single cream
2 tablespoons chopped parsley and chives

Boil or steam the potatoes with a little salt for 15–20 minutes, until tender. Drain, set aside and keep warm. Heat the oven to Gas 6/400°F/200°C. Put the skate in a wide pan, just cover with water and add the vinegar and salt. Bring just to the boil, cover and poach in barely simmering water until the fish becomes opaque and begins to come away from the rays, which takes about 5–10 minutes. Butter an oven dish, carefully lift out the wings with a spatula and lay them in it. Surround with the potatoes. Season with salt and pepper. Pour the cream over the wings, sprinkle with the herbs and put into the oven for 5–10 minutes.

Dogfish with wine
Chien de mer au vin

The dogfish is a small shark with strong teeth, hence its English and French names. It has several aliases in both languages. We call it rock salmon and huss while they call it *roussette* and *aiguillat*. Whatever the name, it is a fish that appeals to children and bone-haters alike because, being cartilaginous, it has only a central spine. In this recipe it is cooked with potatoes in a little wine flavoured with onions and herbs.

25 g (1 oz) butter
1 tablespoon oil
2 onions, chopped
700–900 g (1½–2 lb) dogfish, cut in 4 slices
1 clove garlic, chopped
1 teaspoon dried mixed herbs
1 bay leaf
450 g (1 lb) potatoes, thinly sliced
150 ml (¼ pint) dry white wine
150 ml (¼ pint) water
salt
freshly milled black pepper

Heat the oven to Gas 4/350°F/180°C. Choose a wide, lidded, heavy pan that can go from stove to oven. Heat the butter and oil and add the onions and fry them until golden. Add the fish slices and let them seal on either side. Top with the garlic, herbs, bay leaf and potatoes. Pour in the wine and water. Bring to boiling point, season with salt and pepper, put on the lid and transfer to the oven. Bake for 40 minutes.

Pheasant with potatoes
Faisan au bonhomme normand

This is an unpretentious but delicious way of cooking a pheasant. It emerges from the pot succulent and tender on its bed of potatoes. If the *bonhomme* is feeling rich, he uses 3 or 4 tablespoons of calvados instead of the cider. If you follow his example, omit the reducing process.

25 g (1 oz) butter
1 teaspoon oil
1 pheasant
150 ml (¼ pint) strong dry cider
700–900 g (1½–2 lb) potatoes,
  cut in even-sized pieces
salt
freshly milled black pepper
1–2 tablespoons crème fraîche
juice of ½ lemon

Heat the oven to Gas 5/375°F/190°C. Melt the butter with the oil in a heavy-based casserole and brown the pheasant all over. Remove to a plate. Pour in the cider, taking care it doesn't splutter and burn you, and boil hard until it has reduced by half. Add the potatoes, turn them over and over and put the pheasant on top. Season with salt and pepper, cover the casserole and put into the oven for 45–60 minutes. Put the pheasant and potatoes on to a warm serving dish. Transfer the casserole to the top of the stove, boil the liquid hard for 2 or 3 minutes, then stir in the crème fraîche. When it bubbles and thickens, stir in the lemon juice and either pour over the bird or serve in a sauceboat.

Cabbages to chicory

Cabbage or greens with butter

Red cabbage with apples

Poor man's soup

Cabbage soup and *la graisse normande*

Pork potful

Brussels sprouts with butter

Brussels sprout soup

Brussels sprouts with potatoes

Cauliflower in cider sauce

Cauliflower salad

Cauliflower fried in butter

Chicory with butter and egg

Chicory salad with chives

Chicory with cream

Beetroot and chicory salad

Chicory gratin

Mussel and chicory salad

Chicory tart

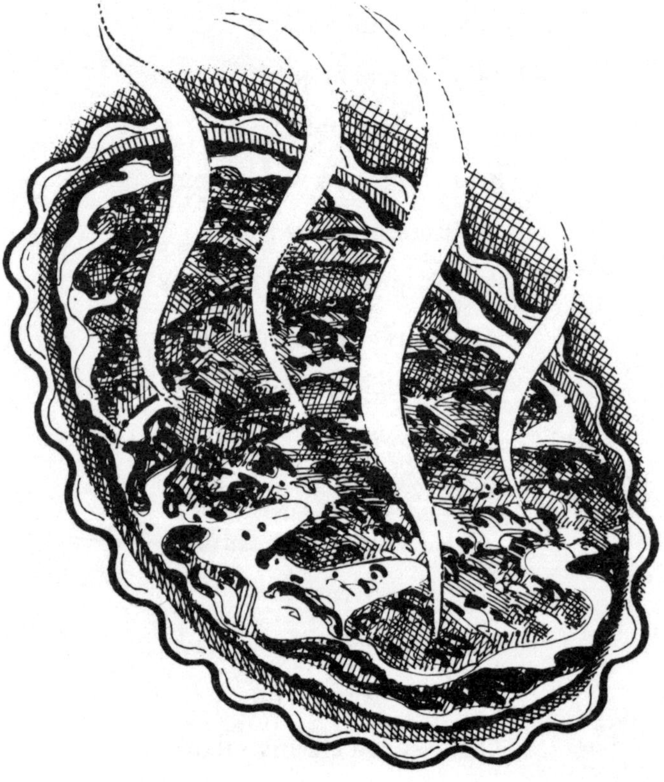

Cabbages, greens, Brussels sprouts and cauliflowers are cultivated on a vast scale in northern France, in field after field, row after row. All members of the same family, they have somehow failed to ignite the imagination yet, properly cooked, they can equal in flavour many more exotic vegetables, with the added advantage that, because they are classed as poor relations, they are usually quite cheap.

CABBAGES

Cabbages and greens are perhaps the most despised, everyone having memories of watery, overcooked soggy leaves on many a school plate. But chosen carefully, they are delicious. The best is the Savoy, with its crinkly outer dark green leaves and bright green centre. Tight, white cabbages lack the Savoy's flavour and are better shredded and added to salads but the red cabbage makes a hearty accompaniment to game and winter stews.

When buying cabbages or greens – which include specially grown spring greens, Brussels tops or the sprouts of cabbage plants – make sure they are very fresh, rejecting any that are limp and yellowing. Press the centre of a cabbage; it should feel tight and firm. Store in a cool, dark place. Greens should be eaten within a day or two but a cabbage will keep for several days in the refrigerator.

Prepare by washing under running cold water, slice a cabbage into quarters, greens into ribbons, and cut away only the hard and woody stalks, the rest can be added to the pot.

Cabbage or greens with butter
Chou au beurre

Cabbages and greens need the minimum amount of time and should be tender but still retain a hint of crispness.

1 Savoy cabbage or 450 g (1 lb) greens	salt
25 g (1 oz) butter	pepper
	freshly grated nutmeg

Steam or boil the prepared cabbage or greens in a very little, salted water for 5–8 minutes. Drain well. Return to the pan, add the butter, season with salt and pepper and add the grated nutmeg. Toss well and serve immediately.

Red cabbage with apples
Chou rouge à la mode de Normandie

Red cabbage needs long, slow cooking. In Normandy they cook it with apples, as they do in many parts of France. As it cooks it turns from deep red to purple; without the vinegar it would turn blue. In the Ardennes, they cook green cabbage in the same way but halve the cooking time and flavour it with juniper berries.

1 red cabbage, weighing approximately 900 g (2 lb)
2 tablespoons oil
300 ml ($\frac{1}{2}$ pint) water or red wine
salt
freshly milled black pepper
1 tablespoon of wine vinegar or cider vinegar
4 crisp eating apples peeled, quartered and cored
1 tablespoon brown sugar

Cut the cabbage in four and cut out and discard the hard core; wash it well and cut it in fine strips. Heat the oil in a heavy-based pan and add the cabbage, turning it over and over for a minute or two. Add the water or wine, season with salt and pepper and add the vinegar. Cover and put over a low heat for 45 minutes. Add the apples and brown sugar and cook for a further 15 minutes.

Poor man's soup
Soupe du pauvre

Recipes for cabbage soups flavoured with potato and bacon abound all over northern France. This one from Brittany is made with a variety called *bricolins*, *bricolis* or *piochons*, sold in bunches very cheaply. It is perhaps a close cousin to wild cabbage – its other name is *choux à vache*, cow's cabbage – or to our own sprouting greens. The soup, with its flavours of garlic and thyme, becomes one for the rich when mixed with a little crème fraîche.

- 25 g (1 oz) butter or 2 tablespoons oil
- 100 g (4 oz) streaky bacon, chopped
- 2 onions, chopped
- 225 g (8 oz) potatoes, sliced
- 225 g (8 oz) Brussels tops or spring greens, sliced
- 1 tablespoon tomato purée
- 2–3 sprigs of fresh thyme or ½ teaspoon dried
- 1 clove garlic, chopped
- 1 litre (1¾ pints) stock or water
- salt
- freshly milled black pepper
- 2–3 tablespoons crème fraîche (optional)
- handful parsley, chopped

Heat the butter or oil in a large pan and fry the bacon and onions until just beginning to brown. Add the potatoes, cover, and let the vegetables sweat for 5–10 minutes over a low heat. Add the Brussels tops or spring greens, tomato purée, thyme and garlic. Stir in the stock or water, bring to the boil, season with salt and pepper, cover and simmer gently for about 1 hour. Put through a *mouli-légumes* or food processor, or use a hand-held mixer to purée the soup. Check the seasoning and stir in the crème fraîche, sprinkle over the parsley and serve at once.

Cabbage soup and *la graisse normande*
Soupe à la normande

In Normandy, the cook who is making soup in a hurry, with no time to sweat the vegetables to bring out their flavour, puts them straight into the pot, covers them with water and gives taste by adding a dollop of *graisse normande*, otherwise called *graisse de Cherbourg*. Although once everyone made their own, nowadays most people buy it from the butcher or *charcuterie*. Made of clarified beef and pork fat, flavoured with herbs and vegetables, it is also used to roast meat, flavour stews or spread on to bread.

- 3 large leeks, finely sliced
- 700 g (1½ lb) medium-sized potatoes, quartered
- 2 tablespoons *graisse normande* (see below)
- 2 litres (3½ pints) water
- salt
- freshly milled black pepper
- 450–700 g (1–1½ lb) white cabbage, cut into strips
- 225 g (8 oz) French beans, chopped
- 1 stick celery, chopped

Put the leeks and potatoes into a large saucepan with the *graisse normande*. Add the water and bring to the boil. Season with salt and pepper and simmer, covered, for 30 minutes. Add the cabbage, beans and celery then boil steadily, uncovered, for a further 45 minutes until the potatoes have almost dissolved. Serve without puréeing.

Graisse normande

Most recipes specify huge amounts of pork flay and ox kidney fat, neither of which are easy to obtain from the modern butcher's shop or supermarket meat counter. The fat must be trimmed and chopped and slowly melted with the flavouring ingredients over a period of several hours. However, the whole process can be made very easy by reducing quantities and using suet instead of beef kidney fat, and lard instead of pork flay. The quantities given will produce 450 g (1 lb). It will keep for ages in the fridge.

In Brittany they make a similar preparation called *graisse de Cornouaille* which consists of lard flavoured with a mixture of finely chopped shallots, onions, parsley, salt and pepper. Spread on bread it is a popular snack for peasant and labourer alike.

1 tablespoon water
225 g (8 oz) beef suet
100 g (4 oz) lard
½ leek, coarsely chopped
1 small onion, stuck with 2 cloves
1 carrot, quartered
1 small turnip, quartered
sprig of parsley
sprig of thyme
1 bay leaf
pinch of salt
freshly milled black pepper

Put the tablespoon of water and the two fats in a heavy-based pan over a low heat. As soon as they begin to melt add all the other ingredients, cover and leave over the lowest possible heat or put into a low oven, Gas 2/300°F/150°C, for 1–1½ hours. Set aside to cool and strain into a sterilized jam jar, filling right to the top. When cold, cover tightly and keep in a cool place.

Pork potful
Potée de l'Argoat

I give this recipe from the Argoat, the interior of Brittany, for the adventurous to try. Potées, which stem from the days of subsistence farming, were a cross between a soup and a stew and were simmered all day suspended over the fire in an earthenware pot which was sometimes glazed on the inside. In order to prevent the pot cracking in the heat, its base would be rubbed with garlic. The ingredients included whatever meat and vegetables were to hand. This one is made with lightly salted shin of pork, pigs' tails, ears and trotters bulked out with a variety of vegetables including cabbage and leeks. The men coming in from the fields would ladle it directly into their bowls on top of slices of bread.

First a firm cabbage is quartered and blanched for 10 minutes, then drained. At the same time a shin of pork, two tails, two trotters and two ears are put into a large pot, covered with cold water and slowly brought to the boil. After simmering for 10 minutes they are drained. The pot is rinsed out and filled with 5 litres (1 gallon) of water which is brought to the boil. The meat is returned and left to simmer for 1½ hours with sprigs of thyme, a bay leaf and 2 large onions each stuck with 2–3 whole cloves. It must be skimmed at intervals. At this point the following roughly chopped vegetables are added: 900 g (2 lb) leeks, 450 g (1 lb) carrots, 225 g (8 oz) turnips, 1 swede or kohlrabi and the quarters of cabbage. The pot is seasoned with salt and pepper and left to simmer for another hour. Finally 900 g (2 lb) of quartered potatoes are added and left to cook a further 30 minutes. When it is ready to eat, the meat is removed and cut into pieces and returned to the pot. Meat, vegetables and soup are served in large deep bowls on top of slices of bread.

BRUSSELS SPROUTS

As my mother will tell you, I adore Brussels sprouts. These miniature cabbages come, as their name implies, from Brussels where they have been grown for hundreds of years, gradually infiltrating into northern France. Overblown and overcooked they can be horrid, but when the buds are tight and a deep green, they make succulent mouthfuls. They are at their sweetest early in the season, after Christmas they develop a bitter taste.

Choose Brussels sprouts that are firm and tight and a healthy-looking green, and avoid those which are beginning to yellow and fade and smell faintly bitter. Prepare them by removing any loose outer leaves and if you suspect that insects may be lurking within, soak them in salted water. Some people insist on cutting a cross on their base, they say it makes them cook evenly, but I find no difference whether you do or not.

Brussels sprouts with butter
Choux de Bruxelles au beurre

This is the simplest and best way of dealing with sprouts when they are to be served as an accompanying vegetable. You can if you like tart them up a little by adding a handful of almond slivers fried until golden brown in a little butter, or at Christmas time add them to a bowl of skinned, boiled and drained chestnuts.

450 g (1 lb) Brussels sprouts
25 g (1 oz) butter
salt
freshly milled black pepper
nutmeg

Steam or boil the sprouts, covered, in a little salted water until just tender. (Steaming will take about 10 minutes, boiling about 5.) Drain. Melt the butter in the pan and when it is sizzling, add the sprouts. Toss over a high heat until they are just beginning to turn brown. Season with salt, pepper and a little grated nutmeg. Serve piping hot.

Brussels sprout soup
Crème bruxelloise

Potatoes and Brussels sprouts flavoured with bacon enriched with an egg yolk combine to make a creamy, pale green, Flemish soup. Serve the soup with fried croûtons.

1 tablespoon oil
2 rashers smoked streaky bacon, chopped
1 onion, chopped
225 g (8 oz) Brussels sprouts
225 g (8 oz) potatoes, peeled and sliced
600 ml (1 pint) water or stock
sprigs of parsley
salt
freshly milled black pepper
150 ml ($\frac{1}{4}$ pint) milk
knob of butter
1 egg yolk

Heat the oil in a heavy-based saucepan and add the chopped bacon. Toss over a medium heat until the fat begins to run, then add the chopped onion, lower the heat and cook gently for 5–10 minutes. Add the prepared sprouts and potatoes to the pan. Pour in the water or stock, add the parsley and season with salt and pepper. Bring to the boil, cover and simmer for about 1 hour. Purée the soup. Stir in the milk and bring back to the boil, remove from heat and stir in the knob of butter and the egg yolk. Taste and if necessary add more salt and pepper.

Brussels sprouts with potatoes
Purée de choux de Bruxelles aux pommes de terre

When you grow tired of sprouts on their own or want something different from mashed potatoes, try instead this mixture of the two which goes well with sausages or pork dishes.

1 tablespoon oil
1 onion, chopped
450 g (1 lb) Brussels sprouts
450 g (1 lb) potatoes, quartered
salt
25 g (1 oz) butter
milk
pinch of nutmeg
freshly milled black pepper

Heat the oil in a saucepan, add the chopped onion and let it soften and turn golden. Add the sprouts and potatoes, pour over sufficient water just to cover and season with salt. Simmer, covered, for about 30 minutes, until sprouts and potatoes are soft. Drain well. Mash and add butter and beat in enough milk to form a thick purée. Add nutmeg and season generously with salt and pepper.

CAULIFLOWER

The cauliflower is, I suppose, the king of the cabbage family, and the Bretons, who produce the bulk of France's cauliflowers, have adopted it as one of their symbols – along with the artichoke – but they are also grown and appreciated all over northern France, in particular in Flanders around St-Omer, Dunkerque, Leffinckouque and Rosendaël and in Barfleur in Normandy. Now an attractive rendezvous for yachtsmen, it was from here that William the Conqueror is supposed to have sailed in 1066 but in gastronomic terms, the words *à la Barfleur* on the menu signify a dish with a cauliflower base.

The true cauliflower is a summer vegetable and the winter variety which comes from Italy is actually a form of broccoli, but so closely related to the cauliflower that from the cook's point of view there is no point in distinguishing between the two. In Brittany they might eat it like we do, coated in a béchamel sauce, but often they add a garnish such as hard-boiled eggs and brown the dish under the grill or they decorate the cauliflower with prawns and *langoustines*, or feature it in a salad with potatoes, mayonnaise and prawns. A delicious accompaniment to roast lamb are *pannequets au chou-fleur*, small pancakes filled with cauliflower and cheese sauce which are rolled and tied then dipped in egg, grated cheese and breadcrumbs before being deep-fried until crisp and golden.

When choosing cauliflowers go for firm ones with clear, white or cream florets, avoiding those which are flaky or mottled with any hint of mould. The outer leaves help to keep the vegetable fresh, so shun the greengrocers who cut them away, they will be hiding the fact that the leaves are wilting and trying to pretend the cauliflower is fresh. It will just be stale and horrid.

Prepare it by dividing into florets and only discard the woody part of the stem and the tough outer leaves. All the rest is edible. Wash quickly under running cold water and either steam or boil it in the minimum of salted water until just tender but still with a bite. Drain well and serve either with melted butter or a béchamel sauce (see Etceteras). Or make a gratin by stirring grated cheese into the sauce, pouring it over the cauliflower, sprinkle with more cheese and put under a hot grill until bubbling and golden.

Cauliflower in cider sauce
Chou-fleur à la Normandie

This is Normandy's variation on the theme of cauliflower in a white sauce. Their sauce is flavoured with onions and cider and thickened with spoonfuls of cream. This adaptation is not quite so rich as the original.

1 cauliflower
25 g (1 oz) butter
1 onion, chopped
25 g (1 oz) flour
150 ml (¼ pint) strong dry cider
150 ml (¼ pint) milk
salt
freshly milled black pepper
pinch of nutmeg
2 tablespoons crème fraîche
juice of ½ lemon

Divide the cauliflower into florets and steam or boil in a little salted water until just tender. Meanwhile make the sauce by melting the butter in a small pan and gently frying the chopped onion until soft. Sprinkle in the flour and stir over a low heat for 2 minutes. Gradually stir in the cider followed by the milk and bring to the boil, stirring constantly. Add salt, pepper and nutmeg to taste. Drain the cauliflower and put into a warm serving dish. Stir the crème fraîche into the sauce, add the lemon juice and pour it over the cauliflower.

Cauliflower salad
Chou-fleur en salade

Cauliflower florets are delicious eaten raw and dipped into mayonnaise or lightly cooked as a salad, either to be eaten alone or as part of a mixed Breton hors-d'oeuvre which might include haricot beans, chopped tomatoes, hard-boiled eggs, sliced beetroot and potatoes all arranged next to one another on a long platter.

1 cauliflower, divided into florets
1 tablespoon cider vinegar
3–4 tablespoons oil
salt
freshly milled black pepper
handful chervil, chopped

Lightly steam or boil the cauliflower until just tender but still with a bite. Put into a bowl and while it is still warm sprinkle with the vinegar and oil and mix lightly. Season with salt and pepper. Allow to cool and just before serving sprinkle with the chopped chervil.

Cauliflower fried in butter
Chou-fleur au beurre

Cauliflower florets cooked this way have a slight, nutty flavour, especially if you add a tablespoon or two of slivered almonds to the pan.

1 cauliflower	salt
50 g (2 oz) butter	freshly milled black pepper

Divide the cauliflower into florets and steam or boil in salted water until just beginning to become tender. Drain well. Melt the butter in the pan and when it sizzles add the drained florets. Toss them over a high heat until golden brown, season with salt and pepper and serve.

CHICORY

The azure blue flowers of wild chicory open to greet the morning sun and close as soon as the heat becomes too fierce, hence its English name of Jack-go-to-bed-at-noon. All that remains to be seen are woody stems and crumpled leaves close to the ground. The shoots from these plants, called *barbe-de-capuchin*, friar's beard, were dug out by wily peasants in the spring and used to make salads, but it took a Belgian in the eighteenth century to discover the art of cultivating the plump vegetable we know today, with its furl of white leaves tinged with gold. Now it is grown all over northern France but principally in Flanders and Picardy.

It is known as *chicon*, *witloof* (white leaf), or *barbe-de-bouc*, goat's beard, which is a name used in English as well. But officially in France, its name is *endive* which is what *we* call the frizzy green salad vegetable known by them as *chicorée*. The whole thing is thoroughly confusing and stems it seems from the fact they are related plants with very similar Latin names. However, this knowledge does help to explain the origins of *chicorée à torrefiée* or *chicorée à café*, so popular in the north of France, which is not made from chicory (Fr. *endive*) but endive (Fr. *chicorée*). Got it! Chicory-flavoured coffee is very bitter, which perhaps gives the northern French an excuse to add a dash of gin to their morning brew! This same plant is used to flavour a drink made in Picardy called *frenette*, which is a kind of beer made from ash leaves.

The French and Belgians have devised several ways of preparing chicory and perhaps the most famous is in a gratin with or without a wrapping of ham. In Flanders they serve *witloof* with crushed hard-boiled eggs mixed with melted butter or in a salad with potatoes, onions and herring. Gently stewed they make a pleasant accompaniment to game, poultry or fish and in the Ardennes they might add some diced raw country ham and flavour the dish with nutmeg. *Pâtisseries* sell *feuilletés flamands*, puff pastry rolls filled with chicory, ham and cheese.

Whiteness is the key to freshness. Chicory is raised under a covering of straw in specially heated, roofed, forcing beds, so that the shoots, deprived of light, will remain white. Once they come out of the dark they begin to turn green and develop an unpleasant bitter flavour, so even when they are sold they are kept wrapped in deep blue or purple paper. Buy heads just tipped with golden yellow and spurn any which are green. Try to make sure there is no brown discoloration at the base or on the leaves. Chicory can be stored for a few days in the dark or in the bottom drawer of the fridge. Prepare by wiping with kitchen paper, trimming the base and cutting away any brown patches.

Chicory with butter and egg
Chicons à la flamande

This is a popular starter in northern France. The chicory is cooked slowly in the oven until it is meltingly tender and then eaten with parsleyed butter and crushed hard-boiled egg. This sauce sometimes accompanies asparagus, so the dish is also known as *chicons en asperge*. Eat it as a starter or light supper or lunch dish. Without the eggs, chicory cooked in this way can be served as a vegetable accompaniment.

8 heads chicory
2 lemons
1 teaspoon sugar
salt
pepper
4 eggs
150 g (6 oz) butter
handful parsley, chopped

Heat the oven to Gas 4/350°F/180°C. Put the heads of chicory into an ovenproof dish with a lid and add the juice of the lemons, sugar, salt and pepper. Cover and bake for 1 hour. Meanwhile, hard-boil the eggs for 9 minutes, run them under cold water and peel them. Just before serving, melt the butter, stir in the parsley and pour into a sauceboat. Cut the eggs in half and put in a bowl.

To serve, let everyone help themselves to an egg, crush it on their plate, mix with melted butter and then take the chicory, dipping each mouthful into the sauce.

Chicory salad with chives
Salade de chicons à la ciboulette

We ate a similar salad to this in a small hotel in Crécy-sur-Serre one wet autumn evening. The dining room was full of English people en route for Calais and we all spoke in whispers until the wine began to take effect which made the atmosphere jollier. The salad was robust and included diced potato which, like the bacon, had been cooked unashamedly in lard. This is a more elegant version using walnut oil, wine or raspberry vinegar and a sprinkling of snipped chives. Serve it as a starter.

450 g (1 lb) chicory, sliced
2 tablespoons walnut oil
100 g (4 oz) streaky bacon, chopped
1 tablespoon wine or raspberry vinegar
100 g (4 oz) croûtons
salt
freshly milled black pepper
1 tablespoon chopped chives

Put the sliced chicory in a salad bowl. Heat the oil and fry the bacon until it is crisp. Add to the salad. Put the vinegar in the pan, let it sizzle and scrape all the juices into the salad. Add croûtons, season with salt and pepper and sprinkle the chopped chives over the salad.

Chicory with cream
Chicons à la crème

As an accompanying vegetable to fish or poultry, chicory is delicious gently stewed in butter and lemon juice. The crème fraîche adds a touch of luxury but if you feel this is too rich, leave it out.

50 g (2 oz) butter
4–6 heads chicory
salt
juice of ½ lemon
2 tablespoons crème fraîche (optional)
handful parsley, chopped

Melt the butter in a saucepan, put in the heads of chicory, add salt and lemon juice, cover and cook very gently for 10–15 minutes, until tender, shaking the pan from time to time. Add the crème fraîche (if using), stir gently and serve dusted with the parsley.

Beetroot and chicory salad
Salade de betteraves et chicons

Chicory makes a good winter salad, either on its own in a mustardy vinaigrette or perhaps with sliced hard-boiled eggs or, as in this recipe, with beetroot, whose sweetness contrasts in a satisfying way with chicory's slight bitterness. Add the beetroot just before serving so that its pink juices have no time to spread over the pale chicory.

4 heads chicory, sliced
150 g (6 oz) beetroot, cooked and peeled
1 heaped teaspoon mustard
1 tablespoon cider vinegar
salt
freshly milled black pepper
5–6 tablespoons oil

Put the sliced chicory into a salad bowl. Just before serving cut the beetroot into small cubes and sprinkle it over the chicory. Make a vinaigrette by mixing the mustard with the vinegar, salt, pepper and oil. Pour over the salad and serve at once.

Chicory gratin
Chicons au gratin

Variations on this recipe come from all over northern France. Usually, though not always, they include ham, but the method of gently stewing the chicory before baking it in a white sauce, covered in grated cheese, remains constant. Near the coast, you might discover a handful of prawns have been added to the sauce.

4 heads chicory
salt
1 sugar lump
juice of ½ lemon
150 ml (¼ pint) milk
25 g (1 oz) butter
25 g (1 oz) flour
freshly milled black pepper
¼ teaspoon grated nutmeg
100 g (4 oz) cheese, grated
4 slices cooked ham
mustard, mild or spicy according to taste

Heat the oven to Gas 6/400°F/200°C. Blanch the trimmed heads of chicory in boiling salted water with the sugar and lemon juice for 10 minutes. Drain the chicory well but reserve 150 ml (¼ pint) of the cooking liquid.

Make the sauce by putting the reserved cooking liquid with the milk into a small saucepan with the butter and flour. Put over a medium heat and bring to the boil, beating all the time with a wire whisk. As it thickens, lower the heat and continue to beat the sauce so that no lumps form. Add pepper and nutmeg and half the grated cheese. Remove from the heat and beat until cheese melts. Spread the slices of ham with mustard, and wrap a slice round each head of chicory. Put a little of the sauce over the base of a gratin dish. Lay the chicory and ham on top, with the overlaps underneath, and pour over the remaining sauce. Sprinkle over the rest of the cheese and put into the oven for about 20 minutes until the top is bubbling and golden.

Mussel and chicory salad
Salade d'endives aux moules

Use fresh mussels for this salad if you have time; if not, mussels canned in brine or frozen can be used but allow time for the latter to thaw thoroughly. Fresh mussels must be scrubbed and washed in two or three changes of water and then steamed open in a little water or white wine. As soon as they open, remove from heat and once cool take the mussels from their shells.

4 heads of chicory, finely sliced
juice of 1 lemon
1 tablespoon crème fraîche
salt
freshly milled black pepper
450 g (1 lb) fresh or frozen mussels or 1 can mussels in brine, drained
2 tomatoes, quartered
handful parsley, chives and chervil, chopped

Put the chicory in a shallow dish, add the lemon juice, crème fraîche, salt and pepper and mix gently. Add the mussels, decorate with the tomatoes and sprinkle with the parsley, chives and chervil.

Chicory tart
Flamiche aux endives

The first time we ate *flamiche* was in a most unlikely setting. We were visiting friends who live in a hilltop farmhouse in the fertile pastures close to Toulouse, in south-west France. Here they breed cows and we were all invited to dinner with the local practitioner of artificial insemination. It was obvious as soon as we arrived that his wife was entertaining us on sufferance and she took herself off to bed as soon as the meal was finished. She was a lady from the north and despite her bad temper had cooked a delicious meal which began with a leek *flamiche*. This version is made with chicory, but almost any vegetable will do, including pumpkin.

225 g (8 oz) shortcrust pastry
225 g (8 oz) streaky bacon, chopped
25 g (1 oz) butter
450 g (1 lb) heads chicory, sliced
2 eggs plus 2 yolks
300 ml ($\frac{1}{2}$ pint) crème fraîche
100 g (4 oz) mature cheddar, grated
salt
freshly milled black pepper

Heat the oven to Gas 6/400°F/200°C. Roll out the pastry to fit a 30 cm (12 in) flan tin. Fry the bacon with the butter until soft. Stir in the sliced chicory and let it stew gently for 10–15 minutes. In a large bowl beat the eggs, extra yolks and crème fraîche; stir in cheese and the chicory and bacon. Season with salt and pepper. Pour into the pastry shell and bake for 35–40 minutes until puffed and golden brown. The *flamiche* can be kept warm for a while in a turned-off oven.

Camembert de Normandie
appellation d'Origine
Marie Harel

Cheese

In the north of France all the important cheeses are made with cows' milk, though you will come across goats' cheeses which are locally produced, often by newcomers to the area, and shops and markets sell a huge assortment of fresh cream and curd cheeses usually in *faisselles*, perforated plastic pots, the modern replacement to the stoneware pots of the past.

Cheeses from Picardy and the Nord tend to be strong and pungent whereas those of Normandy are subtle and creamy, while those of Brittany . . . well that's another story.

Cheeses from Picardy and the Nord

Here, the most famous cheese is Maroilles, only produced within the Thiérache, a region partly in the Nord and partly in the Aisne. The cheese dates at least from the tenth century when it was first made in the abbey of Maroilles. It used to be called Craquegnon because of its crust which protected the inner soft cheese and made it possible to keep through the winter. The cheese is square-shaped with a reddish rind and a pale yellow interior. It is washed regularly in beer or brine during the ripening process and has a very strong smell and robust flavour. Like many northern cheeses it is referred to as *le puant*, the stinker. *Goyère au Maroilles* is a kind of tart made with a mixture of Maroilles and soft cream cheese, fromage blanc. It is eaten as soon as it comes out of the oven with a beer heated by dipping a hot poker into the glass.

There are many versions of Maroilles, usually called after the town or village in which they are made, such as the *baguettes avesnoise*, *laonnaise* and *de Thiérache*. One of the best known is Le Dauphin. Legend has it that the Dauphin, accompanying Louis XIV on a visit to the area, was offered a Maroilles flavoured with tarragon, parsley and pepper. He liked it so much that they began to make it in dolphin-shaped moulds (a play on the meaning of the word *dauphin*) and called it after him. Nowadays it is commercially produced and more likely to be in the shape of a rectangle, shield, heart or crescent.

Similar to Le Dauphin are the various *boulettes*, which are conical or round and flavoured usually with tarragon and parsley, sometimes with chives, and pepper and crushed cloves. One, Boulette de Thiérache is nicknamed *le suppositoire du diable*. You might come across *caffuts* which are moulded into *boulettes* but are in fact made from left-over cheeses, mixed with herbs.

If you want to try something even stronger and smellier go for the *puant de Lille*, the stinker of Lille, also known as *gris de Lille*, *vieux puant*, *gris puant*, or *puant macéré*. This variation of Maroilles is subjected to a second salting and fermentation. (Don't confuse it with Vieux Lille, a full flavoured, red gold Mimolette that spends six months ripening with beer.) Or try Fort de Béthune, otherwise called Fromage Fort de Flandre, which is so strong and stinking of ammonia that it is sold in pots to hold in the aroma.

Milder cheeses include French versions of Dutch Gouda, Mimolette and Edam. Or you might find Bergues sold in Dunkerque which originates from the nearby fortified Flemish town of that name; this cheese is low fat and is traditionally matured in ancient burial barrows. A cheese similar to Port-Salut, with a golden rind, is Mont-des-Cats, called after the abbey in which it is made. Belval is a semi-soft mild cheese when it is young but ripened Belval is sold as Fromage d'Hesdin and has a stronger flavour. And from Picardy comes Rollot de Montdidier, hard to find, made in round or heart-shaped moulds and less pungent than Maroilles.

Normandy cheeses

The Pays d'Auge in Basse-Normandie produces some of France's most famous cheeses, the first of which is Camembert. Unfortunately because the name was not protected versions of this cheese are made in many other parts of France. For a true Camembert look out for the VCN (*Véritable Camembert de Normandie*) label and seek out the superior Camembert Fermier which is made with unpasteurized milk and to be found in local French markets from late spring through to autumn. A perfect Camembert should be succulent and delicate, any hint of ammonia and it is spoilt, in fact they say it should smell like the feet of a god! Like so many French cheeses its invention is attributed to a farmer's wife. This one, named Marie Harel, was aided by a priest she was hiding during the Revolution. He felt the cheese she made was lacking in subtlety and taught her some of the secrets he had learnt when he lived in the Brie area of Île-de-France. She sold this much improved cheese in the nearby market town of Vimoutiers where her statue now stands in the main square and which boasts a Camembert museum open from April to October.

Pont-l'Evêque, Normandy's oldest cheese, a descendant of *angelot* dating from the Middle Ages, is square with a ridged creamy orange crust, which is cut away before eating. It has a sweet, tangy flavour that belies its strong and pungent smell. Eat soon after purchase because it doesn't keep well. Pavés, (which literally means paving stones) of which there are many, are similar to but larger than Pont-l'Evêque, the best are strong and spicy, while Trouville is a local cheese similar to Pont-l'Evêque.

Livarot, with its whiff of ammonia mixed with brine, is reputed to be one of France's best pungent cheeses, but its flavour is spicy and delicate though slightly stronger than Pont-l'Evêque. In the nineteenth century it was known as *la viande de l'ouvrier*, the workman's meat. It is thicker than, but about the same shape as a Camembert, with a golden-orange middle and pink crust. It used to be wrapped with five strips of sedge and was nicknamed *le colonel*, but nowadays coloured raffia is more often used. The name is protected and the area limited in which it may be produced. Petit Lisieux is a smaller, flatter version of Livarot. It is possible to go on a conducted tour of the *Conservatoire des Techniques Fromagères* in Livarot and see Livarot, Camembert and Pont-l'Evêque being made.

In Haute-Normandie the principal cheeses are produced in the Pays de Bray and Neufchâtel-en-Bray is known as the dairy of Paris. It was here somewhere around the tenth century where Neufchâtel was invented. In its oldest form it was known as *bondon* because it was shaped like a small barrel bung, but it is hard to find today. Depending on its size or shape it is called *bondard*, *double bonde*, *bonde*, *carré de Bray*, *coeur de Bray* etc. and it is now made across the centre of the Pays de Bray between Aumale and Rouen. Neufchâtel cheeses are snowy white and downy with a hint of red, saltier than Brie, tart and rich. When fresh, *fleuri*, they are eaten with fruit but once mature, *affiné*, they are eaten on their own, often accompanied by a sweet cider.

Three other well-known cheeses come from the Pays de Bray. The first is Boursin, a fresh cream cheese either plain or flavoured with garlic and parsley or rolled in peppercorns; at its best it is rich, creamy and tangy. The other two are Demi-sel, a foil-wrapped mild, half-salted soft cream cheese and Petit Suisse. This last was the brainchild of a Swiss cheesemaker, who in the nineteenth century worked for a dairy farmer's wife, Madame Hérould. He suggested mixing fresh cream with the developing curds. The little cheeses were sent to Paris where they came to the attention of Charles Gervais who decided to set up a factory to make them near Gournay. Madame Hérould became rich but what happened to the Swiss cheesemaker nobody knows. Nowadays Petits Suisses are made all over France but most still come from Gournay-en-Brie. Commerically produced they lack the finesse of the originals but even so these soft, creamy curds are delicious eaten with sugar or fruit. The same place produces Gournay, a small, round Neufchâtel-type cheese sometimes called Malakoff when sold young.

Normandy produces many other lesser cheeses, each with their own local characteristics and most often called after the town or village in which they originate.

Cheese and the Bretons

Cheesemaking never caught on in Brittany despite the large number of dairy cows and although nowadays cheeses are produced there, none of them originated in the region. In fact the old name for cheese was *beurre pourri*, putrid butter.

Brittany's most famous cheese is Curé, also called Nantais or Nantais du Curé; the method of making it was introduced by a priest fleeing the famine of the war in Vendée, south of the Loire in 1794. Carré Breton is similar. A few Port-Salut-type cheeses are produced in various Trappist monasteries and convents, and there are Breton factory versions of Emmenthal and Saint-Paulin.

In the absence of cheese, Bretons make wonders with curds and creams. First there are *cailles* made by heating milk to blood temperature, adding a coagulating agent like rennet – although in the old days it was most likely to be the flowerhead of an artichoke or thistle – and setting aside for the curds to form. The curds are eaten with boiled potatoes, buckwheat pancakes or chestnuts, or gently heated they are eaten as a soup. *Caillebottes* are curds drained in moulds, sometimes in the form of little baskets made from reeds, which are served, unmoulded, covered with cream dusted with sugar and are delicious with strawberries or raspberries.

Cream is used to make *crémets*, known as *crémets de Bretagne* or *crémets nantais*, which are a mixture of crème fraîche and stiffly beaten egg white, drained in moulds, then turned out and served covered with fresh cream and vanilla sugar.

Maingaux, *maingneau*, *maigneaux* or *mingots rennais* is a farm-produced cream mixture made by whipping together sour and fresh cream. Everyone has their own version but some say to be successful it must be whipped using a wooden whisk. Others say it should be made with a mixture of yesterday's cream, today's cream and even tomorrow's. It is used to garnish puff pastries or eaten with strawberries, raspberries or sweet pancakes. You can make it yourself by beating 300 ml (½ pint) crème fraîche with the same amount of whipping or double cream.

Camembert pancakes
Pannetots de camembert

Pannetot is just a rather charming name for a small pancake. These are filled with a cheese sauce made with Camembert but of course almost any other kind of cheese could be used.

25 g (1 oz) butter
12 g (½ oz) flour
150 ml (¼ pint) milk
150 g (6 oz) Camembert, outer rind removed
8 small pancakes

Heat the oven to Gas 5/375°F/190°C. Melt half the butter, stir in the flour and cook for 2 minutes, stirring all the time. Gradually mix in the milk to make a thick sauce. Crush the cheese with a fork in a bowl and stir in three-quarters of the sauce. Spread this mixture over the pancakes, roll them up and lay them side by side in a buttered ovenproof dish. Cover with the remaining white sauce. Dot with the rest of the butter. Bake for 10 minutes until hot through and bubbling.

Camembert canapés
Canapés normands

For a simple cocktail snack, butter small biscuits or bread croûtons and top with camembert mashed to a pulp. Decorate with slivered toasted almonds.

Cheese eggs
Oeufs farcis du pays de Bray

Eggs stuffed with Neufchâtel cheese make a pleasant lunch or supper dish, especially if served on a bed of spinach.

4 hard-boiled eggs
1 tablespoon chopped parsley
1 Neufchâtel cheese
300 ml (½ pint) béchamel sauce (see Etceteras)

Heat the oven to Gas 5/375°F/190°C. Cut the eggs in half and scoop out the yolks. Put the yolks into a bowl with the parsley and 75 g (3 oz) of the cheese. Mash together, and return the mixture to the hollows in the whites. Lay the eggs in a buttered oven dish. Make the béchamel sauce and pour it over the eggs. Dot with the remaining cheese. Bake for 10–15 minutes.

Cheesy potatoes
Pommes braytoises

Jacket potatoes stuffed with cheese are tasty and filling and can be eaten on their own for a snack or accompanying a roast.

4 baking potatoes
100 g (4 oz) Neufchâtel or Camembert
1 tablespoon crème fraîche
2 egg yolks
salt
freshly milled black pepper

Heat the oven to Gas 6/400°F/200°C and bake the potatoes until soft, about 1–1½ hours depending on size. Meanwhile grate the cheese into a bowl. When the potatoes are done, cut them in half and scrape the pulp into the bowl, keeping the skins intact. Heat the grill. Mix the cheese and potato with the crème fraîche and egg yolks. Season with salt and pepper. Fill the skins and put under the grill to brown.

Breton creams
Crémets

Nowadays *crémets* are commercially produced but you can make your own. They are delicious with summer fruits like raspberries or strawberries. Holed cheese moulds can be bought in kitchen shops and muslin from dress material shops.

300 ml (½ pint) crème fraîche
2 egg whites
150 ml (¼ pint) double cream
vanilla sugar

Whip the crème fraîche until it doubles in volume and forms soft peaks. Beat the egg whites until stiff and gently fold them into the crème fraîche. Line a holed cheesemould with muslin, put in the mixture and set aside to drain in a cool place overnight. Next day unmould, mask with the double cream and serve with the vanilla sugar in a bowl.

Etceteras

From pastry to vanilla sugar
by way of an omelette and pancakes . . .

Shortcrust pastry
Pâte brisée

Below is the simplest sort of short pastry. It can be made with concentrated butter, in which case allow only 75 g (3 oz). Freshly made pastry tends to shrink if rolled out and cooked immediately, so make it ahead and put it in the fridge in a bag for half an hour or so before using.

225 g (8 oz) flour
100 g (4 oz) butter
pinch of salt
2–3 tablespoons cold water

Either rub the flour and butter together until the mixture resembles breadcrumbs, or put them into a food processor and blend until mixed. Add the salt and mix in sufficient water to form a firm, pliant dough. Remove, roll into a ball on a floured board and set aside to rest.

Sweet shortcrust pastry
Pâte sucrée

This sort of pastry is usually mixed on a marble slab. The sieved flour is hollowed in the centre and all the other ingredients added and mixed together with the fingers and finally the flour is drawn in. The result is a crumbly mixture which must be pressed together using the heel of the hand. The dough is then left to rest for at least an hour before using. The method below uses a food processor which is one of the most useful of today's gadgets.

75 g (3 oz) concentrated butter, softened
1 egg
50 g (2 oz) caster sugar
225 g (8 oz) flour

Cut the butter in pieces and put it, the egg and the sugar into the bowl of a food processor. Blend until mixed. Tip in the flour and blend until it forms a ball of dough. Remove, roll into a ball on a floured board and flatten it into a thick disc. Put it into a plastic bag and refrigerate for at least 1 hour. Roll out carefully on a floured board. Line flan tin, pressing together any breaks or tears as although it is quite pliable it can also be a little fragile.

Baking blind

To avoid soggy pastry when cooking flans or tarts with a moist filling, if you have the time it is worth partially cooking the pastry base before adding the filling. This is done by pricking the base with a fork then lining it with a sheet of foil or greaseproof paper. Cover the protected base with a layer of rice or dried beans and bake on a baking sheet for 10 minutes in a pre-heated oven, Gas 6/400°F/200°C. Remove the foil/paper and rice/beans and cook a few minutes longer until the base has lost its glazed appearance. Add the filling and continue the cooking at the temperature and for the time specified in the recipe. (Beans and rice can be stored and used again. For recipes which require a fully cooked pastry case, continue the cooking for a further 15–20 minutes, lowering the heat if the edges are becoming too brown.)

Breadcrumbs

Breadcrumbs in the recipes are dried unless otherwise stated. These can be made and stored in an airtight jar.

To make a supply, remove the crusts from stale bread and either grate it first, or slice it and grate it after drying. Heat the oven to Gas 3/325°F/160°C. Put crumbs/bread on to a baking sheet and leave in the oven until very dry. Alternatively, freshly grated crumbs can be left in a warm place, on top of the stove or in the airing cupboard, for a day or two until very dry.

Bread croûtons

Bread croûtons are made by frying slices of French bread or small bread squares in hot oil or butter until golden brown. Alternatively, sprinkle them with oil – small croûtons are most easily coated if you put the oil into a bowl and toss them in it – and bake at the top of a hot oven, Gas 7/425°F/220°C, for 5–10 minutes.

Crème fraîche

This French soured cream is now widely available and comes to us all the way from Normandy. It has a higher fat content than our own soured cream but at least one supermarket chain is now importing a low-fat version. Crème fraîche has a pleasant, nutty flavour and keeps well; the thick version won't curdle even when boiled. If unobtainable in your area, you can make your own by mixing up to double the amount of double cream with ordinary soured cream or smetana. Stand the mixture in a warm place for several hours, then refrigerate.

Béchamel sauce
Sauce béchamel

This famous sauce is claimed by the Bretons to have been invented by one of their ancestors. His name was Antinous Béchamel, Marquis de Nointel, who lived in Rennes where he collected the king's taxes, which didn't endear him to the local population. He was a keen cook and a handsome man and he invented his beautiful white sauce, so the story goes, in order to win the favours of a young lady. The result was not quite as he planned. The sauce became a world beater but his sweetheart married another. The original recipe calls for a scruple of nutmeg, an atom of cinnamon and an idea of ginger. Adjust your pinches accordingly!

1 teaspoon oil
25 g (1 oz) butter
25 g (1 oz) flour
300 ml (½ pint) milk
salt
freshly milled black pepper
1 clove head, crumbled
pinch of nutmeg
pinch of cinnamon
pinch of ground ginger

Heat the oil and butter over a low heat and stir in the flour. Stir for 2 minutes to cook the flour. Gradually mix in the milk and bring to the boil, stirring all the time as the sauce thickens to avoid lumps. Simmer gently for several minutes and then add the salt, pepper, clove, nutmeg, cinnamon and ginger.

Mother Poulard's omelette
Omelette de la Mère Poulard

If you ever visit Mont-St-Michel, apart from the wonder of the place and the huge numbers of tourists who come in car and coach loads, you might well be struck by the metallic sounds of rhythmic beating coming from the kitchen of the Hôtel Poulard. If you can push your way through the crowds and reach the windows, you will see what at first glance look like animated waxworks, dressed in nineteenth-century costume. A man and a woman stand behind a table, beating eggs in big, copper bowls, while another man is cooking an omelette in plenty of butter in a large pan over a huge open fire. Then, you realize, they are real people, making real omelettes which are served in the adjoining restaurant at hugely real prices.

Madame Poulard was a clever lady. She perfected and became famous for one simple dish and she refused to tell anyone else exactly how she did it. Her omelette was puffed and golden with a delicious moist and creamy centre. No one could guess how she achieved this and suggested she must add cream or flour. But when she was an old lady, she did write down a sort of recipe which contained the words: 'I break some good eggs in a bowl and beat them well,' and so by breaking the first classic rule of omelette making – which is to beat the eggs as little as possible – she became famous. The following is enough for one person.

2 large eggs
pinch of salt
50 g (2 oz) butter

Have the eggs at room temperature. Break them into a bowl, add salt and beat with a wire whisk until the mixture is light and frothy. This will take at least 5 minutes; if your wrist aches, have a pause before continuing to beat. (Or use an electric beater or mixer!) Melt the butter in a frying pan until it is white and frothy and is no longer sizzling, *a fini de chanter*. Tip in the eggs and, as the base begins to set, lift the edges to allow the runny centre to flow underneath. After a minute or so, remove from the heat and set aside to allow the omelette to rise. Return to the heat, cook a few seconds more, then fold in half while the centre is still very moist. Slide on to a hot plate and eat at once.

Pancakes

What is the difference between a *galette* and a *crêpe*? Both names are used in France for pancakes, but the word *galette* comes from the Celtic-speaking Haute-Bretagne, and *crêpe* is the French word which was used in Basse-Bretagne as well as Normandy and the rest of France. Pancakes are a way of life in Brittany but they appear all over northern France; in Picardy you'll probably come across *galopins*, which are thickened with stale brioche or bread and elsewhere in the Nord they make thick, filling pancakes often with beer instead of milk and water and call them *koukebaeke* or *couqueback*.

Nowadays, *galette* usually means a savoury pancake made with buckwheat flour, whereas the word *crêpe* generally refers to a pancake, most often sweet, made with wheat flour. *Galettes* made purely with buckwheat, salt and water were once the daily bread of most Bretons; they were eaten most simply spread with butter or jam or cut into strips and soaked in a bowl of fresh or soured milk. All sorts of fillings have since been devised and are served in *galettières* all over Brittany and parts of Normandy. Often an egg is cooked in the centre; or they are filled with slices of fried *andouille*, ham, sausage or pâté; or rolled round grilled sausages or sardines. They make a cheap and filling snack, eaten at an outside table, accompanied by a bowl of local cider or *lait ribot* (once the name of buttermilk but now used for a thin yoghurt-type drink).

The best way to learn how to make *galettes* or *crêpes* is to watch one of the practitioners making and selling his wares in a Breton market. He has the panache of a magician as he greases the griddles using a mixture of egg yolk and lard to prevent them sticking, then spreads the batter with a special T-shaped rake (known variously as a *raclette*, *rouable*, *rozell* or *rastell*). The half-cooked pancake is transferred from one griddle to another, he breaks in an egg or adds a filling, then folds the edges over, making four half-moons which leave the centre slightly exposed, and all the time carrying on a bantering conversation with his queue of customers.

Galettes

A batter made entirely of buckwheat flour is hard to handle, so below is a compromise. The addition of wheat flour (our ordinary flour) makes a less fragile mixture. It is important not to overgrease the pan, so make a ball with a wodge of kitchen paper, dip it into the oil and then wipe it over the base of the pan.

50 g (2 oz) buckwheat flour
50 g (2 oz) plain flour, sieved
pinch of salt
1 egg
150 ml (¼ pint) milk
150 ml (¼ pint) water
50 g (2 oz) concentrated butter, melted
groundnut oil

Put the flours into a large bowl with the salt. Make a well in the centre and break in the egg. Mix with a wooden spoon, gradually incorporating the milk and water. Beat well and add the butter. Beat again, by which time the mixture should be like thick cream. Set aside for at least 2 hours.

To cook, thoroughly heat the griddle or a heavy frying pan for about 5 minutes. Wipe it over with a wodge of kitchen paper dipped in the oil and test if it is hot enough by adding a drop of batter, which should immediately sizzle. When this happens, pour in 2–3 tablespoons of batter and spread it thinly over the pan using a wooden spatula. Cook until the underside is crisp and flip the pancake over. Cook for a further 30 seconds or so, and transfer to a warm plate.

Crêpes

For savoury *crêpes* follow the recipe for *galettes* but use all plain, sifted flour.

To make sweet *crêpes* add 1–2 tablespoons caster or vanilla sugar and a tablespoon of calvados, rum, brandy or orange flower water. Or flavour them with cinnamon or aniseed. Spread the cooked pancakes with either butter, jam, chestnut purée or cream, or a little honey. Then fold over into four. You can also fill them with apple, pear or strawberry slices cooked until soft in a little butter and sugar. For a special occasion flame the folded pancakes with spirit.

Crêpes-dentelle

Quimper, the old capital of Brittany's Cornouaille, is reputedly the place where the first Cornish Celts, fleeing from the Anglo-Saxons, landed some time in the Dark Ages. Later it became famous for its pottery founded in the seventeenth century by a Provençal, Jean-Baptiste Bousquet. The pretty bowls and plates decorated with Breton figures surrounded by a blue border are quite expensive, but the souvenir trade has solved the problem by transferring the design to tins of biscuits and chocolates.

Quimper's other speciality is the *crêpe-dentelle* which is famous all over the world, wherever Bretons have landed. Its invention is attributed to a Madame Tanguy who ran a *crêperie* there towards the end of the nineteenth century. But others say she stole the idea from Marie-Anne-Catherine Cornic, who was affectionately known as Madame Katel and ran a little grocer's shop in the rue des Gentilhommes. The recipe is one of those culinary secrets which the experts are not prepared to share. Basically it is made with a vanilla-flavoured batter but with equal weights of flour and sugar. Such a lot of sugar makes the pancake hard to cook and success depends on the skill of the operator. The cooked pancake is cut into strips, which are then rolled into flat cylinders around the blade of a knife.

Crêpes-dentelles, which can be bought in packets or tins all over France, are eaten, often accompanied by sweet wine or champagne, either on their own or as part of a dessert. Enjoy them on the spot when you are in Quimper!

Rice pudding
Bourgoule

What most of us think of as an essentially English pudding also appears in Normandy. It has various local names such as *tord-goule*, *tergoule* or *terrinée*. The secret of a really creamy pudding is long slow cooking; it used to be cooked all night in the embers of the fire or in that proverbial baker's oven from which it emerged with a deep brown crust. In Normandy it is eaten hot, warm or cold accompanied with *sablés normands* (see below).

75 g (3 oz) carolina rice
pinch of salt
50 g (2 oz) caster sugar
½ teaspoon ground cinnamon
1 litre (1¾ pints) milk

Heat the oven to Gas 2/300°F/150°C. Put all the ingredients into a buttered shallow ovenproof dish and stir well. Bake for 3½–4 hours, stirring every hour until rice has absorbed all the milk and the top is a deep golden brown.

Normandy shortbread
Sablés normands

Sablés, which are often served in Normandy with rice pudding (see above), are a kind of shortbread often flavoured with calvados. Their creamy flavour depends on using a good Normandy butter.

150 g (6 oz) flour
100 g (4 oz) Normandy butter, cut in pieces
50 g (2 oz) caster or vanilla sugar
1 teaspoon calvados
1 egg yolk

Put the flour, butter, sugar and calvados into a food processor and blend until they form a lump of dough. Remove, roll into a ball and refrigerate in a plastic bag for 30 minutes. (Without a food processor, cream the butter, sugar and calvados, then use your fingers to rub in the flour to form the dough.) Heat the oven to Gas 4/350°F/180°C. Line a baking sheet with greaseproof paper and sprinkle it lightly with flour. Divide the dough into four and, working on a floured board, roll into balls and press and roll these with a rolling pin into flat discs about 12 cm (5 in) in diameter. Use the edge of a knife blade to tidy the edges. Cut each disc into four triangular shapes, put them on the floured paper and brush with the egg yolk. Bake for 10–15 minutes until golden. Use a palette knife to transfer them to a wire tray to cool.

Fish stock
Court bouillon

When you decide to do something relatively simple like poaching a fish, does your heart sink as you realize you must first make a fish stock? Nothing complicated about that, but it does require time. The answer is to make more than you need and store the rest in pots in the freezer, to be used as and when required. Below is a basic recipe. As they do in France, you can vary the herbs to suit what you have on hand.

2 kg (4½ lb) fish heads and bones
1 onion, sliced
1 carrot, sliced
1 leek, sliced
sprigs of celery, thyme and parsley
1 bay leaf
1 teaspoon black peppercorns
600 ml (1 pint) strong dry cider
1 tablespoon cider vinegar
2 litres (3½ pints) water

Put everything into a large saucepan. Bring to the boil, remove the scum that forms with a slotted spoon, then cover, lower the heat and simmer for no more than 30 minutes. Strain and put into pots and freeze until wanted.

Soaking and cooking pulses

Some pulses, such as dried lentils, can be cooked just as they are, but most need to be soaked for at least 2–3 hours in cold water before cooking. If you're planning ahead the simplest solution is to leave them soaking overnight. However, the process can be speeded up by putting them into a large saucepan, cover with cold water, bring to the boil and let them bubble for 5 minutes, then turn off the heat and leave them to steep for 40 minutes.

Whichever method you use, drain them and discard the soaking liquid and cook them in plenty of fresh water. Don't add salt until the end because beans never soften if cooked in salted water; tomatoes have the same effect, but it's worth adding herbs and an onion or shallot to impart flavour to the beans. Cooking times vary according to the varity, anything from 45 minutes to 1½ hours.

Haricot bean purée
Purée à la bretonne

Haricot beans are delicious made into a purée and eaten as an accompaniment to lamb or beef, or simply with poached or fried eggs. Simply drain cooked beans, put them through a *mouli-légumes* (leaving the skins behind). Mix them with a nut of butter and a tablespoon or two of cream or milk and season to taste with salt and pepper.

Vanilla sugar

Vanilla pods, which look like dried up and blackened worms, have magic properties. They lend an incomparable flavour and can be used again and again: simply rinse them and store in a dry place. But better still keep a couple of vanilla pods in a jar of caster sugar and keep it in the store cupboard. The pods can be used as and when needed, rinsed, wiped and returned to the jar, and the sugar itself can be used in any recipe which calls for them both, and will give the finished dish a subtlety which vanilla essence lacks. Only replace the pods when they cease to be effective.

Bibliography

Arzel, Florence, *La Cuisine de Bretagne*, Cuisines du Terroir, Denoël, 1984

Ayrton, Elisabeth, *The Cookery of England*, Penguin, 1977

Behague, Dominique, *Gastronomie Normandie*, SAEP

Binns, Richard, *French Leave 3*, Chiltern House, 1983

Carluccio, Antonio, *A Passion for Mushrooms*, Pavilion, 1989

Compas, Ray, *Le Grand livre de la cuisine normande*, Ch. Corlet, 1986

David, Elizabeth, *French Provincial Cooking*, Penguin, 1977

Davidson, Alan, *North Atlantic Seafood*, Penguin, 1986

Dawes, Frank Victor, *Brittany*, Christopher Helm, 1989

Delille, Jacques Andrieu, *La Cuisine belge*, Guide Marabout, 1981

Eperon, Arthur, *Brittany*, Pan, 1990

Eperon, Arthur, *Normandy*, Pan, 1989

Eperon, Arthur, *Pas de Calais & North-West France*, Pan, 1991

Eperon, Barbara, *Normandy, Picardy and Pas de Calais*, Christopher Helm, 1991

FIOM, *Poissons et fruits de mer de France*, SOPEXA

Grigson, Jane, *Fruit Book*, Penguin, 1982

Grigson, Jane, *Charcuterie and French Pork Cookery*, Penguin, 1970

Grigson, Jane, *The Cooking of Normandy*, A Sainsbury Cookbook, 1987

Grigson, Jane, *Vegetable Book*, Penguin, 1980

Hutchins, Sheila, *English Recipes*, Methuen, 1967

Larousse Gastronomique, Paul Hamlyn, 1969

Le Cunff, Louis, *Cuisine et gastronomie de Bretagne*, Ouest-France, 1984

Liégeois, J. C. and Verraest, D., *Gastronomie des Flandres et d'Artois*, SAEP, 1984

Lyon, Ninette, *Le Tour de France gourmand des spécialités régionales*, Marabout, 1985

Michelin *Green Guides*

Morand, Simone, *Cuisine traditionelle de Bretagne*, Jean-Paul Gisserot, 1989

Parker, Audrey, *A Country Recipe Notebook*, Faber, 1979

Perrin-Chattard, Brigitte and Jean-Pierre, *The Best Breton Recipes*, Ouest-France 1984

Rance, Patrick, *The French Cheese Book*, Macmillan, 1989

Root, Waverley, *The Food of France*, Macmillan Papermac, 1983

Schmaeling, Tony, *French Provincial Cooking*, Omega Books, 1982

Sharman, Fay, *The Taste of France*, Macmillan Papermac, 1983

Simon, André, *Guide to Good Food and Wine*, Collins, 1960

Stobart, Tom, *The Cook's Encyclopaedia*, Macmillan Papermac, 1982

Stobart, Tom, *Herbs, Spices and Flavourings*, Penguin, 1987

Tannahill, Reay, *Food in History*, Penguin, 1988

Vence, Céline, *Encyclopédie Hachette de la cuisine regionale*, Livre de Paris/Hachette, 1979

Ward, Greg, *The Rough Guide to Brittany & Normandy*, Routledge & Kegan Paul, 1987

Willan, Anne, *French Regional Cooking*, Cresset Press, 1989

Index

All the entries and page numbers in **bold** type are for the main ingredients and recipes. Other entries, such as ideas for dishes, names of people, places etc., are in lighter type.